A GUIDE TO TROLLOPE

By the same author:
Alexandre Dumas: A Biographical Study (Cassell, 1950)
The Songs of Schubert (Alston Books, 1964)
Elements — Selected Poems (Outposts Publications, 1967)
Travelled Roads and Other Poems (Golden Head Press, 1969)
Handel: A Chronological Thematic Catalogue (Grian-aig Press, 1972)
Handel Before England (Grian-aig Press, 1975)
The Lieder of Brahms (Grian-aig Press, 1979)
Poems of an Agnostic (Outposts Publications, 1979)
Charades, a 3-act Play (New Playwrights' Network, 1980)
Murder for Love (Merlin Books, 1987)
Stories from a Yorkshire Dale (Merlin Books, 1988)

A GUIDE TO TROLLOPE

Arnold Craig Bell

MERLIN BOOKS LTD.
Braunton   Devon

ISBN 0 86303 427-6
Printed in England by Antony Rowe Ltd., Chippenham, Wilts.

CONTENTS

PREFACE

Of all the great English novelists Trollope is far and away the most prolific: the only one comparable from this aspect, in fact, to his French contemporaries Balzac, Dumas and George Sand. Against him even Scott and Dickens wrote at a leisurely pace. His output comprises 48 novels, four volumes of Tales, five books of travel, various sketches and monographs on Cicero and Thackeray. It was this very prolificness which, allied with his method of work as described in his posthumous and fatal *Autobiography*, was the cause of his temporary relegation to all but oblivion after his death in 1882. The ivory tower aesthetes and disciples of the Art for Art's sake school with its languors and lilies and roses (i.e. Oscar Wilde, William Morris, the Rossettis, Meredith, Pater and the rest), revolted by the assertion that a writer was a worker neither more nor less than a cobbler or a tailor or a Civil Servant and should work to a timetable, united to put him into literary purdah; and from roughly the turn of the century until the 1930s, after being the most popular and highest paid author of his time, the name of Trollope vanished almost entirely from the 'greats' of the Victorian literary scene. If his name was ever honoured by critical reference it was invariably a damning one.* 'Superficial, 'commonplace', 'flat', 'void of imagination' were the common run of epithets used to describe his work.

Then came the inevitable revival. A generation which woke up to the fact that its forerunners had been hoodwinked by the pre-Raphaelite cult and Georgian critical imposters began to realize that an aesthetic which exalted Keats, Shelley, Tennyson, Swinburne and Rossetti at the expense of Wordsworth and Byron, and ranked Meredith and Thackeray above Trollope, could be fundamentally wrong. So, with a new appreciation of realism and the ordinary events in the lives of ordinary people as a basis for fiction, Trollope made a gigantic return to his right and proper place as one of the greatest of English novelists.

That he is such no unbiased critic can doubt. I am old-fashioned enough to hold Trollope's own belief, expressed in his *Autobiography*, that before everything a novel must be a narrative about characters who are credible as human beings and have individual lives of their own expressed in their actions, words and thoughts.** And this essential must apply not only to realist fiction but to works of fantasy and imagination like *Wuthering Heights* and *Moby Dick*. Because of this, to me Trollope is the only British novelist (except for George Eliot, Anne Brontë and Elizabeth Gaskell at their best) who can be named in the same breath as Jane Austen. The juxtaposition of their names is not fortuitous. Both have the rare power of creating tension from and belief in characters and scenes that are ordinary, even humdrum — the height of the novelist's art. Is Frank Churchill really in love with Emma Woodhouse? Who gave Jane Fairfax the mysterious piano? Will Lucy Steele's hypocrisy be seen for what it is, or will she take Edward Ferrars

---

* See for example the 1942 edition of the *Everyman Biographical Dictionary of English Literature*. With, incidentally, an even more myopic reference to Anne Brontë.
** Or as Henry James expressed the same thing in different words: 'The only reason for the existence of a novel is that it does attempt to represent life.' *(The Art of Fiction)*

from Elinor? Will Mr Slope triumph over the Proudies and Grantlys and become Dean of Barchester, or will Mrs Proudie sort him out? Will Lady Arabella Gresham succeed in her determination to prevent her son from marrying Mary Thorne? Such purely domestic and provincial dilemmas become in the master hands of Jane Austen and Trollope as gripping and important as any so-called 'novels of high drama'. Like hers, with certain exceptions to be duly noted, his narratives impart a consummate unsurpassed illusion of reality. The characters are people we know or know of; the events happen as they do in our own lives or those of others; there is no forcing of issues, juggling with circumstances, playing with coincidence or falling into jarring exaggeration. All is unforced and natural. He presents us with as truthful a picture of life as lived over a century ago as does Gissing, but with a less grim, more adroit touch.

It has to be admitted, since every writer, however great, has his limitations and weaknesses, that Trollope does not have Jane Austen's almost infallible skill in construction or her trenchant genius for creating a situation or character with never a wasted word. For example: in *Pride and Prejudice* Mr Collins's background is traced in a single paragraph, and it is all we need to know about him. It would have taken Trollope a whole chapter. Sometimes, even in his best novels such as *Doctor Thorne* (and others) we have to plough through wearisomely detailed preliminary chapters before the story gets off the ground. He is frequently prolix, repetitious, pedestrian, flat-footed in style and occasionally downright dull. But if that is on the debit side, on the credit, in addition to the merits I have already described, he has an almost incredible range of character, knowledge and interests — a range arguably wider than that of any other British novelist. From 'Planty Pal' the Prime Minister, to Roger Scatcherd the hard-drinking, self-made stone mason; politicians of all shades of belief and unbelief; squires, fox-hunting gentry, high and low-life wasters and eccentrics, clerics of all grades, artists manqués, bohemians, religious bigots, boarding-house keepers, commercial travellers, the legal fraternity, civil servants, doctors, farmers, financiers, would-be authors — all are caught in his fantastically capacious net. He seems to be familiar with every stratum of society to a degree which no other novelist can rival. And finally, his knowledge of women and feminine psychology is unsurpassed. As Henry James acknowledged, he was *the* master and interpreter of the English girl and woman. Lily Dale, Lucy Robarts, Mary Thorne, Miss Dunstable, Mrs Proudie, Jemima Stanbury, Caroline Waddington, Lady Glencora, Alice Vavasor, Clara Amedroz, Julia Brabazon, Laura Standish, Violet Effingham, Lizzie Eustace, Lucinda Roanoke, Madame Goesler, Mrs Hurtle, Arabella Trefoil, Mrs Bolton — what other novelist can claim so memorable and varied a portrait gallery? Nor, as is only to be expected, are the best of his male characters any less vital and convincing.

To return to and conclude with the problem of his prolificness. So many would-be readers, looking over the list of his titles, can be forgiven for being bewildered and wondering where to begin. To help here, to act as a guide, has been one of the motives of my attempted survey. By providing a summary and criticism of each novel* in chronological order it is my hope that such readers may find this book to be helpful in the matter of their choice. Once caught in the spell I am sure they will not rest until they have

---

*And I may as well state here that I have confined myself to the novels, passing over the short stories, which are of smaller worth.

explored the Trollopian arena to its full extent. And this is important, since to judge and assess Trollope by a mere handful of the Barchester or Palliser novels is to get a one-sided and false view of him. He is not just the 'escapist', 'comfortable', 'safe', 'respectable' writer as dubbed by so many critics. Commentators who describe him as such cannot have read *The Way We Live Now, Mr Scarborough's Family, Sir Harry Hotspur, The American Senator, He Knew He Was Right* or *An Eye For An Eye*. He did not turn a blind eye to the evils of his time, as those novels reveal. Characters like Mrs Bolton in *John Caldigate*, the clerics in *Miss Mackenzie* and the whole story of *Nina Balatka* and *Linda Tressel* show us his detestation of religious bigotry and racial hatred, just as *Rachel Ray, Ayala's Angel* and others his sympathy with the despised, bullied, repressed, dependent Victorian single woman. In the face of such evidence to maintain that Trollope is an escapist writer unconcerned with social evils and injustices is, to quote Samuel Johnson, to 'speak the language of ignorance.'

I conclude with the brief but arguably the best and most trenchant assessment and description of Trollope's genius ever made, and which puts all I have tried to express in a nutshell. Nathaniel Hawthorne said of the novels: 'They . . . . . are just as real as if some giant had hewn a great lump out of the earth and put it under a glass case, with all its inhabitants going about their daily business, and not suspecting that they were being made a show of.' After that there is really no need to say anything. Except perhaps to add that no one who has read his work *in toto* can have any doubt that, even if he is not our greatest novelist, his contribution to English fiction has not been surpassed.

PRELIMINARY

According to geneticists, men and women of genius in whatever field almost invariably inherit their gifts from the paternal side of the family. This may seem to reek of male chauvinism, but is nevertheless true. It will doubtless, therefore, be a source of comfort and joy to feminists to learn that our author was a signal exception to the genetic law in that he derived his genius from his mother — an exception particularly gratifying in a novelist who not only created more credible and lovable female characters than any other novelist, but whose work is full of solicitude and sympathy for that half of our race who in his day and age were in general regarded as inferiors to and mere shadows of their men-folk and treated accordingly.

Frances Trollope, Anthony's mother, was a prolific writer, almost rivalling her son with her forty-odd books. But her novels and travelogues, so popular in her day, are now as completely forgotten as will be so many of those equally highly acclaimed specimens of our own time in the not so distant future. Anthony, her third son, was born on the 24th April, 1815. An unhappy childhood due mainly to his father's financial ineptitude and misfortunes, and years of misery at Winchester and Harrow public schools because of his poverty, and where he showed no talent for anything whatsoever and was the despair of his masters and himself, was followed in 1834 by a brief sojourn in Belgium where his mother had decamped with the family on the bankruptcy of her husband and where she supported them unaided by her pen. It was here that he witnessed the deaths of his father, a brother and his youngest sister.

The turn for the better in his hitherto unhappy existence came at the age of 19 when, by the influence of a family friend, he obtained a post as junior clerk in the Post Office. Then in 1841 he was transferred to Ireland; and it was here, on his own confession that, partly to lose his own unhappy *ego* by creating a world of his own imagining, and partly in emulation of his mother whose most successful novels *The Widow Barnaby* and *The Widow Married* had recently made her name, he made his first ventures into print with *The Macdermots of Ballycloran* (1847) and *The Kellys and the O'Kellys* (1848). Not only did his career as a writer begin in Ireland but, following his marriage in 1844, so too did a new-found happiness and a zest for life that was never to leave him. Poverty and that crippling sense of inferiority engendered by it were put behind him, and in his own words 'From the day on which I set foot in Ireland, all these evils fell away from me. Since that time who has had a happier life than mine?' He came to love the Irish people, and they accepted him as they did few Englishmen, and in this new atmosphere of mutual affection and esteem he bloomed and blossomed. His job, too, contributed both to his mental and physical well-being, taking him out of doors to all kinds of strange isolated places where he met characters who were to be treasured in his memory and recreated by his genius. He took up riding and became a passionate devotee of fox hunting, and his intimate knowledge of the sport and its followers was to provide him with a richly authentic background to several of his novels.

But in the spring of 1851 the authorities transferred him back to England where he was allotted the job of organizing postal deliveries in the rural south-west counties. At the time the change seemed to him catastrophic. But as with so many such instances in life, the ill wind blew an unsuspected future good — the good in his case taking the form of the idea of writing about a cathedral city and its clerics. From this inspired idea came those stories which have done more than any of the others to place him among the most popular of the great classical novelists.

From the time of the writing, publication and success of *The Warden* his life became one hectic round of writing, hunting and travelling. Dumas alone among writers can rival him in this last capacity. He visited the West Indies, the United States, Egypt, South Africa, Australia; and he wrote while he travelled, and made notes during his various stays and worked them into novels on his return. When he was too old to hunt, famous and well-off, he took to haunting the better London clubs, playing whist with social friends and dining with literary ones. But he never stopped writing; and at his death at the age of 67 from a stroke in the December of 1882, he had placed his name to 48 novels and made according to his own meticulous calculations, £68,939. 17s.5d. by his writing.

APPRENTICE WORKS

It was only natural that, settled in Ireland at the age of twenty-six and finding happiness there for the first time in his life, the young Anthony, feeling the urge to create, should write about the scenes and people he found around him. It is the mistake of many a literary beginner. It takes time and experience to bring home the fact that scenes and people are better described in absence and from a time-distance perspective. In this instance the young inexperienced would-be author was so passionately moved by the poverty and misery of the Irish people and by the callous indifference of the English to their plight that he felt urged to put the situation on paper for the world to be made aware of. He witnessed the appalling famines of 1846 and 1847 and was never to forget them.

The first outcome of this was *The Macdermots of Ballycloran*, written 1843-45, to be followed by the second, *The Kellys and the O'Kellys*, two years later.

In writing these he made two typical apprentice errors. The first, as I have already stated, was to choose a subject altogether too close for him to be able to treat it with that first essential of the novelist — dispassionate objectivity. The second error was to dress up what were really impassioned polemics in the guise of fiction. As treatises he might have made a first-rate job of them; as novels they fall between the two stools of fiction and polemic. If one has to choose, the earlier story is perhaps the better of the two, at any rate being more dramatic, daringly seasoned as it is by seduction, murder, a bastard child and a mother who hankers after her daughter's lover. But even with these ingredients the author can make little of it, and his attempts to be dramatic merely highlight another all-important factor of the novelist's art, namely, that it is not so much what is narrated that counts as the manner in which it is done. Had Trollope written the story in his maturity and away from the scenes described he might well have made a good novel of it. For its inception was promising. Walking with a friend in the countryside of Leitrim they 'turned up through a deserted gateway, along a weedy grass-grown avenue' to find themselves looking at 'the modern ruins of a country house . . . . . and while I was still among the ruined walls and decayed beams I fabricated the plot of *The Macdermots of Ballycloran.*'

But when it came to that acid test of the novelist, the sheer mental and physical concentration of putting the plot on paper, of arranging his material and developing his characters, he found that the story 'hung fire'. And when at length he did finish it and it was published by Newby, his pessimism as to its success was only too well justified, and this not only on account of its weaknesses but because the only Irish stories the British public wanted to read were light-hearted amusing ones after the style of Charles Lever. Such a savage exposure of Irish wrongs and injustice as were to be found in Trollope's pages was altogether too much of a laceration of the British conscience.

Much of the above criticism applies also to the second story, *The Kellys and the O'Kellys*. Despite the fact that, with a description of a hunt, a country house with its various characters and intrigues, a sub-plot and the character of Fanny Wyndham as Trollope's first attempt at a portrait of an English girl — all presages of later masterpieces — the story doesn't really get off the ground or convince. The ideas are there without the genius to exploit them. That was only to come with the 1850s and the first of the Barsetshire chronicles.

Following the two Irish novels the last year of the 1840s was rounded off by his third fictional attempt — *La Vendée*: 'a dull historial tale in the manner of Alexandre Dumas' according to James Pope Hennessy.* Anything less 'in the manner of Alexandre Dumas' it would be difficult to imagine than this lifeless chronicle of the 1848 Paris revolution, lacking as it does all Dumas's verve and characterization. The fact is Trollope simply couldn't inject interest into scenes, incidents and people he knew nothing about, and later he was to admit that he 'knew, in truth, nothing of life in the La Vendée country.'

If, as must be admitted, these three apprentice works are in less or more degree expendable, Trollopians, tracing their author's development, can console themselves by anticipating the next decade which, marked by his return to England, was to see the appearance of the first of his masterpieces.

THE WARDEN

The end of his Irish-found happiness occasioned by a sudden and unexpected recall to England by the Post Office came as a blow; and the mundane fact that his new job, that of reorganizing the postal methods of the West Country, was more important than his present one and something of a rise did little to relieve his disappointment and unease. But as events transpired the move turned out to be a perfect example of the proverb concerning ill winds blowing good fortune. For had Trollope not been recalled to England at this juncture the odds are he would never have had the idea of the Barsetshire chronicles, or for that matter perhaps of the best of the very English novels of his maturity, thus making posterity the poorer for the loss of such as *The Belton Estate, He Knew He Was Right* and *The Way We Live Now*.

How the idea of *The Warden* (or *The Precentor* as it was originally entitled) came to him is best told by Trollope himself in his *Autobiography*.

In the course of my job with the General Post Office I visited Salisbury, and whilst wandering there one midsummer evening round the purlieus of the cathedral I conceived the story of *The Warden*, — from whence came that series of novels of which Barchester, with its bishops, deans and archdeacon, was the central site. I may as well declare at once that no one at their commencement could have had less reason than myself to presume himself to be able to write about clergymen. I have often been asked in what period of my early life I have lived so long in a cathedral city as to have become intimate with the ways of a Close. I have never lived in any cathedral city, — except London, never knew anything of any Close, and at that time had enjoyed no peculiar intimacy with any clergyman. My archdeacon, who has been said to be lifelike, and for whom I confess that I have all a parent's fond affection, was, I think, the simple result of an effort of my moral consciousness.

---

*Anthony Trollope, Jonathan Cape, 1971.

But although it was Salisbury that inspired the idea, Winchester was the Barchester foremost in Trollope's mind when he wrote the Barsetshire series.

Although *The Warden* is one of the shortest of his novels and one of the few to appear in one volume, it took him longer to write than any of the others — over twelve months. The reason for this lies partly in the fact that with it he was starting a new line of country and gradually discovering his true path, and so hesitant; partly because he had to keep tabs on the actual scandal involving the hospital of St Cross, Winchester, which formed the basis of actuality for his story, and make sure of the facts; and partly because his full-time job with the Post Office which he carried out with more than scrupulous conscienciousness, combined with the time-consuming efforts to find a suitable home for himself and his family as he moved about, left him precious little leisure for spare time occupations, whether hunting or writing. And in fact it was not until more than a year after its conception in the Close of Salisbury cathedral that on July 29, 1852, he began the actual writing of the novel; and even then he had to lay it aside owing to the fact that in the autumn of the following year he was posted yet again to Ireland. And it was actually there, in Belfast, that he finished his novel towards the end of 1853.

The story is in essence simple; and indeed the novel is one of the finest examples of the difficult art of simplicity in all fiction. The diffident, gentle Mr Septimus Harding, one of Trollope's most endearing characters and with the Revd Crawley the only example of a genuinely religious unworldly cleric among the many clerics he has given us, lives happily in his little Barchester world as precentor of the cathedral and warden of the historic almshouse, asking no more of life than to be left in peace to organize the music for the services, administer to the comfort of the twelve old beadsmen who live in the almshouse, to play his violoncello in his home and to enjoy the affection of his unmarried daughter, Eleanor, his son-in-law, archdeacon Grantly, and his father-in-law, the old bishop, all of which blessings have been his for many years. But the story opens with a cloud on his horizon no bigger than a man's hand but which nevertheless threatens his position and, more importantly for him, his peace of mind.

The young local doctor, John Bold, is one of those men who go through life if not exactly with a chip on their shoulder, at least with an obsession for discovering injustices somewhere and trying to put them right out of principle. ('The Barchester Reformer' Trollope calls him, with a hint of sarcasm in the title.) He becomes convinced that Mr Harding has no right to his sinecure of warden with its attendant £800 a year, that Hiram's ancient will has been misinterpreted and that the old beadsmen are being scandalously robbed by a smug too-affluent Church. So, even though he is in love with Mr Harding's daughter, so strong are his convictions that he persists with his legal investigations. Once this becomes known all round Barchester, sides are taken with deadly earnest. Archdeacon Grantly, the strong man of the clerical Barchesterites, leaps belligerently into the fray and sets a counter-legal action moving. The all-powerful, infallible 'Jupiter' (Trollope's sardonic name for *The Times*) even devotes leading articles to the brouhaha; so that what began as a mere local storm in a teacup becomes almost a national campaign. With the result that when, driven by the grief and shame of her father, Eleanor daringly (for a Victorian girl) goes to see John Bold and begs him on her knees and with tears to desist from his 'cause', and he accedes, he finds he is powerless to put an end to the affair which now drives on under its own momentum. Finally, the poor old warden, driven out of all peace of mind and half convinced that his accusers are right and that he is not in fact due to his £800 stipend, unheeding the loud protests of the archdeacon, resigns the living and retires from his wardenship to live in comparative poverty with Eleanor.

So simple a story, so drab and local a series of events would, judged superficially, hardly seem to have the ingredients for fiction any more than George Eliot's *Tales of Clerical Life* which appeared a few years later (1857) and may well have been part-inspired by Trollope's Barchester novels. But such is his skill and his genius for portraying character that we are more enthralled by it than by many a novel deliberately aiming to hold us by a series of thrilling incidents and dramatic situations. Moreover Trollope, while refraining from any propaganda and without taking sides, saw in the story a means of drawing attention to the undisputable fact that under the aegis of the Church of England many clerics, like the monks in medieval times, were living cushy lives and drawing stipends for sinecures just such as Mr Harding was doing. But he was equally sardonic about the hypocrisy of the Press in beating such clerics with its too-powerful self-righteous bludgeon of propaganda.

So much for the outline and generalities. Let us now look at the novel in more detail and examine its merits and faults. The latter first. These were to remain with Trollope all his creative life, and with rare exceptions (to be duly noted) he never grew out of them: never probably thought of them as such. These briefly are a tendency he found irresistible to exchange confidences with the reader (a fault shared by all the Victorian novelists, who regarded themselves as mentors and guardians of public morality) and to indulge at length in side issues and so laying himself open to the charge of padding and longueurs. Even this novel, short as it is, could have been made even shorter and better. His attack on the 'Jupiter', for example, is amusing enough, but he goes on about it at far too great length and in too much detail (see chapter 14). Then he makes matters worse by devoting a whole chapter (15) to its editor and to an attack on Carlyle and Dickens under the names of Dr Anticant and Mr Sentiment. Even if the criticism is true it is utterly out of place as far as the story is concerned.

Still, these faults are minor ones and detract very little from the excellence of the whole as some of those in the longer novels do. Intelligent first readers of the book must have told themselves that a new genius had appeared on the scene, a genius who could make ordinary men and women going about their everyday concerns as familiar as their own friends and their problems and emotions more interesting than the improbable heroes and heroines of far-fetched romances. In short, the successor to Jane Austen had been found.

For characters there is first of all the dear old warden himself, diffident, retiring and humble. Mr Harding has one very personal mannerism, a special and individual trait, one which only a born novelist, that is to say a writer who makes a study of human beings and their little foibles, could have imagined. It will be remembered that the cello was Mr Harding's instrument: and so we get:

> The warden still looked mutely in his face, making the slightest possible passes with an imaginary fiddle bow, and stopping, as he did so, sundry imaginary strings with the fingers of his other hand. 'Twas his constant consolation in conversational troubles. While these vexed him sorely, the passes would be short and slow, and the upper hand would not be seen to work; nay the strings on which it operated would sometimes lie concealed in the

musician's pocket, and the instrument on which he played would be beneath his chair; but as his spirit warmed to the subject — as his trusting heart, looking to the bottom of that which vexed him, would see its clear way out, — he would rise to a higher melody, sweep the unseen strings with a bolder hand, and swiftly fingering the cords from his neck, down along his waistcoat, and up again to his very ear, create an ecstatic strain of perfect music, audible to himself and to St. Cecilia, and not without effect.

'I quite agree with Cox and Cummins,' continued the archdeacon. 'They say we must secure Sir Abraham Haphazard. I shall not have the slightest fear in leaving the case in Sir Abraham's hands.'

The warden played the slowest and saddest of tunes. It was but a dirge on one string.

This mannerism receives its ultimate expression in the scene where the old man, at the height of desperation, steals a march on the archdeacon and goes to London to seek an interview with the great lawyer who has undertaken his defence — Sir Abraham Haphazard himself. Shaking like a leaf, Mr Harding beards the lion in his den. It soon becomes apparent to the great Sir Abraham that he has to deal with an idiot: for when he tells the Warden that his case is as good as won, all he can get from the lunatic is a request that it should be given up, thrown to the winds simply because he has come to believe that the accusations of his enemies are just and his conscience forces him to resign his position even though it means poverty for himself and his daughter. When the legal giant remonstrates:

Mr. Harding, seated in his chair, began to play a slow tune on an imaginary violoncello.

"Nay, my dear sir," continued the attorney-general, "there is no further ground for any question; I don't see that you have the power of raising it."

"I can resign," said Mr. Harding, slowly playing away with his right hand, as though the bow were beneath the chair in which he was sitting . . . .

"Have you not a daughter, Mr. Harding — an unmarried daughter?"

"I have," said he, now standing also, but still playing away on his fiddle with his hand behind his back. "I have, Sir Abraham; and she and I are completely agreed on this subject . . . . My friends and I differ on this subject, and that adds much to my sorrow; but it cannot be helped."

And as he finished what he had to say, he played up such a tune as never before had graced the chambers of any attorney-general . . .

Some critics have held that Mr Harding is too good to be true and that he is a sentimentalized character. We all know of course that such honest, diffident people are rare among our species, but they have existed from time to time and indeed still do, though perhaps more rarely, even though they may not be musical and play the cello.

The archdeacon is placed beside Mr Harding as an obvious contrast, and Trollope's analysis and description, with their hint of irony, are a sheer delight.

Though doubt and hesitation disturbed the rest of our poor warden, no such weakness perplexed the nobler breast of his son-in-law. As the indomitable cock preparing for the combat sharpens his spurs, shakes his feathers, and erects his comb, so did the archdeacon arrange his weapons for the coming war, without misgiving and without fear. That he was fully confident of the justice of his cause let no one doubt. Many a man can fight his battle with good courage, but with a doubting conscience. Such was not the case with Dr. Grantly. He did not believe in the Gospel with more assurance than he did in the sacred justice of all ecclesiastical revenues.

When he put his shoulder to the wheel to defend the income of the present and future precentors of Barchester, he was animated by as strong a sense of a holy cause, as that which gives courage to a missionary in Africa, or enables a sister of mercy to give up the pleasures of the world for the wards of a hospital. He was about to defend the holy of holies from the touch of the profane; to guard the citadel of his church from the most rampant of its enemies; to put on his good armour in the best of fights; and secure, if possible, the comforts of his creed for coming generations of ecclesiastical dignitaries. Such a work required no ordinary vigour; and the archdeacon was, therefore, extraordinarily vigorous. It demanded a buoyant courage, and a heart happy in its toil; and the archdeacon's heart was happy, and his courage was buoyant.

He knew that he would not be able to animate his father-in-law with feelings like his own, but this did not much disturb him. He preferred to bear the brunt of the battle alone, and did not doubt that the warden would resign himself into his hands with passive submission.

And when, despite his father-in-law's misgivings he insists on addressing the twelve deluded beadsmen in order to point out to them the folly of their ways in supposing they could remove their present warden and claim the mythical £100 a year for each of them, we are given this picture of him in full flight.

As the archdeacon stood up to make his speech, erect in the middle of that little square, he looked like an ecclesiastical statue placed there, as a fitting impersonation of the church militant here on earth; his shovel hat, large, new, and well-pronounced, a churchman's hat in every inch, declared the profession as plainly as does the Quaker's broad brim; his heavy eyebrows, large open eyes, and full mouth and chin expressed the solidity of his order; the broad chest, amply covered with fine cloth, told how well to do was its estate; one hand ensconced within his pocket, evinced the practical hold which our mother church keeps on her temporal possessions; and the other, loose for action, was ready to fight if need be in her defence; and, below these, the decorous breeches, and neat black gaiters showing so admirably that well-turned leg, betokened the decency, the outward beauty and grace of our church establishment.

He is, in fact, the personification of the Church militant and capitalistic before being shorn of its power by Acts of Parliament enforced by general growing unbelief fomented by the influences of Darwin, Marx, Huxley, Samuel Butler and others like them. Trollope held the opinion that archdeacon Grantly was among the greatest of his many triumphs of characterization, and he was justified in his belief.

In addition there are one or two remarkably felicitous descriptions worthy of Dickens. In general it must be confessed that, in contrast to Dickens, description of people and places was not one of Trollope's strong points. He lacked Dickens's eye and ear for the memorable phrase, the vivid stroke that brings the place or person unforgettably before our eyes, just as, to be fair, Dickens lacked Trollope's genius for creating convincing ordinary people with no eccentric exaggerated quirks or easy catch-phrases. But here Trollope surpasses himself. The chapter describing poor Mr Harding's long day alone in London before his late evening interview with Sir Abraham Haphazard is full of light humorous touches, and the description of the cheap eating house in the Strand where he has a mutton chop to help him to pass the time is not unworthy of Dickens.

A final word. Trollope has no sentimental illusions as to the poor dependent beadsmen whose conduct in fact reveals his profound knowledge of human nature. Their reactions when they learn of the possible wealth (to them) which may accrue to them should they win their case are human nature exemplified. Their greed — that innate greed that lurks in almost every human heart to have more, to claim something, however unnecessary — leaps to the fore. They are all ancient and decrepit; none of them can expect more than a few years of life; they have, if not everything they would like, at least the essentials for their comfort — food, drink, a roof over their heads, no worries about the future. But when they are told that someone is sorry for them and that they might have been robbed of money that was due to them, their reactions are absolutely true to life. They become a world in microcosm, and innate cupidity takes over their better natures. As in the world, the more rebellious and greedy of them organize a petition and shame the reluctant rest into putting their marks to it. All except old Bunce. You will always find in any society the odd grateful and contented man, the die-hard conservative, the man who accepts his place, the hater of trade union and closed shop mentality even though they may be to his own advantage. Such is old Bunce. Loyal to the end to Mr Harding, he pours scorn on the others and accuses them of being traitors to their warden who has looked after them so well. The two extremes of human nature are shown in Bunce and Bell when Mr Harding takes his moving farewell of them.

As they left the hall-door, Mr. Harding shook hands with each of the men, and spoke a kind word to them about their individual cases and ailments; and so they departed, answering his questions in the fewest words, and retreated to their dens, a sorrowful repentant crew.

All but Bunce, who still remained to make his own farewell. 'There's poor old Bell,' said Mr. Harding; 'I mustn't go without saying a word to him; come through with me, Bunce, and bring the wine with you;' and so they went through to the men's cottages, and found the old man propped up as usual in his bed.

'I've come to say good-bye to you, Bell,' said Mr. Harding, speaking loud, for the old man was deaf.

'And are you going away, then, really?' asked Bell.

'Indeed I am, and I've brought you a glass of wine; so that we may part friends, as we lived, you know.'

The old man took the proffered glass in his shaking hands, and drank it eagerly. 'God bless you, Bell!' said Mr. Harding; 'good-bye, my old friend.'

'And so you're really going?' the man again asked.

'Indeed I am, Bell.'

The poor old bed-ridden creature still kept Mr. Harding's hand in his own, and the warden thought that he had met with something like warmth of feeling in the one of all his subjects from whom it was the least likely to be expected; for poor old Bell had nearly outlived all human feelings. 'And your reverence,' said he, and then he paused, while his old palsied head shook horribly, and his shrivelled cheeks sank lower within his jaws, and his glazy eye gleamed with a momentary light; 'and your reverence, shall we get the hundred a year, then?'

How gently did Mr. Harding try to extinguish the false hope of money which had been so wretchedly raised to disturb the quiet of the dying man! One other week and his mortal coil would be shuffled off; in one short week would God resume his soul, and set it apart for its irrevocable doom; seven more tedious days and nights of senseless inactivity, and all would be over for poor Bell in this world; and yet, with his last audible words, he was demanding his moneyed rights, and asserting himself to be the proper heir of John Hiram's bounty! Not on him, poor sinner as he was, be the load of such sin!

Mr. Harding returned to his parlour, meditating with a sick heart on what he had seen, and Bunce with him. We will not describe the parting of these two good men, for good men they were. It was in vain that the late warden endeavoured to comfort the heart of the old bedesman;

poor old Bunce felt that his days of comfort were gone. The hospital had to him been a happy home, but it could be so no longer. He had had honour there, and friendship; he had recognised his master and been recognised; all his wants, both of soul and body, had been supplied, and he had been a happy man. He wept grievously as he parted from his friend, and the tears of an old man are bitter.

The novel ends perhaps a little too Dickensianly slickly and sentimentally with Mr Harding no longer warden but still precentor and, over and above that, rector of the little church of St Cuthbert, so that he is not made to suffer too much from what his disgruntled son-in-law regards as his spineless pig-headedness; his daughter marries John Bold; and though the archdeacon refuses to go to their wedding (he cannot altogether forgive Bold for his arrogance and interference) he allows his wife and family to be present, and all ends happily as a fairy-tale.

Nothing could be more succinct and apt than Henry James's tribute to the novel in his essay (1883) 'Anthony Trollope': 'It is simply the history of an old man's conscience.' Nevertheless, succinct and apt though the tribute is, it misses an important aspect of Trollope's art. While superficially uncomplicated in outline, the novel contains a subtle sophistication all too often missed. The situation of the main antagonists, though simple in itself, vibrates with the overtones of complex motives and moral problems. To put it shortly: Mr Harding, when facing up to the challenge of John Bold, tells himself on searching his conscience that he is in the wrong, and being the dear lovable honest man he is he resigns from the legal battle. John Bold, the prime fermentor of the local storm, and deliberately made by Trollope a somewhat unsympathetic character, in pursuing his ideals and what he believes to be the cause of justice, knows he is in the right. But he is in love with Mr Harding's daughter and realizes he will lose her if he goes on with his legal battle against her father. Thus both the man in the wrong and the man in the right voluntarily forfeit their cause, and the reader, if he is at all discerning, finds himself in the position of pull devil pull baker, sympathizing with the unsympathetic and sympathetic character equally. By this means Trollope gives us in this merely local storm a microcosm of the human world and its complex moral issues. *The Warden*, in fact, is a warning signal of the greater novels yet to come: Trollope is never simple.

In conclusion. *The Warden* is not only a fine novel in its own right: it is important as containing within it the seed of greater stuff to come in the form of its sequels — *Barchester Towers, Doctor Thorne, The Small House at Allington* and *The Last Chronicle of Barset*. One could not better salute it than by repeating Schumann's famous greeting to Chopin's first published opus — 'Hats off, gentlemen, a genius!'

Despite this it is not really surprising that so simple and quiet a tale made little impression on first appearance. Such novels rarely do make a stir. Only 700 copies were sold in four years, and all its author received from Longmans on publication in 1855 was a cheque for £9-odd and one for £10.15s.1d. a year later. 'Stone-breaking would have done better' Trollope recorded sardonically in his *Autobiography*.

BARCHESTER TOWERS

Any would-be reviewer must approach this novel ('written mainly in railway carriages')*
with trepidation. It has become for posterity much as *Pride and Prejudice, David
Copperfield* and *Monte Cristo* for Jane Austen, Dickens and Dumas — viz. if not their
greatest novel certainly their most perennially popular one, the one 'to be read'. While we
may quarrel with posterity's verdict at least as regards Jane Austen, we can surely agree
that as the novels to introduce their authors to new readers they cannot be bettered.

The very title is for once an inspired one — a judgement one can hardly pass on many
of the others, for Trollope was quite unadept at giving titles. In the shadow of the
cathedral its clerics live their lives, carry out their duties, indulge in their petty squabbles
and snobberies, pursue their ambitions, cling to their little cliques and ostracize the rest.
A world in microcosm. The novel is fuller, richer and more varied than *The Warden*
which, good as it is, now that we know this one, can seem only like a prelude to it or an
overture to an opera. We live not only with Mr Harding, Dr Grantly and Eleanor Bold,
whom we already know, but make the acquaintance of the redoubtable Mrs Proudie
whose gigantic shadow obscures her husband, the new Bishop of Barchester; of the
unforgettable Mr Slope, the bishop's chaplain; meet Dr Arabin, the Stanhopes, the
Thornes and the Quiverfuls. Rich company indeed! No other novel is more filled with
characters as real and as ordinary as those in everyday life, and yet so fascinating, so
entertaining that we cannot put the book down. With it Trollope created not only people
but a mythical cathedral city and county. Barchester and Barsetshire join the Lorna
Doone country, the Hardy country, the Brontë country, the Catalans and the Château
d'If in being given 'a local habitation and a name.' But whereas the others really exist and
are visited by thousands yearly, Trollope's country is no more than a figment of his
mind. Yet maps have been made of it and serious arguments entered into by devotees as
to which city should have the honour of being the original and as to the true topography
of Puddingdale, St Ewolds, Plumstead Episcopi, Silverbridge and other parishes round
about, and who will not be convinced that Barsetshire and its inhabitants never existed.

The opening chapter, unlike so many of Trollope's, is one of the finest in fiction,
terse, dramatically satisfying and gets the story off to a flying start. The old bishop of
Barchester is dying; long live the new bishop! Ah, but who is to be the new bishop? Dr
Grantly, torn between grief at the loss of his father and the hope of being called to fill his
place, is at one moment on his knees praying and the next pushing the reluctant and
slightly scandalized Mr Harding into sending telegrams to a certain influential
government VIP. The whole character of the man is embodied here. But all is in vain.
The government falls and with it the VIP on whom Dr Grantly could count for support,
and the unknown Dr Proudie is made bishop. The first shot in the internecine war is
fired. The community soon discovers that their new bishop wears petticoats. Mrs
Proudie! With what joy we welcome the heavy solidity, the devouring propensities, even
the bigoted Sabbatarianism of this she-dragon. She is one of the outstanding examples

---

*Autobiography

which exemplify the difference between life and art. When we are moved to our depths by the sheer tragic power of works like *King Lear, Wuthering Heights* or *Die Winterreise*, those depths are not of despair; rather we are conscious of a sense of catharsis generated by the sheer artistic power of such works. Similarly with characters in a play or novel. In real life Miss Bates would be a loquacious mindless bore we would go miles out of our way to avoid; but such is Jane Austen's art that our eyes light up at her entry on to the scene. Similarly Mrs Proudie would be an intolerable ogress no one would wish to know: in the novel her bouts of strength with her husband and Mr Slope give us a salty tang of sheer delight.

In Obadiah Slope we are reminded of Uriah Heep. Both have the same repulsive oiliness and general aroma of redness about them. But there all comparison ends. The whole difference between Trollope and Dickens is contained in the two creations. We are given no analysis of Heep to explain his inveterate fawning "umbleness'. We have to accept him on Dickens's terms as the ready-made stock villain of the piece to be knocked down and triumphed over by (of all the unlikely people) Mr Micawber. He is a cardboard figure, all black and flat with no redeeming features at all. Now if Trollope had invented him we should have been given another side to his nature. For example, he loves Agnes Wickfield. Now there is no reason on earth why such a man, black as he is painted, should not be really and honestly and decently in love and in his love reveal a better side to his character. And I have no doubt but that in Trollope's hands we should have been shown this other aspect of Heep who would then become a figure in the round, not flat; grey perhaps, but not all black, a human being, not just a caricature of one. Generalizing, one may say that Dickens's characters, while more vivid in outline than Trollope's, are soft in the middle. Trollope's, on the contrary, though they may not be so memorable in outline, are human all through. Which is precisely how Mr Slope is made to appear. Uriah Heep, as he pursues his nefarious schemes, has no pangs of conscience, whereas Mr Slope, when he is caught in the toils by Madeline Neroni's sexual appeal on the one hand and by Eleanor Bold's £1,200 a year on the other, is full of misgivings. So, as he rides slowly along, 'very meditative', Trollope gives us this:

> And here the author must beg it to be remembered that Mr. Slope was not in all things a bad man. His motives, like those of most men, were mixed; and though his conduct was generally very different from that which we would wish to praise, it was actuated perhaps as often as that of the majority of the world by a desire to do his duty. He believed in the religion which he taught, harsh, unpalatable, uncharitable as that religion was. He believed those whom he wished to get under his hoof, the Grantlys and Gwynnes of the church, to be the enemies of that religion. He believed himself to be a pillar of strength, destined to do great things; and with that subtle, selfish, ambiguous sophistry to which the minds of all men are so subject, he had taught himself to think that in doing much for the promotion of his own interests he was doing much also for the promotion of religion. But Mr. Slope had never been an immoral man. Indeed, he had resisted temptations to immorality with a strength of purpose that was creditable to him. He had early in life devoted himself to works which were not compatible with the ordinary pleasures of youth, and he had abandoned such pleasures not without a struggle. It must therefore be conceived that he did not admit to himself that he warmly admired the beauty of a married woman without heartfelt stings of conscience; and to pacify that conscience, he had to teach himself that the nature of his admiration was innocent.
>
> And thus he rode along meditative and ill at ease. His conscience had not a word to say against his choosing the widow and her fortune. That he looked upon as a godly work rather

than otherwise; as a deed which, if carried through, would redound to his credit as a Christian. On that side lay no future remorse, no conduct which he might probably have to forget, no inward stings. If it should turn out to be really the fact that Mrs. Bold had twelve hundred a year at her own disposal, Mr. Slope would rather look upon it as a duty which he owed his religion to make himself the master of the wife and the money; as a duty too, in which some amount of self-sacrifice would be necessary. He would have to give up his friendship with the signora, his resistance to Mr. Harding, his antipathy — no, he found on mature self-examination, that he could not bring himself to give up his antipathy to Dr. Grantly. He would marry the lady as the enemy of her brother-in-law if such an arrangement suited her; if not, she must look elsewhere for a husband.

And when he decides to oppose Mrs Proudie and, in order to curry favour with the affluent widow, to manoeuvre her father back into his former position as warden, Trollope puts his case with admirable force and conciseness.

Moreover, to give Mr. Slope due credit, he was actuated by greater motives even than these. He wanted a wife, and he wanted money, but he wanted power more than either. He had fully realised the fact that he must come to blows with Mrs. Proudie. He had no desire to remain in Barchester as her chaplain. Sooner than do so, he would risk the loss of his whole connection with the diocese. What! was he to feel within him the possession of no ordinary talents; was he to know himself to be courageous, firm, and, in matters where his conscience did not interfere, unscrupulous; and yet be contented to be the working factotum of a woman-prelate? Mr. Slope had higher ideas of his own destiny. Either he or Mrs. Proudie must go to the wall; and now had come the time when he would try which it should be.

With one exception the rest of the families — the Thornes, the Quiverfuls, — merge into the scene like Cotswold stone in Somerset. One cannot pass over the poverty-stricken Quiverfuls with their rabbit warren of a family. Only a great novelist could have given us that desperate journey by Mrs Q to the palace to beard the terrifying Mrs Proudie in her den and demand justice for her poor inoffensive husband and 'sacrificing her last half-crown to the avarice of Mrs Proudie's metropolitan sesquipedalian serving man'; or that delightful domestic touch when, with victory over the scheming Slope made certain and Quiverful knows that — thanks to his wife's courage and Mrs Proudie's determination — he is really to be given the wardenship, 'the two, unmindful of the kitchen apron, the greasy fingers, and the adherent Irish stew, threw themselves warmly into each other's arms.'

The exception to which I referred is the Stanhopes. Where and how, one asks oneself, was Trollope inspired to create them? From sheer inspiration they all exist. They stand out from the decorous clerical atmosphere like beings from another planet, incongruous in the Barchester society as an excrescence on some otherwise decorous tree. Reading of their doings, overhearing their talk, I am invariably made to think of their creator as an inspired chef who, in the midst of his routine efforts is suddenly seized by an overpowering urge to try something different, to introduce an outrageously pungent seasoning into his well-attested routine concoction — with stunning results. Such are the Stanhopes, a nineteenth century more genteel and intelligent version of our own Bright Young Things, hippies, parasites and lay-abouts who, indifferent to public opinion, are completely without social consciousness or conscience, and have no intention of adding their quota to society by working for a living. What a family! — one can't help thinking. There is Dr Vesey Stanhope, the easy-going father who, although ostensibly a churchman, has let his family grow up without any discipline or moral tone and now reaps the fruit of his conduct. There is his wife, the *far niente* of whose long residence in Italy has demoralized her and 'entered into her very soul, and brought her to regard a state of inactivity as the only earthly good.' Next, Charlotte, the eldest and unmarried, the manager of the family much as the manager of a football team, and unscrupulous (as witness her plot to lure Eleanor into the family via marriage with her brother.) Ethelbert ('Bertie'), the said brother, the youngest and only boy, with his outrageous dress, silky beard and bright blue eyes, is a perfect specimen of the indestructible, easy-going, couldn't-care-less artistic parasite who has no intention of making any effort to earn his keep but lives from day to day on his debts and paternal expectations. And lastly there is the unique and incomparable Madeline, alias Madame Neroni, alias the Signora, the crippled cast-off of an Italian adventurer. Although the second in age after Charlotte I have left her to the last because she is the gem of the Stanhope collection. With her we have, memorably, the one and only deliberately created, unashamedly admitted sexy woman of English nineteenth century fiction.* Fabulously beautiful and highly intelligent, but unable to get about on account of her twisted leg and so to enjoy the normal pleasures of a woman's life, she devotes her whole attention to adorning herself and deliberately making herself fascinating to the male sex and distasteful to the female as if to revenge herself for the cruel ill-usage she had endured from her husband (the marriage, Trollope hints, was a shot-gun one). Trollope goes to town with his description of her.

Madame Neroni, though forced to give up all motion in the world, had no intention whatever of giving up the world itself. The beauty of her face was uninjured, and that beauty was of a peculiar kind. Her copious rich brown hair was worn in Grecian *bandeaux* round her head, displaying as much as possible of her forehead and cheeks. Her forehead, though rather low, was very beautiful from its perfect contour and pearly whiteness. Her eyes were long and large, and marvellously bright; might I venture to say, bright as Lucifer's, I should perhaps best express the depth of their brilliancy. They were dreadful eyes to look at, such as would absolutely deter any man of quiet mind and easy spirit from attempting a passage of arms with such foes. There was talent in them, and the fire of passion and the play of wit, but there was no love. Cruelty was there instead, and courage, a desire of masterhood, cunning, and a wish for mischief. And yet, as eyes, they were very beautiful. The eyelashes were long and perfect, and the long steady unabashed gaze, with which she would look into the face of her admirer, fascinated while it frightened him. She was a basilisk from whom an ardent lover of beauty could make no escape. Her nose and mouth and teeth and chin and neck and bust were perfect, much more so at twenty-eight than they had been at eighteen. What wonder that with such charms still glowing in her face, and with such deformity destroying her figure, she should resolve to be seen, but only to be seen reclining on a sofa.

---

* In making this claim for Madeline I am not forgetting Hetty Sorrel who is obviously what we today would call a sex-kitten. But while she fits the designation perfectly, as her sensual appeal to and seduction by Arthur Donnithorne show, George Eliot never does more than give ingenuous mealy-mouthed epithets to describe her such as 'kitten-like', 'pretty', 'sweet', and in one passage sums up her physical charms (with the contemptuous irony of the physically unattractive intellectual woman) with 'the dear, young, round, soft, flexible thing!' And any normal naughty sexual thoughts she might have are never so much as hinted at.

No wonder Longman's reader took exception to the Stanhope episodes, considered the novel 'inferior to *The Warden*', and while admitting that 'there are parts of it that I would be disposed to place on a level with the best morsels of contemporary novelists, there are others — and unfortunately these predominate — the vulgarity and exaggeration of which, if they do not unfit them for publication, are at least likely to be repulsive to readers.' Such were the puerile decencies and proprieties of nineteenth century publishers and their readers that they tried to persuade Trollope to excise the whole of the Stanhope incidents, and even objected to Mrs Proudie. Thank God he stuck to his guns, for they constitute the most piquant flavours of his dish. The potent sexuality of the mysterious signora brings even the clerics buzzing round her — even the ascetic Dr Arabin. The famous sofa on which she is condemned to lie and to be carried round on and on which she displays her allure is the cause of one of the funniest scenes in fiction when it becomes the means of tearing Mrs Proudie's regalia to such a devastating extent that the infuriated lady has to storm from the room and rerobe herself. Her tragi-comic "Unhand it, sir!" made to the innocent Bertie is equalled only by Lady Bracknell's later "A handbag!"

It was inevitable that her foremost victim should be Mr Slope. Dr Proudie's chaplain is, under his greasy pious exterior, a full-blooded normally sensual man, and her overt attractions had titillated his sexual desire. Even though he knows she has a hypothetical husband somewhere, that he is doing wrong to himself and his cloth in paying court to her, and despite his conscience and Mrs Proudie's stern warnings, he cannot stay away from her. But unlike the signora's creator, Mr Slope does not fully understand her character.

> The signora was subdued by no passion. Her time for love was gone. She had lived out her heart, such heart as she had ever had, in her early years, at an age when Mr. Slope was thinking of the second book of Euclid and his unpaid bill at the buttery hatch. In age the lady was younger than the gentleman; but in feelings, in knowledge of the affairs of love, in intrigue, he was immeasurably her junior. It was necessary to her to have some man at her feet. It was the one customary excitement of her life. She delighted in the exercise of power which this gave her; it was now nearly the only food for her ambition; she would boast to her sister that she could make a fool of any man, and the sister, as little imbued with feminine delicacy as herself, good naturedly, thought it but fair that such amusement should be afforded to a poor invalid who was debarred from the ordinary pleasures of life.
>
> Mr. Slope was madly in love, but hardly knew it. The signora spitted him, as a boy does a cockchafer on a cork, that she might enjoy the energetic agony of his gyrations. And she knew very well what she was doing.

Also he does not know she has guessed that he is equally after the widow Bold and her money and plans to make him pay for his audacity by publicly humiliating him. Chapter 27, 'A Love Scene', describing Mr Slope's wooing, is enough to make any novel a classic.

Trollope shows us that he has reached maturity as a novelist not only by superb characterization but by sheer narrative skill as well. There is no creaking in this machinery. The episodes dovetail as in a masterly Sheraton piece of furniture. Slope visits Harding and puts the bishop's offer in such a way that he can only refuse it; visits Eleanor in order to ingratiate himself with her; visits Quiverful off his own bat and all but promises him the wardenship, then, with the widow's comfortable income in mind, persuades the bishop to give it to Harding after all. But he reckons without Mrs Proudie, who brings about his fall from grace. It is technical perfection all the way.

A more serious note is struck with the introduction of Dr Francis Arabin. Some of the more impatient readers may fancy that chapter 20 slows the action unnecessarily and is just another of Trollope's laborious background building attempts. Without denying that it might have been cut slightly to good effect, the chapter is evidence of Trollope's interest in the intellectual problems of his day over and above his genius as a story teller and portrayer of character. Indeed it seems to me that he is the only Victorian novelist, George Eliot, Kingsley and Elizabeth Gaskell apart, who raises any of the more important issues of sociology such as, for example, religion, politics, bastardy, adultery, crime, to name only a few. Admittedly from an artistic point of view a good novel which avoids such issues is to be preferred to an indifferent one which includes them. The novels of Jane Austen, *Wuthering Heights* and *Wives and Daughters*, for example, are far greater works of art than, say, *Mary Barton, Ruth, Yeast* or *Oliver Twist;* and George Eliot is a living warning against being so intellectual and moralistic, learned and didactic as to be prosy and sermonizing and allowing her very intelligence to obstruct and deviate tediously from a plain tale. Nevertheless there is a happy medium, and Trollope achieves this as no other novelist does. The chapter in question is just such an example. From it we learn how thoroughly he has considered religious belief and its various doctrines, and how they can affect a young man's character and future way of life. Newman is mentioned, and the Oxford Tractarian movement which shook the Establishment to its foundations, and via Arabin that 'agony of doubt' sown in the minds of his followers when Newman embraced Catholicism. Should he — Arabin — follow his leader? His struggle is told simply and persuasively; and we may smile as we read Trollope's verdict — the verdict of a thoroughly British individualist. 'It was from the poor curate of a small Cornish parish that he first learnt to know that the highest laws for the governance of a Christian's duty must act from within and not from without; that no man can become a serviceable servant solely by obedience to written edicts; and that the safety he was about to seek within the gates of Rome was no other than the selfish freedom from personal danger which the bad soldier attempts to gain who counterfeits illness on the eve of battle.' Catholics may, and no doubt will, deny this, but to the typical British nonconformist spirit it forms the nub of his repulsion of 'the scarlet woman'.

Then Trollope shows that Arabin's religious convictions helped to shape his attitude (a typically Victorian one) to women, and, while making him diffident and completely ignorant of feminine nature, make him also begin to think, as he sees the marital happiness and family life of the archdeacon, that something might be missing from his life. The reader can only regret that when he does eventually realize he is in love it should be with Eleanor Bold — 'my heroine' as Trollope more than once refers to her. A more irritating heroine has surely never been given us, even by Dickens, Thackeray or Hardy. My God! the modern reader must be driven to exclaiming, how these Victorian women are given to weeping! There is scarcely a scene in which she is involved but she dissolves into floods of tears. She weeps when she is sad or annoyed (and she is mostly both) and she weeps when she is happy. I have been driven to counting the occasions when she lets the flood gates open, and they amount to no less than twelve times. She weeps twice in *The Warden* and ten times in *Barchester Towers*. She weeps when Mr Slope, in their first interview, refers to 'her early sorrow' of widowhood; she weeps when the same gentleman advises her to see the bishop herself in order to plead for her father's reinstatement as warden to the hospital; she 'sobbed as though her heart would break' when Dr Grantly warns her against the enticements of Mr Slope; weeps when her father confesses he has suspected her of a preference for that oily character; 'could not abstain from bursting into tears' after she had slapped the same gentleman's face when he had the audacity to propose to her; 'burst out into a flood of tears' when she learns from Bertie Stanhope of his sister Charlotte's secret plan to get him to marry her; weeps in front of her sister-in-law when recounting her troubles and wakes her infant merely to hug him in order to find some comfort; weeps when Mr Arabin makes his clumsy apology to her; and finally, 'she wept with grief and wept with joy' when she learns that her husband-to-be has been made the new dean in preference to her father. In fact the pages are soggy with her facile tears.

Yet Trollope obviously loved his 'heroine', describes her as 'a lady at any rate past the wishy-washy bread-and-butter period of life' and insists that she is both beautiful and intelligent. But his claim is simply not credible, and we can only wonder that so intellectual and ascetic a man as Arabin should fall in love with her. No doubt the Victorians, who revelled in this sort of thing, saw in her weepings the sign of a tender heart; but our own more hard-bitten age can only wish Trollope (along with Dickens, Thackeray and his contemporaries generally) had been more parsimonious with the emotional floodgates. And though we can forgive her much for slapping Mr Slope's face, we cannot but feel she is not really worthy of that marvellous contretemps at the Ullathorne banquet where she finds herself hedged in by Mr Slope, Mr Arabin and Bertie Stanhope, and Miss Thorne introduces the hostile Slope and Arabin to each other over her, and when 'the two gentlemen bowed stiffly to each other across the lady whom they both intended to marry, while the other gentleman who also intended to marry her stood behind, watching them.'

There are other minor blots. We encounter the puerile trick, against which Henry James, an admirer of Trollope, so rightly protested, of underlining the trade or profession of some of the characters by giving them schoolboy-punning names like Subsoil and Greenacres for farmers, Rerechild, Bumpwell and Fillgrave for doctors, Slow and Bideawhile for solicitors. And the celebrated consultant Sir Omicrom Pie is always popping in and out.

Then we have the Victorian intrusions and finger-shaking of the author. These can usually be side-stepped comfortably, but in this novel there are two which are difficult to swallow. Giving us Eleanor Bold's thoughts on the two men with whom she is on particularly friendly terms — viz. Mr Arabin and Bertie Stanhope — Trollope writes:

> Alas for the memory of poor John Bold! Eleanor was not in love with Bertie Stanhope, nor was she in love with Mr. Arabin. But her devotion to her late husband was fast fading when she could revolve in her mind, over the cradle of his infant, the faults and failings of other aspirants to her favour. Will anyone blame my heroine for this? Let him or her rather thank God for all His goodness, for His mercy endureth for ever.

One can only blink, gulp, writhe and pass quickly on.

Just as bad, if not worse, is the lengthy aside (chapter 15) in which Trollope expatiates on his code of literary ethics and delivers protest against the deliberate attempts of novelists to keep their readers in suspense — a protest he was to repeat in *Dr.*

Wortle's School (q.v.). This revulsion against all mystery and suspense, which he regarded as factitious, was a passion with him. With him, to lay a false trail was the work of a cheap-jack. I suspect that almost one hundred per cent of today's readers, nurtured on thrillers of one kind or another, will disagree, and violently disagree, with this Trollopian theory. If we confine his fulminations to the cheap sensational ultra-romantic novelettes of his own time, we may go along with him. But when it comes to not even permitting the reader to be left in doubt as to the outcome of a woman's having more than one possible lover, one can only feel a keen sense of disappointment and a wish to have been innocently cheated. This is merely human nature, and no less a classic than Jane Austen understood this and played on it deliberately and with unsurpassed skill. Suppose she had shared Trollope's opinion in this and warned the reader in advance not to be alarmed: that Wickham would not hoodwink Elizabeth Bennet into marrying him and throwing over Darcy, nor Anne Elliot fall for the wiles of her cousin, nor the charms of Mrs Clay seduce Sir Walter, how cheated the reader would feel. A little dangling is a useful thing! But the adamantine Anthony refuses to budge and concludes his literary sermon and chapter with: 'I would not for the value of this chapter have it believed by a single reader that my Eleanor could bring herself to marry Mr. Slope, or that she should be sacrificed to a Bertie Stanhope. But among the good folk of Barchester many believed both the one and the other.' Readers may be forgiven if they mentally tell the shade of Anthony that they would prefer to have been left in the same state of mind as 'the good folk of Barchester.'

But these blemishes are small enough when placed alongside the splendid whole. And rather than leave any reader or would-be reader of the novel in a trough of criticism, let me conclude by drawing his or her attention to that superb chapter XXX entitled 'Another Love Scene'. It concerns Eleanor and Mr Arabin.

Mr. Arabin had heard from his friend of the probability of Eleanor's marriage with Mr. Slope with amazement, but not with incredulity. It has been said that he was not in love with Eleanor, and up to this period this certainly had been true. But as soon as he heard that she loved someone else, he began to be very fond of her himself. He did not make up his mind that he wished to have her for his wife . . . . . . but he experienced an inward indefinable feeling of deep regret, a gnawing sorrow, an unconquerable depression of spirits, and also a species of self-abasement that he — he Mr. Arabin — had not done something to prevent that other he, that vile he, whom he so thoroughly despised, from carrying off this sweet prize.

This is a subtle analysis of a man's heart, be he clergyman or layman. Trollope then goes on to show us his profound understanding of women's hearts as well. Arabin and Eleanor are alone together in the room. She is angry with him for believing she could ever fall for Slope and for believing Dr Grantly's accusations. After some trite conversation Arabin plucks up courage to try to explain and apologize; but being intellectual and a bachelor of forty with no experience of women, he does it so clumsily that he succeeds only in making matters worse and so offends her in his self-defence that she jumps up from her chair, leaves him in anger and goes out into the garden. Desperate to placate her, win her good will and let her know of his love for her, he follows her.

But 'understanding little of the nature of a woman's feelings' he proceeds so awkwardly and self-consciously that, although longing to forgive him in spite of her anger, she is unable to do so. Having made her understand that he thinks more of her than of any other woman and so softened her towards him, he makes a dreadful masculine blunder.

Poor Mr. Arabin! It would not come out of him, that deep true love of his. He could not bring himself to utter it in plain language that would require and demand an answer. He knew not how to say to the woman by his side, 'Since the fact is that you do not love that other man, that you are not to be his wife, can you love me, will you be my wife?' These were the words which were in his heart, but with all his sighs he could not draw them to his lips. He would have given anything, everything for power to ask this simple question; but glib as was his tongue in pulpits and on platforms, now he could not find a word wherewith to express the plain wish of his heart.

And yet Eleanor understood him as thoroughly as though he had declared his passion with all the elegant fluency of a practised Lothario. With a woman's instinct she followed every bend of his mind, as he spoke of the pleasantness of Plumstead and the stones of Oxford, as he alluded to the safety of the Romish priest and the hidden perils of temptation. She knew that it all meant love. She knew that this man at her side, this accomplished scholar, this practised orator, this great polemical combatant, was striving and striving in vain to tell her that his heart was no longer his own.

She knew this, and felt a sort of joy in knowing it; and yet she would not come to his aid. He had offended her deeply, had treated her unworthily, the more unworthily seeing that he had learnt to love her, and Eleanor could not bring herself to abandon her revenge. She did not ask herself whether or no she would ultimately accept his love. She did not even acknowledge to herself that she now perceived it with pleasure. At the present moment it did not touch her heart; it merely appeased her pride and flattered her vanity. Mr. Arabin had dared to associate her name with that of Mr. Slope, and now her spirit was soothed by finding that he would fain associate it with his own. And so she walked on beside him inhaling incense, but giving out no sweetness in return.

'Answer me this,' said Mr. Arabin, stopping suddenly in his walk, and stepping forward so that he faced his companion. 'Answer me this one question. You do not love Mr. Slope? you do not intend to be his wife?'

Mr. Arabin certainly did not go the right way to win such a woman as Eleanor Bold. Just as her wrath was evaporating, as it was disappearing before the true warmth of his untold love, he re-kindled it by a most useless repetition of his original sin. Had he known what he was about he should never have mentioned Mr. Slope's name before Eleanor Bold, till he had made her all his own. Then, and not till then, he might have talked of Mr. Slope with as much triumph as he chose.

'I shall answer no such question,' said she; 'and what is more, I must tell you that nothing can justify your asking it. Good morning!'

And so saying she stepped proudly across the lawn, and passing through the drawing-room window joined her father and sister at lunch in the dining-room. Half an hour afterwards she was in the carriage, and so she left Plumstead without again seeing Mr. Arabin.

His walk was long and sad among the sombre trees that overshadowed the churchyard. He left the archdeacon's grounds that he might escape attention, and sauntered among the green hillocks under which lay at rest so many of the once loving swains and forgotten beauties of Plumstead. To his ears Eleanor's last words sounded like a knell never to be reversed. He could not comprehend that she might be angry with him, indignant with him, remorseless with him, and yet love him. He could not make up his mind whether or no Mr. Slope was in truth a favoured rival. If not, why should she not have answered his question?

Poor Mr. Arabin — untaught, illiterate, boorish, ignorant man! That at forty years of age you should know so little of the workings of a woman's heart!

Such a chapter is only one of the many reaons why *Barchester Towers*, 'warts and all', remains one of the outstanding perennial classics of English fiction.

Not only so, but to close on a commercial note which certainly does not go against the Trollopian grain, with the novel Trollope established himself both with critics and public as a new novelist to be reckoned with, and from now on he was in a position to demand good solid payment from his publishers.

THE THREE CLERKS
and
THE STRUGGLES OF BROWN, JONES AND ROBINSON

It is difficult to believe that after fulfilling himself so completely with *Barchester Towers*, Trollope should proceed to turn out these two dismal failures.

The former novel, one might have supposed, being autobiographical in that under the name of Charles Tudor it relates something of his own early life and emotions as a drudge in the General Post Office, would be full of youthful charm, with amusing incidents and portraits of existence in the Civil Service. But Trollope altogether lacked that bonhomie, that racy touch and scapegrace element which make, for example, Dumas's account in his *Mémoires* of his brief career as a clerk in the Paris of the 1820s such amusing reading. Indeed the whole subject, at least as treated by Trollope, strikes the reader as being utterly unsuitable material for fiction and to make him wish that he had taken Dumas's line and introduced the whole episode as frank memorabilia in his *Autobiography*. It might have leavened that dull, prosy, close-fisted, all too money-conscious piece of reminiscence. As fiction it can only be placed among his worst failures. The writing is pedestrian and the characterization insipid and full of improbabilities. We simply cannot believe, for example, that the competent Alaric Tudor could have been so corrupt and inept. And the author's attempts at satire in the characters of Sir Gregory Hardlines and Sir Warwick Westend (the facetious nomenclature alone makes one wince) are unbelievably banal. Then in Katie Woodward we have the first of the several Trollopian young women who, jilted by their fiancés, feel they must henceforth be dedicated to virginity. While making full allowance for the inhuman ostracism they had to endure from the social mores of their time in such circumstances, one tends to lose patience with the feebleness of character of the women who meekly accept their situation. It is true that at his greatest Trollope was able to make a true heroine out of the circumstance — witness Lily Dale and Alice Vavasor — but his worst can only provide us with the present Katie and the future Emily Wharton. This quasi-obsession is difficult to explain in a novelist whose psychological insight and unsurpassed knowledge of young women and youthful love are in general so uncannily right.

The second novel is even worse; and arguably with *The Two Heroines of Plumplington* and *The Fixed Period* the most dismal failure of all his works. And yet, blatantly revealing his critical obtuseness, he could write of it: 'It was meant to be funny, was full of slang, and was intended as a satire on the ways of the trade. I still think there is some good fun in it, but I have heard no one else express such an opinion . . . . '

Apparently Trollope intended it as a skit on the new 'up-to-date' methods of advertising following hard on the much publicized Great Exhibition of 1852, and it may have been suggested by Richard Doyle's *Foreign Tours of Messrs. Brown, Jones and Robinson* published two years earlier.

Unfortunately, while he had a lively sense of fun under his bearded and rather unprepossessing exterior, Trollope had no talent whatever for literary humour. His attempts at it almost ruined *Can You Forgive Her?* and spoilt other novels, and here his jejune efforts at facetiousness make the book unreadable.

Begun in 1857 it was not finished until three years later and — incredibly — immediately on his completion of *Orley Farm* — one of his best novels. It was accepted reluctantly by the editor of *Cornhill*, and on appearance universally damned. For once contemporary opinion was right. Yet in the face of this Trollope persuaded Smith, Elder to publish it in one volume in 1870, and got £600 for it. He was indeed right when he wrote of it in his *Autobiography*: 'I think it was the hardest bargain I ever sold to a publisher.'

And it may as well be confessed here and the reader warned, that such lapses from grace went on occurring all through Trollope's career. At any time a masterpiece could be preceded or followed by a novel that is third-rate; so that it is virtually impossible to tell (unlike Dickens in this) whether masterpiece or failure came early or late in his vast creative output. *Hard Times*, for example, could only have come late, and *Pickwick Papers* early with Dickens; whereas — to take examples at random — *He Knew He Was Right* or *Marion Fay* might have been written at any time in Trollope's career.

Like Thackeray's *The Virginians* and Charlotte Brontë's *The Professor*, these two novels of Trollope can only be described as expendable. Yet unbelievably, discussing *The Three Clerks* in his *Autobiography*, with *The Warden* and *Barchester Towers* behind him Trollope could write: 'It was certainly the best novel I had yet written.' and goes on to declare his belief that he considered it superior to *Doctor Thorne*. Authors are notoriously lacking in self-criticism, but of them all, from this aspect at any rate, Trollope must undoubtedly take first place.

DOCTOR THORNE

Bearing in mind my last words on the two previous novels, one need not be surprised to find the splendid *Doctor Thorne* being written immediately after the immature, derivative *The Three Clerks*. For Sadleir the novel is one of the most perfect Trollope ever wrote, and a 'rave'.* I cannot quite go all the way with him here although I admit it must be given a place among his best dozen. Certainly the plot, supplied by Anthony's brother Tom, is a gift for any novelist and opens up endless possibilities. Let us begin by considering the story from this aspect.

Mary Thorne, the heroine, is a bastard child of Doctor Thorne's elder brother Henry and Mary, the sister of Roger Scatcherd, a stone mason. In revenge for the seduction of his sister Scatcherd kills her seducer and is imprisoned for manslaughter. After the birth of the child Mary is forgiven by her former lover and he takes her away to America as his wife to start a new life there. But he refuses to accept her child, who is left behind in the care of Doctor Thomas Thorne, Henry's younger brother and a bachelor. When Scatcherd eventually comes out of prison he is kept in ignorance of these events, and for all he knows the child has vanished for good, and the young ward in the doctor's care is simply a 'niece' he has chosen to adopt.

Now comes the strange reversal of fate. The uncouth, hard-working, hard-drinking stone mason becomes a railroad builder and contractor and makes a fortune. The Greshams of Greshamsbury, once the proud and wealthy owners of Gresham Park and mansion, through the foolish conduct of the present squire, John Newbold Gresham, lose nearly all their money, and the estate becomes mortgaged up to the hilt, with the result that his son and heir, young Frank, has precious little birthright to look forward to when his father dies. His mother, therefore, the haughty, snobbish, purse-proud, rank-conscious Lady Arabella, who is related to the even more haughty, snobbish, purse-proud, rank-conscious Courcy Castle lot, parrots incessantly to him that it is up to him to retrieve the family fortunes and to *marry money*. It is her watchword, her slogan, her bible. He must either marry money or be ruined. Unfortunately for her Frank has already lost his heart to Mary Thorne, Doctor Thorne's 'adopted niece,' who has no money at all and whose birth is shrouded in suspiciously shameful anonymity.

Such is the scene when the curtain goes up, and to make a résumé of the story, what happens is that in his will Roger Scatcherd, failing an heir, leaves most of his vast fortune to 'his sister Mary's eldest child,' whoever and wherever he or she may be. This, as the reader is aware, is no other than Mary Thorne, and the impoverished Greshams' fortunes are saved by the very girl whom Lady Arabella has hounded and rejected and made unhappy. It is Nemesis with a vengeance, but a kind one: sheer irony, in fact.

Let us now look and see how Trollope handles the plot. The 'warts' are more prominent than in *The Warden* and *Barchester Towers*. The first chapter is tedious in the extreme with its prosily detailed account of the Gresham family and antecedents plus a lengthy description of their estate that is flat and leaves no impression on the mind; and

---

*M. Sadleir; *Trollope; A Commentary* (1922)

the second chapter, dealing with the Thornes, is no better. To add insult to injury in the reader's mind, Trollope confesses that he realizes this himself, and in a spasm of critical awareness admits in the first paragraph of the second chapter: 'I quite feel that an apology is due for beginning a novel with two long dull chapters full of description . . . ' But then he tries weakly to defend himself by saying in so many words that he cannot believe thoroughly in his characters unless and until he has explored fully their backgrounds, and he concludes: 'This is unartistic on my part, and shows want of imagination as well as want of skill . . . . ' He knows, yet he persists! It is a thousand pities that Chapman & Hall's reader did not demand some abridgment as a price of publication and, if Trollope insisted he didn't know how to do it, order him a course of Jane Austen, who could have done it twice as effectively in half the space.

There are later faults too, all characteristically Trollopian in that they consist of too much detail and spinning out, and unnecessary episodes. Roger Scatcherd's son, Louis, is, one feels, totally unnecessary, and one asks why bring him in at all merely to let him die of delirium tremens very conveniently before he is twenty-five so that Mary can inherit his father's fortune? Why not have left Roger childless and so simplified the story? But no: Trollope can never resist giving another turn to the screw. The three-decker novel must be filled and the publisher and reader given their money's worth. (How much artistic deleteriousness that Victorian monstrosity has to answer for.) Again, the Moffat episodes have no bearing on the story and would seem to be dragged in solely to provide Trollope with those two amusingly feminine letters (1) from Lady Amelia de Courcy to Miss Augusta Gresham in which the former asks the latter for her advice as to the propriety of her marrying the commoner, Mortimer Gazebee, and (2) from Miss Augusta Gresham to Lady Amelia de Courcy in which the former strongly deprecates the proposed match with all the snobbery of rank. After which Trollope wickedly relates how, not long after this correspondence, the Lady Amelia herself is led to the altar by — Mortimer Gazebee! It is a superb attack on (to give the title of chapter 39) 'What the world says about blood', a savage exposure of feminine hypocrisy and aristocratic cant. And then some critics have been known to assert that Trollope has no bite!

He drags in another tilt too which shows him yet again to be ahead of his time in his detestation of that piece of religious cant, especially when perpetrated in public functions, known as 'grace before meat'. It occurs during the first evening of Frank Gresham's stay at Gatherum Castle as the guest of the Duke of Omnium where he has gone much against his will but at the insistence of his mother for the sole purpose of carrying out her command to 'marry money' by trying to hook the wealthy Miss Dunstable. Suddenly, in the midst of the hubbub of guests all talking loudly while inwardly longing to sit down to their host's food and wine, Mr Athill, a parson, is called on to say a grace. Trollope's comments, while they may be a piece of personal digression and as such open to criticism, are splendidly to the point and must have horrified many of his readers. But how honestly right they are!

All these are undoubtedly blots on the craftsmanship of the novel; but if the reader is prepared to overlook them and persevere he will find rich reward for his tolerance and be able to enjoy that constant quality in Trollope which helps to outweigh his defects, namely, the characterization. While I think Sadleir's eulogy of Mary Thorne as his most lovable heroine is somewhat overdone, she is certainly refreshing after Eleanor Bold (she weeps only twice!). Where E.B. would have run out of the room 'in floods of tears',

Mary stands up to the dictatorial Lady Arabella with firmness, dignity and spirit, and wins our hearts. And her refusal at first to take the boyish Frank Gresham's overtures seriously is not, one feels, as one sometimes does in Trollope, done merely to keep the story going, but because she is indeed much more mature than he is and sees him simply as a boy friend she has known most of her life. Her eventual discovery that she does love him as time passes and he shows his determination and single-mindedness in face of his family's opposition is beautifully told. The chapter 'The Donkey Ride' in which he proposes to her for the second time, in its deftness and unusual quiet humour, must be accounted one of the best scenes ever to come from Trollope's fertile pen.

Mary's uncle, the doctor, is too a finely drawn character, blunt and direct and not afraid to speak his mind to the money bags who use him, but kind and thoughtful at the same time.

Another character to win all our sympathy is the wealthy much sought after Miss Dunstable. She knows that all the men who propose to her are after her money, with the result that under her gay laughing exterior she is hard-headed and occasionally bitter and sad. The way in which she deals with Frank Gresham's half-hearted proposal is one of the highlights of the novel and worth quoting. They have been purposely left together by Lady de Courcy in the hope that the heiress to the thousands made by her father with his famous 'Oil of Lebanon' might be well and truly hooked at last. Frank begins his dangerous course by being sentimental.

'Oh, Miss Dunstable! you do not in the least understand what my feelings are.'

'Don't I? Then I hope I never shall. I thought I did. I thought they were the feelings of a good, true-hearted friend; feelings that I could sometimes look back upon with pleasure as being honest when so much that one meets is false. I have become very fond of you, Mr. Gresham, and I should be sorry to think that I did not understand your feelings.'

This was almost worse and worse. Young ladies like Miss Dunstable — for she was still to be numbered in the category of young ladies — do not usually tell young gentlemen that they are very fond of them. To boys and girls they may make such a declaration. Now Frank Gresham regarded himself as one who had already fought his battles, and fought them not without glory; he could not therefore endure to be thus openly told by Miss Dunstable that she was very fond of him.

'Fond of me, Miss Dunstable! I wish you were.'

'So I am — very.'

'You little know how fond I am of you, Miss Dunstable,' and he put out his hand to take hold of hers. She then lifted up her own, and slapped him lightly on the knuckles.

'And what can you have to say to Miss Dunstable that can make it necessary that you should pinch her hand? I tell you fairly, Mr. Gresham, if you make a fool of yourself, I shall come to a conclusion that you are all fools, and that it is hopeless to look out for any one worth caring for.'

Such advice as this, so kindly given, so wisely meant, so clearly intelligible, he should have taken and understood, young as he was. But even yet he did not do so.

'A fool of myself! Yes; I suppose I must be a fool if I have so much regard for Miss Dunstable as to make it painful to me to know that I am to see her no more: a fool: yes, of course I am a fool — a man is always a fool when he loves.'

Miss Dunstable could not pretend to doubt his meaning any longer; and was determined to stop him, let it cost what it would. She now put out her hand, not over white, and, as Frank soon perceived, gifted with a very fair allowance of strength.

'Now, Mr. Gresham,' said she, 'before you go any further you shall listen to me. Will you listen to me for a moment without interrupting me?'

Frank was of course obliged to promise that he would do so.

'You are going — or rather you were going, for I shall stop you — to make to me a profession of love.'

'A profession!' said Frank making a slight unsuccessful effort to get his hand free.

'Yes; a profession — a false profession, Mr. Gresham, — a false profession — a fake profession. Look into your heart — into your heart of hearts. I know you at any rate have a heart; look into it closely. Mr. Gresham, you know you do not love me; not as a man should love the woman whom he swears to love.'

Frank was taken aback. So appealed to he found that he could not any longer say that he did love her. He could only look into her face with all his eyes, and sit there listening to her.

'How is it possible that you should love me? I am Heaven knows how many years your senior. I am neither young nor beautiful, nor have I been brought up as she should be whom you in time will really love and make your wife. I have nothing that should make you love me; but — but, I am rich.'

'It is not that,' said Frank, stoutly, feeling himself imperatively called upon to utter something in his own defence.

'Ah, Mr. Gresham, I fear it is that. For what other reason can you have laid your plans to talk in this way to such a woman as I am?'

'I have laid no plans,' said Frank, now getting his hand to himself. 'At any rate, you wrong me there, Miss Dunstable.'

'I like you so well — nay, love you, if a woman may talk of love in the way of friendship — that if money, money alone would make you happy, you should have it heaped on you. If you want it, Mr. Gresham, you shall have it.'

'I have never thought of your money,' said Frank, surlily.

'But it grieves me,' continued she, 'it does grieve me, to think that you, you, you — so young, so gay, so bright — that you should have looked for it in this way. From others I have taken it just as the wind that whistles;' and now two big slow tears escaped from her eyes, and would have rolled down her rosy cheeks, were it not that she brushed them off with the back of her hand.

'You have utterly mistaken me, Miss Dunstable,' said Frank.

'If I have, I will humbly beg your pardon,' said she. 'But — but — but —'

'You have; indeed you have.'

'How can I have mistaken you? Were you not about to say that you loved me; to talk absolute nonsense; to make me an offer? If you were not, if I have mistaken you indeed, I will beg your pardon.'

Frank had nothing further to say in his own defence. He had not wanted Miss Dunstable's money — that was true; but he could not deny that he had been about to talk that absolute nonsense of which she spoke with so much scorn.

'You would almost make me think that there are none honest in this fashionable world of yours. I well know why Lady de Courcy has had me here: how could I help knowing it? She has been so foolish in her plans that ten times a day she has told her own secret. But I have said to myself twenty times, that if she were crafty, you were honest.'

'And am I dishonest?'

'I have laughed in my sleeve to see how she played her game, and to hear others around playing theirs; all of them thinking that they could get the money of the poor fool who had come at their beck and call; but I was able to laugh at them as long as I thought that I had one true friend to laugh with me. But one cannot laugh with all the world against one.'

'I am not against you, Miss Dunstable.'

'Sell yourself for money! why, if I were a man I would not sell one jot of liberty for mountains of gold. What! tie myself in the heyday of my youth to a person I could never love, for a price! perjure myself, destroy myself — and not only myself, but her also, in order that I might live idly! Oh, heavens! Mr. Gresham! can it be that the words of such a woman as your aunt have sunk so deeply in your heart; have blackened you so foully as to make you think of such vile folly as this? Have you forgotten your soul, your spirit, your man's energy, the treasure of your heart? And you, so young! For shame, Mr. Gresham! for shame — for shame!'

Frank found the task before him by no means an easy one. He had to make Miss Dunstable understand that he had never had the slightest idea of marrying her, and that he had made love to her merely with the object of keeping his hand in for the work as it were; with that object, and the other equally laudable one of interfering with his cousin George.

And yet there was nothing for him but to get through this task as best he might. He was goaded to it by the accusations which Miss Dunstable brought against him; and he began to feel, that though her invectives against him might be bitter when he had told the truth, they could not be so bitter as those she now kept hinting at under her mistaken impression as to his views. He had never had any strong propensity for money-hunting; but now that offence appeared in his eyes abominable, unmanly, and disgusting. Any imputation would be better than that.

'Miss Dunstable, I never for a moment thought of doing what you accuse me of; on my honour, I never did. I have been very foolish — very wrong — idiotic, I believe; but I have never intended that.'

'Then, Mr. Gresham, what did you intend?'

This was rather a difficult question to answer; and Frank was not very quick in attempting it. 'I know you will not forgive me,' he said at last, 'and, indeed, I do not see how you can. I don't know how it came about; but this is certain, Miss Dunstable; I have never for a moment thought about your fortune; that is, thought about it in the way of coveting it.'

'You never thought of making me your wife, then?'

'Never,' said Frank, looking boldly into her face.

'You never intended really to propose to go with me to the altar, and then make yourself rich by one great perjury?'

'Never for a moment,' said he.

'You have never gloated over me as the bird of prey gloats over the poor beast that is soon to become carrion beneath its claws? You have not counted me out as equal to so much land, and calculated on me as a balance at your banker's? Ah, Mr. Gresham,' she continued, seeing that he stared as though struck almost with awe by her strong language; 'you little guess what a woman situated as I am has to suffer.'

'I have behaved badly to you, Miss Dunstable, and I beg your pardon; but I have never thought of your money.'

'Then we will be friends again, Mr. Gresham, won't we? It is so nice to have a friend like you. There, I think I understand it now; you need not tell me.'

'It was half by way of making a fool of my aunt,' said Frank, in an apologetic tone.

'There is merit in that, at any rate,' said Miss Dunstable. 'I understand it all now; you thought to make a fool of me in real earnest. Well, I can forgive that; at any rate it is not mean.'

It may be, that Miss Dunstable did not feel much acute anger at finding that this young man had addressed her with words of love in the course of an ordinary flirtation, although that flirtation had been unmeaning and silly. This was not the offence against which her heart and breast had found peculiar cause to arm itself; this was not the injury from which she had hitherto experienced suffering.

At any rate, she and Frank again became friends, and, before the evening was over, they perfectly understood each other. Twice during this long *téte-à-téte* Lady de Courcy came into the room to see how things were going on, and twice she went out almost unnoticed. It was quite clear to her that something uncommon had taken place, was taking place, or would take place; and that should this be for weal or for woe, no good could now come from her interference. On each occasion, therefore, she smiled sweetly on the pair of turtle-doves, and glided out of the room as quietly as she had glided into it.

But at last it became necessary to remove them; for the world had gone to bed. Frank, in the meantime, had told to Miss Dunstable all his love for Mary Thorne, and Miss Dunstable had enjoined him to be true to his vows. To her eyes there was something of heavenly beauty in young, true love — of beauty that was heavenly because it had been unknown to her.

'Mind you let me hear, Mr. Gresham,' said she. 'Mind you do; and, Mr. Gresham, never, never forget her for one moment; not for one moment, Mr. Gresham.'

Frank was about to swear that he never would — again, when the countess, for the third time, sailed into the room.

'Young people,' said she, 'do you know what o'clock it is?'

'Dear me, Lady de Courcy, I declare it is past twelve; I really am ashamed of myself. How glad you will be to get rid of me to-morrow!'

'No, no indeed we shan't; shall we, Frank?' and so Miss Dunstable passed out.

Then once again the aunt tapped her nephew with her fan. It was the last time in her life that she did so. He looked up in her face, and his look was enough to tell her that the acres of Greshamsbury were not to be reclaimed by the ointment of Lebanon.

Nothing further on the subject was said. On the following morning Miss Dunstable took her departure, not much heeding the rather cold words of farewell which her hostess gave her; and on the following day Frank started for Greshamsbury.

I know of no other British novelist (not even Jane Austen) who could narrate such a scene between a young man and a woman so simply yet so realistically. Miss Dunstable is one of the best drawn of Trollope's characters, and we shall be having more of her in *Framley Parsonage*. Finally there is that personage unique in Trollope and nineteenth century fiction — Roger Scatcherd, the crude, uncultured, aggressive, self-made man. The description of him as he lies dying from literally drinking himself to death, knowing he is dying and yet refusing to give up his brandy, is a grim piece of realism Dickensian in its vividness. When Doctor Thorne remonstrates with him and tries to tell him that with his wealth he could be or do anything:

'No,' and the sick man shrieked with an energy that made him audible all through the house. 'I can do nothing that I would choose to do; be nothing that I would wish to be! What can I do? What can I be? What gratification can I have except the brandy bottle? If I go among gentlemen, can I talk to them? If they have anything to say about a railway, they will ask me a question: if they speak to me beyond that, I must be dumb. If I go among my workmen, can they talk to me? No; I am their master, and a stern master. They bob their heads and shake in their shoes when they see me. Where are my friends? Here!' said he, and he dragged a bottle from under his very pillow. 'Where are my amusements? Here!' and he brandished the bottle almost in the doctor's face. 'Where is my one resource, my one gratification, my only comfort after all my toils? Here, doctor; here, here, here!' and, so saying, he replaced his treasure beneath his pillow.

There was something so horrifying in this, that Dr. Thorne shrank back amazed, and was for a moment unable to speak.

'But, Scatcherd,' he said at last; 'surely you would not die for such a passion as that?'

'Die for it? Aye, would I. Live for it while I can live; and die for it when I can live no longer. Die for it! What is that for a man to do? Do not men die for a shilling a day? What is a man the worse for dying? What can I be the worse for dying? A man can die but once, you said just now. I'd die ten times for this.'

'You are speaking now either in madness, or else in folly, to startle me.'

'Folly enough, perhaps, and madness enough, also. Such a life as mine makes a man a fool, and makes him mad, too. What have I about me that I should be afraid to die? I'm worth three hundred thousand pounds; and I'd give it all to be able to go to work to-morrow with a hod and mortar, and have a fellow clap his hand upon my shoulder, and say: "Well, Roger, shall us have that 'ere other half-pint this morning?"

I'll tell you what, Thorne, when a man has made three hundred thousand pounds, there's nothing left for him but to die. It's all he's good for then. When money's been made, the next thing is to spend it. Now the man who makes it has not the heart to do that.'

One can only marvel at what must have been purely intuitive understanding of the mentality and make-up of a class of man so far removed from his own. No other novelist of his time can approach Trollope in this.

With all its faults *Doctor Thorne* is one of the books every Trollopian should have on his bookshelf.

A last word of general interest about the novel. It was while he was working on *Barchester Towers* and *Doctor Thorne* that Trollope, realizing that the greater part of his time and energy was being devoured by his job, leaving him little enough of either for his writing, devised two methods for combating this. The first was to set himself a rigid timetable: one which necessitated his rising at 5 a.m. and, after a cup of strong coffee, seating himself at his desk at 5.30 then, with his watch placed beside him, writing until 9.30, putting on paper 250 words every quarter of an hour without fail, thus ensuring the production of something like 4,000 words every day.

His second way out was this: unable often to carry out his timetable on account of the inordinate amount of travelling enforced by his work, he evolved a 'tablet' (as he called it) which enabled him to write on it in trains or on board ship almost as easily as on his desk; and it was mostly in this way that *Doctor Thorne* was written. For it was while he was writing it that he was instructed by his government employers to go to Egypt in order to renew a treaty with Said Pasha concerning the conveyance of Indian mail by the new Cairo-Suez railway. In his own words written during a rough passage between Marseilles and Alexandria: 'I wrote my allotted number of pages every day . . . . more than once I left my paper on the cabin table, rushing away to be sick in the privacy of my state room . . . . but I still did my work.' His 'work' averaged 40 pages a week, either on the ship or in Egypt.

As I stated in the Foreword, such a process of creation made the aesthetes of the 1880s squirm, and they denounced it and author hook, line and sinker. How, they demanded, could anything but hackwork be produced in such a mechanical way? Their frail talent made it impossible for them to understand that such self-discipline could go hand in hand with sheer professionalism and genius: forgetting too that, minus the watch, Balzac, Dumas and George Sand turned out even more pages than Trollope. Moreover they overlooked Trollope's own words about his fiction and creative work in general.

I was moved by a decision to excel, if not in quality, at any rate in quantity. An ignoble ambition for an author, my readers will no doubt say. But not, I think, ignoble if an author can bring himself to look at his work as does any other workman. My novels, good or bad, have been as good as I could make them. Had I taken three months of idleness between each they would have been no better. Feeling convinced of that, I finished *Doctor Thorne* one day, and began *The Bertrams* on the next.

And

> The novelist desires to make his readers so intimately acquainted with his characters that the creatures of his brain should be to them speaking, moving, living human creatures. This he can never do unless he knows his fictitious personages himself, and he can never know them unless he can live with them. They must be with him as he lies down to sleep and as he wakes from his dreams. He must learn to hate them and to love them . . . . It is so that I have lived with my characters and thence has come whatever success I have obtained.

The secret of fictional creation and the answer to Trollope's critics lie in those words. But the final, incontrovertible answer, surely, must be: if such a method gave us the Barchester chronicles and the dozen best of the other novels, of what validity are the arguments against it?

THE BERTRAMS

When some now-forgotten writer, struggling with a novel, asked Dumas with some envy "How do you manage to write so much so easily?" he replied ingenuously, "Ask a plum tree how it grows plums." The same metaphor can be applied to Trollope, and he had no idea which of his plums were good and which were indifferent: or rather, since that is not quite true, he knew which were good but not those which were not so good. That he had no self-criticism is not surprising in a writer who rated *Ivanhoe* and *Henry Esmond* above *Pride and Prejudice*.

But let us not carp and condemn too critically. After all, the marvel in either case is that the plum trees should have produced so many splendid plums and so comparatively few poor ones. It must be admitted right away, however, that *The Bertrams*, 'begun in Egypt the day *Doctor Thorne* was finished,' is decidedly one of the plums to be thrown away. Anyone picking up the novel and dipping into the first chapters to catch the flavour and style of it will almost certainly put it back on the shelf. And in fact the first half of the novel is so flat, stale and unprofitable that it reads like a bad imitation of Trollope — a sort of hybrid between Trollope, Scott and Thackeray. We can feel no interest whatever in the two Oxford undergraduates, George Bertram and Arthur Wilkinson, or the former's friend Harcourt, the barrister. In addition, the manipulation of the story is incredibly amateurish for a novelist who had *Doctor Thorne* and *Barchester Towers* behind him. Chapter 16, for example, begins by asking the reader to 'pass over two years', then after adding apologetically 'It is a terrible gap in the story', concludes with the lame excuse that 'in these days the unities are not much considered,' only to be followed by 'But something must be told of the occurrences of these two years.' Then adding insult to injury, chapters 17 and 18 are titled respectively 'Retrospective — First Year' and 'Retrospective Second Year.' Such crudities can only irritate a reader.

I have mentioned the influences of Scott and Thackeray, both of whom Trollope strangely admired beyond all others. That of Scott can be seen in the stock character of old Bertram, the close-fisted rich man who holds the purse strings; that of Thackeray in Sir Lionel Bertram, the elderly sponger and social parasite, and in the far too frequent mawkish would-be moralistic addresses to the reader — especially the female reader — which are splashed about the pages.

Such clumsy second-rate writing is a pity in that (1) the basic plot is a good one and opens up splendid possibilities (2) from chapter 24 onwards the story gets off the ground, catches genuine Trollopian fire and is worth reading. Cut to its bare bones the plot is this: George Bertram falls in love with and becomes engaged to his cousin, Caroline Waddington. He is anxious that she should make a good impression on his brilliant friend, Harcourt, so he introduces him to her. Harcourt is not only impressed by her 'Junoesque beauty' but is a little too impressed, Trollope hints. The engaged couple have differences and quarrels which end in their engagement bring broken off, and Harcourt, now Sir Henry Harcourt, the rising politician and solicitor-general, is only too happy to step into the breach and take over, partly smitten by her beauty and partly in the hope of thereby inheriting at least something of her uncle's fortune. After some hesitation, knowing that she does not love Harcourt as she had loved George Bertram, Caroline marries him, seduced by his success (a favourite theme with Trollope). Unhappiness for all three follows: she finding him to prove a typically tyrannous Victorian husband and herself not only not able to love him but to be still in love with her former lover. In the end she leaves him in the face of his threats and social ostracism; Harcourt, with both his political career and domestic life in ruins, commits suicide; and after some years, too late for essential happiness, Bertram and Caroline marry and live in unimpassioned domestic quietude.

So much for the plot, which as I have said is all but thrown away in its poor manipulation. But as I have also said, there are a few highlights. These come in the chapters narrating Bertram's inability to keep away from his former fiancée even when she is married. He dances with her at Mrs Madden's ball, to the annoyance of Harcourt, who forbids her ever to dance with him again. He even visits her at her home in Eaton Square where on two occasions he finds her alone. On the first occasion both admit in low, almost frightened voices that they made a mistake in separating, and imply a still-existing love. The second occasion he intends to be his farewell, having decided to go away and place himself beyond temptation, but he finds her in dangerous tears after a savage quarrel with her husband. The inevitable happens: they confess their love, he kisses her and leaves her. The next chapter, 'A Matrimonial Dialogue', must be counted among the best things Trollope has given us. If his readers were jolted by his audacity in allowing a man to make love to a married woman, the powerful frankness of its sequel must have shocked them. For when Harcourt, later that same day, returns and accuses her of admitting Bertram, of allowing him to pay court to her, even of allowing herself to think of him as her lover, she has the brazen audacity to admit his charges to his face.

> After this there was a slight pause, and then she added: 'Now, Sir Henry, I think you know it all. Now may I go?'
> He rose from his chair and began walking the length of the room, backwards and forwards, with quick step. As we have before said, he had a heart in his bosom; he had blood in his veins; he had those feelings of a man which make the scorn of a beautiful woman so intolerable. And then she was his wife, his property, his dependant, his own. For a moment he forgot the Hadley

money-bags, sorely as he wanted them, and the true man spoke out with full, unabated anger.

'Brazen-faced harlot!' he exclaimed, as he passed her in his walk, 'unmitigated harlot!'

'Yes, sir,' she answered, in a low tone, coming up to him as she spoke, laying her hand upon his arm, and looking still full into his face — looking into it with such a gaze that even he cowered before her. 'Yes, sir, I was the thing you say. When I came to you, and sold my woman's purity for a name, a house, a place before the world — when I gave you my hand, but could not give my heart, I was — what you have said.'

'And were doubly so when he stood here slobbering on your neck.'

'No, Sir Henry, no. False to him I have been; false to my own sex; false, very false to my own inner self; but never false to you.'

'Madam, you have forgotten my honour.'

'I have at any rate been able to remember my own.'

They were now standing face to face; and as she said these last words, it struck Sir Henry that it might be well to take them as a sign of grace, and to commence from them that half-forgiveness which would be necessary to his projects.

'You have forgotten yourself, Caroline —'

'Stop a moment, Sir Henry, and let me finish, since you will not allow me to remain silent. I have never been false to you, I say; and, by God's help, I never will be —'

'Well, well.'

'Stop, sir, and let me speak. I have told you often that I did not love you. I tell you so now again. I have never loved you — never shall love you. You have called me now by a base name; and in that I have lived with you and have not loved you, I dare not say that you have called me falsely. But I will sin no more.'

'What is it you mean?'

'I will not deserve the name again — even from you.'

'Nonsense; I do not understand you. You do not know what you are saying.'

'Yes, Sir Henry, I do know well what I am saying. It may be that I have done you some injury; if so, I regret it. God knows that you have done me much. We can neither of us now add to each other's comfort, and it will be well that we should part.'

'Do you mean me to understand that you intend to leave me?'

'That is what I intend you to understand.'

'Nonsense; you will do no such thing.'

'What! would you have us remain together, hating each other, vilifying each other, calling each other base names as you just now called me? And do you think that we could still be man and wife? No, Sir Henry. I have made one great mistake — committed one wretched, fatal error. I have so placed myself that I must hear myself so called and bear it quietly; but I will not continue to be so used. Do you think he would have called me so?'

'Damn him!'

'That will not hurt him. Your words are impotent against him, though they may make me shudder.'

'Do not speak of him, then.'

'No, I will not. I will only think of him.'

'By heavens! Caroline, your only wish is to make me angry.'

'I may go now, I suppose?'

'Go — yes; you may go; I will speak to you tomorrow, when you will be more cool.'

'Tomorrow, Sir Henry, I will not speak to you; nor the day afterwards, nor the day after that. What you may wish to say now I will hear; but remember this — after what has passed today, no consideration on earth shall induce me to live with you again. In any other respect I will obey your orders — if I find it possible.'

She stayed yet a little while longer, leaning against the table, waiting to hear whether or no he would answer her; but as he sat silent, looking before him, but not at her, with his hands thrust deep into his pockets, she without further words withdrew, and quietly closed the door after her.

The episode marks the climax of the novel. After it the rest is a slow anticlimax right to the inevitable 'Conclusion' which, beginning with the banal uncharacteristic sentence 'Methinks it is almost unnecessary to write this last chapter,' proclaims the sort of epilogue it is to be. It is without doubt one of the worst pieces of writing and anticlimax Trollope ever put on paper. Yet I do not imagine for a moment that he was aware of it.

CASTLE RICHMOND

The novel was begun on Trollope's return to Ireland in the summer of 1859 after a year spent travelling around 'The West Indies and the Spanish Main' as he titled his book relating his experiences, and would seem to have been written, in James Pope Hennessy's words, 'as a valediction to Ireland.' For Trollope had persuaded the Post Office to transfer him to England, and sensed that he and Ireland were soon to be parted, perhaps for good.

One has the feeling that Ireland had become for Trollope what Greece had been for Byron — a virus in the blood. Unfortunately Erin failed to inspire the novelist as Greece had inspired the poet. Like the previous stories with an Irish background *Castle Richmond* can be dismissed from serious consideration. If proof were not existent it would be difficult, if not downright impossible, to credit that with *Barchester Towers* and *Doctor Thorne* behind him and *Framley Parsonage* being written concurrently, their creator could turn out a thing as poor as this. Quite apart from the general flatness of the style, a 'novel' which, to quote Michael Sadleir, expatiates on its author's 'belief in God, his conception of the workings of the Supreme Intelligence' can be little better than 'a sermon on humanity's behalf' — an offense unpardonable in a novelist, whose prime attributes must be objective observation and creative ability. Moved by emotional indignation for Irish sufferings in the years of the Great Hunger, Trollope allows his narrative to become bogged down in political events to the exclusion of all interest in the individuals who created them. Apart from the widowed Lady Desmond, the heroine's obsessive mother who has a passion for her daughter's lover, the characters are mere shadows and excite no interest in their fates. Trollope's own comments on the novel are right on the mark for once. 'Castle Richmond . . . . is a weak production. The characters do not excite sympathy. The heroine has two lovers, of whom one is a scamp and the other a prig. As regards the scamp the girl's mother is her own rival . . . . The girl herself has no character; and the mother, who is strong enough, is almost revolting. The dialogue is often lively, and some of the incidents are well told; but the story as a whole was a failure.'

We can fairly leave the work on that summing up by its author. Except to add that Chapman paid Trollope £600 in advance for the novel. Recalling the miniscule amount he had been paid for *The Warden* and the £400 for *Doctor Thorne* and *The Bertrams*, there is surely a moral here: perhaps that once a writer has made his name anything he turns out will be accepted by his publisher and public.

FRAMLEY PARSONAGE

To turn after *Castle Richmond* to this, the fourth of the Barchester series, is to breathe a different air, to read a magically transformed writer. It is only a slight exaggeration to say that the novel is a mirror image of its predecessor; or, to put it in another way — they are like two peas from the same pod. The central 'plots' are identical, being that of a dowerless middle-class girl who is loved by a caste-superior young man against the wishes of his family. In *Doctor Thorne* the set-up is Mary Thorne, Frank Gresham and Lady Arabella; here it is Lucy Robarts, Lord Lufton and Lady Lufton. To choose between the two novels on merit is difficult, but if forced I would go for *Framley Parsonage* if only because, unlike the other, there is no padding, no excess verbiage; for the sake of the heroine, Lucy; more generous space devoted to the ebullient and fascinating Miss Dunstable; the first appearance of the Crawleys and the return — if slight and limited — of Mrs Proudie.

Of all Trollope's heroines Lucy Robarts is, along with Lily Dale, the nonpareil. Similar in many ways to Mary Thorne, she makes an even deeper claim on our affection, I think, by adding that rare, almost non-existent trait in heroines of any time or class — a sense of humour. She can almost bring herself to laugh at her predicament and ask her family to laugh at her too.

Let us look at the story in outline. The Reverend Mark Robarts owed the living of Framley to the good graces of Lady Lufton, with whom he is a favourite. Although a do-gooder and very conscious of her class, she is nothing like her prototype Lady Arabella, nor a bigot. In fact Trollope has drawn her with such skill that in spite of her faults she leaves us with an impression of basic kindliness and — for her time — of tolerance. This kindliness and tolerance are certainly very hardly tried, first by her son Ludovic, then by her cherished protégé, Mark Robarts. To take the former first. Lady Lufton, acting according to the gospel of most aristocratic mothers, has set her heart on her son 'marrying well' i.e. some wealthy woman of his own class, in this instance the young lady in view being Griselda Grantly, daughter of Archdeacon Grantly of *Barchester Towers* fame. But true to form and life, Ludovic, suspecting this, and finding no fascination in Griselda's statuesque impassive beauty, contrarily begins to fall in love with Lucy Robarts, Mark Robarts's sister who has come to live at Framley Parsonage with him and his wife Fanny on the death of her father: this to Lady Lufton's horror, for she sees in Lucy neither beauty nor intelligence nor breeding: and as for class and fortune . . . ! But Lady Lufton is wrong. Lucy may not be a beauty in the accepted sense of the term, but she has under her quiet simple exterior a force of character and charm of her own which make Griselda Grantly insipid in comparison. And here, far from making him blind, love has given young Lord Lufton the perception to see this.

Finding herself baulked in direct appeal to her son, Lady Lufton goes about the business in a typically femine indirect way: she takes Fanny Robarts into her confidence and asks her to point out (tactfully!) to Lucy the 'impropriety' of encouraging her son to fall in love with her. Poor Fanny, trapped and with divided loyalties, does her best to pass on Lady Lufton's wishes to her sister-in-law in 'delicate hints'; but at the first words Lucy flares up in half-indignant, half-humorous denial that she has drunk deeply from the Lufton 'danger bottle' and tries to shrug the caution off. On reflection, however, she has to confess to herself that she has absorbed the 'poison' of the Lufton bottle too deeply into her system for comfort: in other words that she really is in love with Ludovic Lufton, mamma or no mamma. At the same time she realizes there is a disturbing grain of truth in Lady Lufton's second-hand words, that marriage with him would bring her into open antagonism with his mother, would be a 'come-down' for Ludovic and would leave her wide open to the criticism that she had been 'intriguing to catch a lord.' So, like the virtuous, morally conscious, Victorian heroine she is, when soon afterwards Ludovic does propose to her, and when he challenges her to lay her hand on her heart and then tell him she cannot love him, she does so knowing she is telling a lie and plunging both of them into misery. To try to forget his unhappiness in a change of scene he goes salmon fishing in Norway, but not before he has angrily informed his mother that nothing will induce him to take up with Griselda Grantly or to give up Lucy. So, taking advantage of his absence, in a very polite note she asks the girl to come and see her. The interview (chapter 35 — 'The Story of King Cophetua'), like nearly all such between women by Trollope, is superbly done. Lucy comes out of it not only unsubjugated but victrix and with the heightened good opinion of Lady Lufton. The scene is followed by another little gem with her brother and sister-in-law. In reply to Mark's "What did she say?" Lucy replies:

'How green you are, Mark; and not only green, but impolite also, to make me repeat the story of my own disgrace. Of course she told me that she did not intend that I should marry my lord, her son; and of course I said that under those circumstances I should not think of doing such a thing.'

'Lucy, I cannot understand you,' said Fanny, very gravely. 'I am sometimes inclined to doubt whether you have any deep feeling in the matter or not. If you have, how can you bring yourself to joke about it?'

'Well, it is singular; and sometimes I doubt myself whether I have. I ought to be pale, ought I not? and very thin, and to go mad by degrees? I have not the least intention of doing anything of the kind, and, therefore, the matter is not worth any further notice.'

'But was she civil to you, Lucy?' asked Mark: 'civil in her manner, you know?'

'Oh, uncommonly so. You will hardly believe it, but she actually asked me to dine. She always does, you know, when she wants to show her good-humour. If you'd broken your leg, and she wished to commiserate you, she'd ask you to dinner.'

'I suppose she meant to be kind,' said Fanny, who was not disposed to give up her old friend, though she was quite ready to fight Lucy's battle, if there were any occasion for a battle to be fought.

'Lucy is so perverse,' said Mark, 'that it is impossible to learn from her what really has taken place.'

'Upon my word, then, you know it all as well as I can tell you. She asked me if Lord Lufton had made me an offer. I said, yes. She asked next, if I meant to accept it. Not without her approval, I said. And then she asked us all to dinner. That is exactly what took place, and I cannot see that I have been perverse at all.' After that she threw herself into a chair, and Mark and Fanny stood looking at each other.

'Mark,' she said, after a while, 'don't be unkind to me. I make as little of it as I can, for all our sakes. It is better so, Fanny, than that I should go about moaning, like a sick cow'; and then they looked at her, and saw that the tears were already brimming over from her eyes.

After such a brave attempt at indifference and refusal to show how deeply she resented and was hurt by the whole thing we can forgive her her little weep with Fanny.

Of course, in the end, driven by the triple urge of her son, her conscience and her secret admiration for Lucy, Lady Lufton sinks her pride, gives the demanded permission and the wedding bells ring.

But poor Lady Lufton has other worries beside these. Her dearly loved chosen parson is giving her cause for anxiety and dismay. Mark Robarts is what we would term today, I believe, a 'sporty parson'. He loved horses and racing, and yearned to hunt, if 'propriety' had allowed it, and he was fond of good company, especially if aristocratic, and all that went with it. Thus before long, unable to resist flattering invitations, he finds himself in all kinds of trouble — trouble which includes ambitious association with (in his patron's eyes) the iniquitous Gatherum Castle set, imfamous Liberal politicians and even — the crowning worry and disgrace — debt. His is a skilfully drawn portrait of a fundamentally good, well-intentioned young man led astray by weakness of will.

In stark contrast we get the soured, humourless, burningly sincere, one-track-minded Revd Crawley in his poverty-stricken living of Hogglestock. Although a fine scholar he has had no luck in his career, and has seen his old friend Arabin — to say nothing of Mark Robarts — rise to heights of comparative affluence and easy living and social respect while he has been left to stagnate in his wretched parish on little more than a pauper income. And here (chapter 14) Trollope inserts one of his typical digressions to make a blazingly ironical charge against the system of church government with its 'present arrangement of parochial incomes' which he stigmatizes as 'being time-honoured, gentlemanlike, English and picturesque . . . . How pleasant it was [too] that one bishop should be getting fifteen thousand a year, and another with an equal cure of parsons only four! . . . There was something in it pleasant, and picturesque; it was an arrangement endowed with feudal charms . . . . A utilitarian age requires the fatness of the ecclesiastical land in order that it may be divided out into small portions of provender, on which necessary working clergymen may live — into portions so infinitesimally small that working clergymen can hardly live. . . . And with reference to this matter, I will only here further explain that all these words have been brought about by the fact, necessary to be here stated, that Mr. Crawley only received one hundred and thirty pounds a year for performing the whole parochial duty of the parish of Hogglestock. And Hogglestock is a large parish.'

So poor Mr Crawley, with his scholarship, wife and children (two of whom had died) and the 'one barefooted little girl of fourteen to aid them in their small household matters,' became embittered and subject to bouts of depression which not all his deep religious belief could conquer. Nor, ashamed as he was of his threadbare clothes, would his pride allow him to accept Arabin's constant invitations to visit him at his Barchester deanery. 'His poverty had been so terrible to himself that it was not in his heart to love a rich friend,' Trollope concludes his analysis. Not a lovable person at all, the Revd

Crawley: a Puritan to the core with a genius for antagonizing his best friends and rebuffing all well-wishers by his thin-skinned pride and self-respect. Yet more than one commentator has voted him as being the finest drawn, most true-to-life character in all the Trollopian gallery.

Mrs Crawley is a subtle feminine contrast.

> Could we have looked into the innermost spirit of him and his life's partner, we should have seen that mixed with the pride of his poverty there was some feeling of disgrace that he was poor, but that with her . . . . there was neither pride nor shame. The realities of life had become so stern to her that the outward aspects of them were as nothing. She would have liked a new gown because it would have been useful; but it would have been nothing to her if all the county knew that the one in which she went to church had been turned three times. It galled him, however, to think that he and his were so poorly dressed.

So the fruit and jams and sweets brought by the Robarts are smuggled in via her under the poor man's very nose.

Then there is the ever-refreshing Miss Dunstable. As we saw in *Doctor Thorne*, single men coveted her for her wealth, and Frank Gresham's would-be wooing of the lady has been quoted and commented on. But even stranger is the wooing of Sowerby via his sister, Mrs Harold Smith. She, ambitious for her brother's political and social future, a friend of the lady and knowing her, as she thinks, infallibly, urges him to propose to her without any sentimental preliminaries or pretences of love and to tell her that he does so for the sake of her fortune. Miss Dunstable loves frankness and hates hypocrisy! But a man has nothing like the shamelessness or temerity of a woman in such circumstances: he cries off and asks her to do it for him. The chapter 'Magna est Veritas' which describes her attempt, like the later one (38) in which Mary Gresham is audacious enough to suggest to the same lady that she might do worse than marry her uncle, Dr Thorne, is one (of the many) I would select to put before any perceptive reader as proof of Trollope's mastery of dialogue, feminine psychology and his stature as a novelist.

In contrast, and still exemplifying his mastery over his craft, chapter 29, describing Miss Dunstable's 'At Home' reveals his ability to manipulate a bustling crowded scene equally with the duologue. The little side-rivalry between Lord Dumbello and Lord Lufton vis-à-vis Griselda Grantly is a choice bit of social satire.

> 'Are you going to dance, Ludovic?' said Lady Lufton.
> 'Well, I am not sure that I do not agree with Mrs Proudie in thinking that dancing would contaminate a conversazione. What are your ideas, Miss Grantly?' Griselda was never very good at a joke, and imagined that Lord Lufton wanted to escape the trouble of dancing with her. This angered her. For the only species of love-making, or flirtation, or sociability between herself as a young lady, and any other self as a young gentleman, which recommended itself to her taste, was to be found in the amusement of dancing. She was altogether at variance with Mrs Proudie on this matter, and gave Miss Dunstable great credit for her innovation. In society Griselda's toes were more serviceable to her than her tongue, and she was to be won by a rapid twirl much more probably than by a soft word. The offer of which she would approve would be conveyed by two all but breathless words during a spasmodic pause in a waltz; and then as she lifted up her arm to receive the accustomed support at her back, she might just find power enough to say, 'You — must ask — papa.' After that she would not care to have the affair mentioned till everything was properly settled.

'I have not thought about it,' said Griselda, turning her face away from Lord Lufton.

It must not, however, be supposed that Miss Grantly had not thought about Lord Lufton, or that she had not considered how great might be the advantage of having Lady Lufton on her side if she made up her mind that she did wish to become Lord Lufton's wife. She knew well that now was her time for a triumph, now in this very first season of her acknowledged beauty; and she knew also that young, good-looking bachelor lords do not grow on hedges like blackberries. Had Lord Lufton offered to her, she would have accepted him at once without any remorse as to the greater glories which might appertain to a future Marchioness of Hartletop. In that direction she was not without sufficient wisdom. But then Lord Lufton had not offered to her, nor given any signs that he intended to do so; and to give Griselda Grantly her due, she was not a girl to make a first overture. Neither had Lord Dumbello offered; but he had given signs — dumb signs, such as birds give to each other, quite as intelligible as verbal signs to a girl who preferred the use of her toes to that of her tongue. 'I have not thought about it,' said Griselda, very coldly, and at that moment a gentleman stood before her and asked her hand for the next dance. It was Lord Dumbello; and Griselda, making no reply except by a slight bow, got up and put her hand within her partner's arm.

'Shall I find you here, Lady Lufton, when we have done?' she said; and then started off among the dancers. When the work before one is dancing the proper thing for a gentleman to do is, at any rate, to ask a lady; this proper thing Lord Lufton had omitted, and now the prize was taken away from under his very nose.

There was clearly an air of triumph about Lord Dumbello as he walked away with the beauty. The world had been saying that Lord Lufton was to marry her, and the world had also been saying that Lord Dumbello admired her. Now this had angered Lord Dumbello, and made him feel as though he walked about, a mark of scorn, as a disappointed suitor. Had it not been for Lord Lufton, perhaps he would not have cared so much for Griselda Grantly; but circumstances had so turned out that he did care for her, and felt it to be incumbent upon him, as the heir to a marquisate, to obtain what he wanted, let who would have a hankering after the same article. It is in this way that pictures are so well sold at auctions; and Lord Dumbello regarded Miss Grantly as being now subject to the auctioneer's hammer, and conceived that Lord Lufton was bidding against him. There was, therefore, an air of triumph about him as he put his arm round Griselda's waist and whirled her up and down the room in obedience to the music. Lady Lufton and her son were left together looking at each other. Of course, he had intended to ask Griselda to dance, but it cannot be said that he very much regretted his disappointment.

Finally, for good measure, we are given a whole chapter (17) and part of two others (40 and 45) to the reappearance of the ogress, Mrs Proudie. In the first, (describing her 'Conversazione'), she is rather tepid, for Mrs P. outside the environs of her natural reserve of the Bishop's palace is only half Mrs P. The full force of her is only to be felt there in the course of the 'internecine war' (as Trollope names chapter 40) between her and the Grantlys over the Dumbello-Griselda match. The cat fight between her and Mrs Grantly is exhilarating. How Trollope knew and could reproduce feminine snide, guile and scratch!*

Framley Parsonage may not quite rival *Barchester Towers*, but it comes very close to it. And as a coda to the novel which partly, perhaps, because it was serialized by Thackeray in the *Cornhill* became the most popular of them all and did more than all the

---

* It is reported that a London hostess, obviously struck by this aspect of Trollope's art, once asked him "How do you know what we women say to each other when we are away from you in our rooms?"

rest to bring him fame and fortune, there should always be added his own words on it: 'Of *Framley Parsonage* I need only further say, that as I wrote it I became more closely acquainted than ever with the new shire which I had added to the English counties. I had it all in my mind — its roads and railroads, its towns and parishes, its members of Parliament, and the different hunts which rode over it. I knew all the great lords and their castles, the squires and their parks, the rectors and their churches. This was the fourth novel of which I had placed the scene in Barsetshire, and as I wrote it I made a map of the dear county. Throughout these stories there has been no name given to a fictitious site which does not represent to me a spot of which I know all the accessories, as though I had lived and wandered there.'

In conclusion, two facts about the novel should be noted (1) It opened the first number of new *Cornhill Magazine* with Thackeray for its editor (2) Thackeray paid him £1,000 for it.

ORLEY FARM

Framley Parsonage was swiftly followed by another masterpeice, *Orley Farm*. Trollope always considered this to be one of his best works, and for once general opinion has agreed with him. Not only is the plot one of the best of all his plots, but the whole narrative, with two minor flaws to be noted, keeps to his highest level. The first is an almost invariable weakness. The fact that, like the novels of Dickens, it was published in monthly numbers before coming out as a two-volume 'yellow back' partly accounts for the episodic construction, the introducing of unnecessary 'low' (as reviewers referred to them) characters created to fill the requisite number of pages. Here, while the Dickensian Mr Moulder and his circle show yet again Trollope's amazing range of knowledge of different types and classes of human kind, the reader may be forgiven for finding them irritatingly unnecessary to the story and for revealing that their creator lacked the vital Dickensian gift of outrageous comedy. As George Lewes succinctly observed in his review of the novel in the *Cornhill*: 'the funny people are there but not the fun.'

The second flaw is the absurd relationship between Felix Graham and Mary Snow. Why Trollope should ever have thought of introducing the idea of a well-educated and intelligent young man deliberately purposing to marry an ignorant girl with the idea of 'moulding a wife to himself' passes comprehension.

Nevertheless, these weaknesses apart, the novel is a superb piece of plotting, characterization and narrative. In this last aspect it is the nearest approach Trollope ever made to suspense *à la* Wilkie Collins, the difference being that the characters of Lady Mary Mason and the Ormes are quite beyond Collins, who moreover would never have disclosed the secret and crux of the plot half-way through the story. Trollope himself confessed that he had doubts as to whether he had not been guilty of an error of judgement in revealing Lady Mason's guilt before the trial. I do not think he need have worried. On the contrary, the fact that, true to his strict self-confessed principle of never misleading his readers or of deliberately keeping them in suspense he gives away the secret half-way through the story is to me at least one more evidence of his greatness as a writer.

Let us consider the plot briefly. Sir Joseph Mason of Groby Park in Yorkshire, a widower with a son and three married daughters, marries again, and by his young second wife has a son, Lucius. It had always been understood by his eldest son, Joseph, that both his father's properties of Groby Hall and Orley Farm (the last near London) were to go to him. But when after his father's death the will is read, he discovers to his bitter disappointment that by a codicil he has been left only Groby Park — Orley Farm going to his young half-brother Lucius and his mother.

He contests the validity of the will and particularly the codicil, which appeared to have been added in somewhat devious circumstances, and the ensuing legal proceedings became known as The Great Orley Farm Case. But he lost the case and retired, unconvinced and breathing vengeance, to his Yorkshire estate, leaving Lady Mason and her son in full possession of Orley Farm, a holding of some 200 acres.

When the action of the novel begins they have been living there for nearly twenty years. Lucius is now twenty-two and his mother in her forties; and they might have gone on enjoying their rights for the rest of their lives but for a small but fatal error on their part, namely, that of taking away from Mr Dockwrath the let of two fields belonging to the farm. Now Dockwrath, an attorney 'with a small practice and a large family,' had married Miriam Usbech, one of the witnesses in the original Orley Farm Case and who had benefited, thanks to her father, from Sir Joseph Mason's will to the tune of £2,000. Dockwrath is mean, avaricious and ambitious, and treats his wife despicably. When Lucius Mason, on his coming of age, deprives him of the two fields he has had so long thanks to Lady Mason's kindness, he simmers with rage and meditates vengeance. It was this apparently trivial act which resurrected the second Great Orley Farm Case. For Dockwrath, searching among the late Jonathan Usbech's papers, came across some details of the previous litigation which aroused his suspicions, at any rate enough to make him believe that vital facts from the first case had not been brought to light during the trial. Armed with these papers, and seeing in them possibilities of legal kudos and of returning the wrong he fancies he has suffered at the hands of Lucius and his mother, he takes them to Groby Park. Joseph Mason, though now a magistrate and personage of consequence, is still sore about the verdict, and twenty years have not lessened his desire to avenge himself on the Orley Farm occupants and get back what he considers to be his rightful property. Needless to say, he jumps at this opportunity offered by Dockwrath, and between them they reopen the lawsuit.

The unravelling of the mysterious codicil forms the greater part of the story, and one can only admire the skill with which Trollope does it — not least the way in which, little by little, he builds up in the reader's mind doubt as to the innocence of Lady Mason, despite her charm and courage. Why, if she is innocent as the former verdict declared her to be, is she so alarmed by the news that Joseph Mason is instituting fresh proceedings? — her friends Sir Peregrine Orme and his widowed daughter-in-law, Edith, ask themselves. Why does she so urgently ask them to stand by her whatever the verdict? Her son, too, is baffled by her unwillingness to discuss the case openly with him, and her appeal to him not to confront Dockwrath and metaphorically take him by the throat. In passing one notes that Lucius is a serious-minded, moral and earnest young man, and a prig, and his mother is rather afraid of him — two factors which greatly influence the denouement. Puzzled too is Mr Furnival, who had undertaken her defence in the original case, and who has agreed to undertake it yet again, and a suggestion she makes appals him, namely, that they should pay Joseph Mason something to keep him quiet.

In the course of the various proceedings and interviews new emotions are brought into play. Both Mr Furnival and Sir Peregrine Orme find that their solicitude for her leads them to have stronger feelings — feelings which with the former lead to a breakdown in his marital relationship, and with the latter to a proposal of marriage, old though he is. For:

> Lady Mason was rich with female charms, and she used them partly with the innocence of the dove, but partly also with the wisdom of the serpent. But in such use as she did make of these only weapons which Providence had given to her, I do not think that she can be regarded as very culpable. During those long years of her young widowhood in which nothing had been wanting to her, her conduct had been free from any hint of reproach. She had been content to find all her joy in her duties and in her love as a mother. Now a great necessity for assistance had come upon her. It was necessary that she should bind men to her cause, men powerful in the world and able to fight her battle with strong arms. She did so bind them with the only chains at her command, — but she had no thought, nay, no suspicion of evil in so doing. It was very painful to her when she found that she had caused unhappiness to Mrs. Furnival; and it caused her pain now, also, when she thought of Sir Peregrine's new love. She did wish to bind these men to her by a strong attachment; but she would have stayed this feeling at a certain point had it been possible for her so to manage it.

She accepts Sir Peregrine, to the secret dismay of his daughter-in-law and Mr Furnival and the overt antagonism of her son and Sir Peregrine's grandson. The skein is becoming well and truly entangled. Then Trollope lets us into the great secret, and the blow falls. Mary Mason, after long heart-searching with herself and Edith Orme, now her closest friend, realizing that her marriage with a man so much older than herself and so much above her in class would make him appear foolish in the eyes of society and, more telling still, would drag him down with her should she be found guilty, comes to a decision. The scene is one of the highlights of the novel.

> 'Well, Mary, what is it? I know there is something on your mind or you would not have summoned me in here. Is it about the trial? Have you seen Mr. Furnival again?'
>
> 'No; it is not about the trial,' she said, avoiding the other question.
>
> 'What is it then?'
>
> 'Sir Peregrine, it is impossible that we should be married.' And thus she brought forth her tidings, as it were at a gasp, speaking at the moment with a voice that was almost indicative of anger.
>
> 'And why not?' said he, releasing her from his arm and looking at her.
>
> 'It cannot be,' she said.
>
> 'And why not, Lady Mason?'
>
> 'It cannot be,' she said again, speaking with more emphasis, and with a stronger tone.
>
> 'And is that all that you intend to tell me? Have I done anything that has offended you?'
>
> 'Offended me! No. I do not think that would be possible. The offence is on the other side —'
>
> 'Then, my dear, —'

'But listen to me now. It cannot be. I know that it is wrong. Everything tells me that such a marriage on your part would be a sacrifice, — a terrible sacrifice. You would be throwing away your great rank —'

'No,' shouted Sir Peregrine; 'not though I married a kitchen-maid, — instead of a lady who in social life is my equal.'

'Ah, no; I should not have said rank. You cannot lose that; — but your station in the world, the respect of all around you, the — the — the —'

'Who has been telling you all this?'

'I have wanted no one to tell me. Thinking of it has told it me all. My own heart which is full of gratitude and love for you has told me.'

'You have not seen Lord Alston?'

'Lord Alston! oh, no.'

'Has Peregrine been speaking to you?'

'Peregrine!'

'Yes; Peregrine; my grandson?'

'He has spoken to me.'

'Telling you to say this to me. Then he is an ungrateful boy; — a very ungrateful boy. I would have done anything to guard him from wrong in this matter.'

'Ah; now I see the evil that I have done. Why did I ever come into the house to make quarrels between you?'

'There shall be no quarrel. I will forgive him even that if you will be guided by me. And, dearest Mary, you must be guided by me now. This matter has gone too far for you to go back — unless, indeed, you will say that personally you have an aversion to the marriage.'

'Oh, no; no; it is not that,' she said eagerly. She could not help saying it with eagerness. She could not inflict the wound on his feelings which her silence would then have given.

'Under those circumstances, I have a right to say that the marriage must go on.'

'No; no.'

'But I say it must. Sit down, Mary.' And she did sit down, while he stood leaning over her and thus spoke. 'You speak of sacrificing me. I am an old man with not many more years before me. If I did sacrifice what little is left to me of life with the object of befriending one whom I really love, there would be no more in it than what a man might do, and still feel that the balance was on the right side. But here there will be no sacrifice. My life will be happier, and so will Edith's. And so indeed will that boy's, if he did but know it. For the world's talk, which will last some month or two, I care nothing. This I will confess, that if I were prompted to this only by my own inclination, only by love for you —' and as he spoke he held out his hand to her, and she could not refuse him hers — 'in such a case I should doubt and hesitate and probably keep aloof from such a step. But it is not so. In doing this I shall gratify my own heart, and also serve you in your great troubles. Believe me, I have thought of that.'

'I know you have, Sir Peregrine, — and therefore it cannot be.'

'But therefore it shall be. The world knows it now; and were we to be separated after what has past, the world would say that I — I had thought you guilty of this crime.'

'I must bear all that.' And now she stood before him, not looking him in the face, but with her face turned down towards the ground, and speaking hardly above her breath.

'By heavens, no; not whilst I can stand by your side. Not whilst I have strength left to support you and thrust the lie down the throat of such a wretch as Joseph Mason. No, Mary, go back to Edith and tell her that you have tried it, but that there is no escape for you.' And then he smiled at her. His smile at times could be very pleasant!

But she did not smile as she answered him. 'Sir Peregrine,' she said; and she endeavoured to raise her face to his but failed.

'Well, my love.'

'Sir Peregrine, I am guilty.'

'Guilty! Guilty of what?' he said, startled rather than instructed by her words.

'Guilty of all this with which they charge me.' And then she threw herself at his feet, and wound her arms round his knees.

At first he is too stunned to take in what she tells him, or to believe her. The upright, simple-hearted old man finds it beyond his credence that such a woman as Lady Mason, whom he has held in the highest esteem and to whom he is now affianced, could be guilty of such 'a terrible deed.' First, perjury in the previous case, now confessed forgery. But when she confesses her crime to Edith as well, he is forced to face the truth. He forgives her; for like his daughter he realizes she did it all for the sake of her son. Moreover he is deeply appreciative of the fact that she has asked him to break off their engagement because she realizes that, if found guilty, her shame must be shared by her husband, and she wishes to spare him that. Nevertheless, though he forgives her, he cannot forgive her act, and he will no longer see her even though she is living, until the trial, with him and his daughter. He becomes a broken man. Edith's reaction is similar, and yet different. Like her father-in-law she abhors what her friend has done — and of course here we get religious admonishings and biblical quotations — but like the true friend she is she tells her she will stand by her to the end. Thus when the tral comes on, we have the astonishing situation in which the reader, Sir Peregrine and Edith Orme know she is guilty, and the three counsels for her defence are morally certain of her guilt.

The trial itself has been condemned by legal purists as — to quote Michael Sadleir — 'a tissue of mistakes.' The layman need not turn a hair at the various criticisms. From a literary angle it is realistically done. Thanks to the brilliancy of the defence and the ineptitude of the prosecution's witnesses, whose memories are so uncertain as to be invalid (after all, twenty years is a long time to recall details) on the third day the jury brings in the verdict: 'Not Guilty', to the unbounded mortification and rage of Mason and Dockwrath. But the verdict, though clearing her name with the public, means little to her. For on the second day of the trial, trembling and terrified, and after holding out for days against Edith Orme's importuning, she at last agrees with her that Lucius must be told the truth, whatever the verdict. Edith takes it on herself to break the dreadful news to him. Like Sir Percival, he is so shattered that at first he will not believe it, and declares in fact that he will not do so until he is told by his mother. Edith has begged him to be 'merciful', to remember that in spite of her crime she is still his mother and that it was for his sake that she committed it. But as I observed earlier, Lucius is a prig; and when, in tears, contrite and in dread of his censure she throws herself at his feet and 'clasps him round the knees with her arms', all he can allow himself to say and do is to raise her and tell her 'very sternly, standing somewhat away from her, and frowning the while with those gloomy eyebrows,' that though whatever happens he will stand by her, 'the future must be very different from the past,' that there is another world before her — if she can repent of her sin, together with a lot of other moralistic lecturing. And when she comes close up to him and asks in a shaking voice "But you will give me your hand, Lucius?" his reply is: '"Yes, mother, there is my hand. I shall stand by you through it all." But he did not offer to kiss her; and there was still some pride in her heart which would not allow her to ask him for an embrace.' Yet she had committed the crime solely for him! Trollope does not say outright that the young man is a prig, but he cannot resist implying it in his own way, and observes: 'Of all the virtues with which man can endow himself surely none other is so odious as that justice which can teach itself to look down upon mercy almost as a vice.'

The novel ends with Lucius, despite the jury's verdict, quixotically returning Orley Farm to his half-brother and taking his mother to live with him in comparative poverty in a small town in Germany. It may be pointless, but it is interesting to speculate whether a young man of our present materialistic age, in similar circumstances, would be equally quixotic. Did the Victorian code of ethics, with all its intolerance, class distinction, snobbery and ridiculous mis-sense of propriety, have a greater rectitude and code of honour? Lucius's act at least suggests comparisons. If Trollope had any moral point in mind when he wrote the novel it was, I think, to bring home the truth that a wrong done, however well-intentioned, however strongly the doer may feel he has justice on his side, will always recoil and recoil as often as not to hurt others as much as if not more than the perpetrator of it. Here, Lucius and Sir Peregrine Orme feel the blow and the disgrace no less than Mary Mason, and Dockwrath (though one can feel no pity for him) is 'ruined' suing Joseph Mason over their supposed contract that he should be given possession of Orley Farm if his claim succeeded.

But I think the story shows less of any such intention on Trollope's part than it does his warm-hearted sympathy and fellow-feeling for those driven by circumstance to wrong-doing. And he conveys this by making Mary Mason at once the 'villain' and 'heroine' of the novel. Her secret confession of guilt to her nearest and dearest as against the judgement of the court that she is innocent is a superb piece of irony, making the denouement all the more tragic.

Compared with the main plot the side issues, though far from irrelevant and skilfully woven into it, seem small beer, particularly the somewhat Dickensian 'low life' characters Moulder, Kantwise and their milieu. But the Furnivals are well drawn, particularly the daughter Sophia with her calculating eye to the main chance; and the entanglements and disentanglements of the various young lovers — Augustus Staveley, his sister Madeline, Felix Graham and young Peregrine Orme — are interesting and credible (always with the exception already noted of the Mary Snow affair). But it is Lady Mason who carries the story on her shoulders, wins our sympathy and whom we remember most vividly.

Trollope was right. *Orley Farm* must be reckoned among the best of his novels. But it is at the same time something more than a gripping tale. It is a psychological study of a battle between human conscience and social convention. As I have already observed, Trollope had no gift for finding good titles for his novels. Written almost contemporaneously with Dostoievsky's masterpiece, it would have been far more dramatically and justly entitled *Crime and Punishment*.

THE SMALL HOUSE AT ALLINGTON

The novel differs from the rest of the cycle in one main factor: whereas they are comedies, it is a tragedy. In predetermining this Trollope set himself an ambitious task — ambitious in that, like Jane Austen, he knew himself to be essentially a creator of social comedy, taking the word in its broadest sense. Not only was his line dictated by his nature, but also by his public. The Victorians, with their distorted religious and moral sense, reacted against tragedy. For them virtue had always to be rewarded and evil to be meted with their just deserts. To show vice triumphant and virtue defeated was unthinkable in their philosophy, let life prove that philosophy null and void to the hilt. Hence the outcry and tears when Dickens was heartless enough to kill off Little Nell. Steerforth could die grandly and comfortably as his just desert; he had seduced Emily. Though tears might be shed, Dora Spenlow and Joe the crossing sweeper could die, the former being a silly, shallow little creature standing in the way of the saintly dummy, Agnes Wickfield, and the latter because it meant the end of all his miseries and for him to become, in Uriah Heep's unforgettable response when asked by David about the condition of his father, "a partaker of glory, Master Copperfield."

So far Trollope had played up to his public's expectations. In *The Warden* Mr Harding had suffered, but he had come through only slightly scathed. In *Barchester Towers*, though Mrs Proudie had emerged as victrix, Mr Slope had been branded and banished, Eleanor had won her Arabin, the disrupting, vice-promoting Stanhopes had returned to Italy and all had ended well. In *Doctor Thorne* and *Framley Parsonage* similarly all rifts had been closed and wounds healed without any broken hearts. Now that is all to be changed. In *The Small House* there is to be a broken heart, and that the heart of the girl who is arguably not only Trollope's most endearing heroine but, along with Scott's Di Vernon, Anne Brontë's Helen Huntingdon, Jane Austen's Elizabeth Bennett and Elizabeth Gaskell's Margaret Hale the most lovable heroine in nineteenth century fiction — namely Lily Dale.

The first thing to notice (and it is only to be fully appreciated on a second reading) is the skill with which Trollope builds her character. She lives with her mother and sister 'Bell' in the Small House which adjoins and is owned by Mrs Dale's brother-in-law, the squire of Allington, Christopher Dale, who lives in the Great House. Although Bell is generally considered to be the more beautiful of the sisters, Lily is the more vivacious, and it is this out-going vivacity, this high-spirited sense of fun which not only endears her to the reader (none of Trollope's other heroines have this characteristic) but makes the ensuing tragedy so bitter, so unbearable. Our introduction to her is via a conversation with her sister — one of those private dialogues between women of which Trollope was such a master; and only later, after the tragedy, does the reader appreciate the dramatic irony of her very critical comments on Crosbie. "But Mr. Crosbie is only a mere clerk," is her very first gambit. Then later: "You know what I mean by a mere clerk. It isn't much in a man to be in a public office, and yet Mr. Crosbie gives himself airs;" and in conclusion she declares "I'll tell you what he is, Bell; Mr. Crosbie is a swell" — for which Bell takes her to task for using unladylike slang, only to be told that she likes using slang as a change from the dull ordinary words of the dictionary, and still teasing her sister she goes on to call Crosbie "Apollo" with no little irony. At which point, talking of the devil, 'Apollo' himself appears at the french window along with Bernard Dale, their cousin and the squire's nephew. Again unbeknown to the reader the quartet is a fateful one: Lily will love Crosbie too well and Bell will not love Bernard enough. But just now all is well, and Trollope really conveys the sense of young people enjoying their youth and high spirits in one another's company. They play croquet, and Lily ribs Crosbie unmercifully on his poor play ("Apollo can't get through the hoops," she says to Bell afterwards; "but then how gracefully he fails to do it!") then, tiring of that, they go out into the fields where they find the remnants of hay-making, and throw hay over one another and generally romp about like very normal young folk. But in effect it is all skilful preparation for the sombre contrast of events to come.

The novel consists of three main strands: (1) the two Houses at Allington, already mentioned (2) Guestwick Manor, the home of Lord de Guest and his maiden sister, Lady Julia, related by marriage to the Dales (3) Courcy Castle, the home of Lady Rosina De Courcy and her aristocratic but indifferently behaved family. There is in addition a fourth minor establishment, namely, Mrs Roper's boarding-house in London where Johnny Eames is in 'digs'. These different establishments are correlated by Trollope in the most adroit way and with no forcing of incident or relationship such as he was later guilty of in *The Prime Minister*. The characters move naturally from one milieu to the other, carrying the action and emotional interactions along with them. Crosbie had known one or two of the Courcy set in town, and receiving a letter of invitation to visit them from Lady Rosina, he decides to accept it and informs Lily of the fact. On this simple turn of events the whole tragedy hangs. For during a second, longer stay at the Great House as Bernard's guest, Crosbie had fallen in love with Lily and she with him, and they became engaged. But Lily's love is very different from that of Crosbie's. Under her gay exterior she is deeply emotional, and is in fact one of those beings, few and far between, who love once, irrevocably, and never again. This must be stressed, for her tragedy turns on the fact like a linch pin. In the course of the average novel, as in the course of average life, ninety-nine out of a hundred jilted women or men, human nature being what it is, get over their grief. But every now and then we meet with one of those rare, tragic persons, usually a woman, who can love only once and, that love failing them, they find no substitute, no consolation in anyone else. They live on, showing a brave face to the world, but they never fall in love again. Lily Dale was just such a one. When she fell in love with Crosbie she gave him her whole heart, her will, her future, every fibre of her being. The sincerity, the depth of her nature, her adoration and trust are revealed in that brief but poignant scene which must make any sensitive reader's heart turn over, more especially if he is reading the book for the second time (which he should do) and knows the shape of things to come.

> At last Lily got the dancers out upon the lawn, and then they managed to get through one quadrille. But it was found that it did not answer. The music of the single fiddle which Crosbie had hired from Guestwick was not sufficient for the purpose; and then the grass, though it was perfect for purposes of croquet, was not pleasant to the feet for dancing.
>
> 'This is very nice,' said Bernard to his cousin. 'I don't know anything that could be nicer; but perhaps —'
>
> 'I know what you mean,' said Lily. 'But I shall stay here. There's no touch of romance about

any of you. Look at the moon there at the back of the steeple. I don't mean to go in all night.' Then she walked off by one of the paths, and her lover went after her.

'Don't you like the moon?' she said, as she took his arm, to which she was now so accustomed that she hardly thought of it as she took it.

'Like the moon — well; I fancy I like the sun better. I don't quite believe in moonlight. I think it does best to talk about when one wants to be sentimental.'

'Ah; that is just what I fear. That is what I say to Bell when I tell her that her romance will fade as the roses do. And then I shall have to learn that prose is more serviceable than poetry, and that the mind is better than the heart, and — and that money is better than love. It's all coming, I know; and yet I do like the moonlight.'

'And the poetry, — and the love?'

'Yes. The poetry much, and the love more. To be loved by you is sweeter even than any of my dreams, — is better than all the poetry I have read.'

'Dearest Lily,' and his unchecked arm stole round her waist.

'It is the meaning of the moonlight, and the essence of the poetry,' continued the impassioned girl. 'I did not know then why I liked such things, but now I know. It was because I longed to be loved.'

'And to love.'

'Oh, yes. I would be nothing without that. But that, you know, is your delight, — or should be. The other is mine. And yet it is a delight to love you; to know that I may love you.'

'You mean that this is the realization of your romance.'

'Yes; but it must not be the end of it, Adolphus. You must like the soft twilight, and the long evenings when we shall be alone; and you must read to me the books I love, and you must not teach me to think that the world is hard, and dry, and cruel, — not yet. I tell Bell so very often; but you must not say so to me.'

'It shall not be dry and cruel, if I can prevent it.'

'You understand what I mean, dearest. I will not think it dry and cruel, even though sorrow should come upon us, if you — I think you know what I mean.'

'If I am good to you.'

'I am not afraid of that; — I am not the least afraid of that. You do not think that I could ever distrust you? But you must not be ashamed to look at the moonlight, and to read poetry, and to —'

'To talk nonsense, you mean.'

But as he said it, he pressed her closer to his side, and his tone was pleasant to her.

'I suppose I'm talking nonsense now?' she said, pouting. 'You liked me better when I was talking about the pigs; didn't you?'

'No; I like you best now.'

'And why didn't you like me then? Did I say anything to offend you?'

'I like you best now, because —'

They were standing in the narrow pathway of the gate leading from the bridge into the gardens of the Great House, and the shadow of the thick-spreading laurels was around them. But the moonlight still pierced brightly through the little avenue, and she looked up to him, could see the form of his face and the loving softness of his eye.

'Because —,' said he; and then he stooped over her and pressed her closely, while she put up her lips to his, standing on tip-toe that she might reach to his face.

'Oh, my love!' she said. 'My love! my love!'

How often Crosbie was to repeat to himself those words of Lily Dale: "Oh, my love! my love!" in the months to come and during his half-hearted wooing of the cold-blooded Alexandrina De Courcy! The scene stands as one of the rare touches of poetry in Trollope and, in its simple naturalness but blazing intensity, as one of the great love scenes in fiction. Thus the reader is so made to sense Lily's passionate involvement that the laceration she feels on her betrayal — a laceration and loss so intense, so lethal, that she knows she can never love a man again — is not felt to be any exaggeration. And it is precisely in this that Trollope has set himself a challenge which must be one of the greatest a novelist can impose on himself: that of creating a heroine who, before half the story is over, can have no further love interest. And he overcomes the challenge magnificently; does it by showing us how 'the wounded fawn', as he calls her, in spite of being stricken, rallies, and hiding her wound under a will of steel, keeps her interest in the doings of those around her. It is she who, while recovering from her illness, takes poor tongue-tied Dr Crofts (a deliberate contrast to the facile Crosbie, one suspects) on one side and tells him in so many kind words not to be such a fool and to get on with proposing to her sister a second time (she has refused him once, and he is in the doldrums). The contrast between Bell's happiness and her own misery is infinitely pathetic.

And Adolphus Crosbie, the 'Phoebus Appolo' — what of him? Trollope is careful not to make him a typical Victorian arch-villain who goes about deceiving inexperienced young girls: no Lovelace, Lothario or Don Juan, simply a very human, handsome, gregarious, ambitious, society-loving young man who can mix in any society and is popular wherever he goes. Of course he realizes and values his own worth, and he has told himself that if he ever does marry he must marry well to keep up his position. But it is just here that he has failed himself, for he has found Lily Dale attractive and, conquered by her sincerity, direct simplicity and worth (for he appreciates these qualities in her) he has fallen for her and become engaged to her. But after the carefree holidaying in her company and that of Bell and her mother, comes the backlash. Lily has no money of her own and he has only his income, and he is haunted by thoughts of a future consisting of 'a small house, five children and horrid misgivings as to the baker's bill' when he might do much better for himself. Driven to desperation he braced himself to ask the squire over their wine whether he was prepared to 'do anything' for his niece when he married her. (The modern reader must always be surprised by the seemingly inevitable discussion on settlements which occurs in Victorian novels in which parents or guardians were always expected to 'do the handsome thing' by their wards or children when they married). But he is met by an almost brutal refusal, and he is left to chew the cud of doubts and hesitations. Trollope's analysis of his waverings is masterly, and after them we know him to the bone, not as a mere playboy, but as a fundamentally decent but weak-willed, selfish, ambitious young man who knows he is behaving like a heel in so much as thinking of giving Lily up. One has only to compare him with Steerforth in *David Copperfield* to appreciate the subtler genius of Trollope in such matters. We get no single revelatory word from Steerforth or Emily to suggest or explain their emotional relationship. Everything is sacrificed to that element which Trollope so despised, namely, shock, surprise, but which Dickens loved and for which he was prepared to sacrifice all reasonable preparation and reality.

Crosbie, then, is torn by doubt and aftermath reasonings; and of course no lover can mask such feelings from the girl who loves him. So, in that wonderful chapter 'The Last Days', guessing his dilemma, she offers him the chance to break their engagement. But Trollope, knowing too well the moral cowardice of men in such a situation, their horror of giving such insulting offence coupled with their knowledge that the baseness of such behaviour must cling to them like a scar, could not let Crosbie take that way out even though it would have been the less dishonourable way. 'His heart misgave him, and he lacked the courage to extricate himself from his trouble; or, as he afterwards said to himself, he had not the heart to do it.' Their last words together and their goodbye are profoundly moving.

'I have only one minute to speak to you,' said she, jumping up, 'and I have been thinking all night of what I had to say. It is so easy to think, and so hard to speak.'

'My darling, I understand it all.'

'But you must understand this, that I will never distrust you. I will never ask you to give me up again, or say that I could be happy without you. I could not live without you; that is, without the knowledge that you are mine. But I will never be impatient, never. Pray, pray believe me! Nothing shall make me distrust you.'

'Dearest Lily, I will endeavour to give you no cause.'

'I know you will not; but I specially wanted to tell you that. And you will write, — very soon?'

'Directly I get there.'

'And as often as you can. But I won't bother you; only your letters will make me so happy. I shall be so proud when they come to me. I shall be afraid of writing too much to you, for fear I should tire you.'

'You will never do that.'

'Shall I not? But you must write first, you know. If you could only understand how I shall live upon your letters! And now good-bye. There are the wheels. God bless you, my own, my own!' And she gave herself up into his arms, as she had given herself up into his heart.

She stood at the door as the two men got into the gig, and, as it passed down through the gate, she hurried out upon the terrace, from whence she could see it for a few yards down the lane. Then she ran from the terrace to the gate, and, hurrying through the gate, made her way into the churchyard, from the farther corner of which she could see the heads of the two men till they had made the turn into the main road beyond the parsonage. There she remained till the very sound of the wheels no longer reached her ears, stretching her eyes in the direction they had taken. Then she turned round slowly and made her way out at the churchyard gate, which opened on to the road close to the front door of the Small House.

She was never to see him again.

From the Small House he goes to Courcy Castle, there to meet up with the Lady Alexandrina, at whom he had previously made mild passes. She was not only rich but 'the beauty of the family . . . . But the fault of her face was this — that when you left her you could not remember it.' In spite of her unlovable vapid character (and Crosbie knows she cannot compare with Lily) she manoeuvres him so skilfully that she gets him into an inescapable corner, and he leaves Courcy Castle irrevocably compromised. Again, Trollope's description as to how the wealth, snobbery and high living at Courcy Castle slowly but surely seduce Crosbie into the sacrifice of his better judgement and sense of right has all the ring of truth and reality. From this Lily's tragedy follows as night follows day. But it is to be doubted whether she suffers more than her first and only lover. No vengeance on her part or on that of any of her relations or friends (and Johnny Eames's attack on him at the railway station is milk and water compared with it) could have hurt Crosbie more than his marriage to Alexandrina. Even the reader is made to feel a twinge or two for him in his remorse and grief, so terrible is the retribution which overtakes him: and this not because Trollope had any wish to throw a sop to his readers, but logically, growing from the cold-blooded temperament of Alexandrina herself and his own final complete indifference to her.

Mrs Roper's boarding-house, and Johnny Eames's existence there, his disastrous flirtation with Amelia Roper, the marital ups and downs of the Lupex pair and his friendship with the feeble Cradell, form the kernel for the remainder of the action. This was Trollope's first attempt to delineate the seamier side of life, the milieu of the boarding-house denizens of London. The best one can say of it is that it is adequate and reasonably convincing; and after all, there is no reason why it should have been otherwise since Trollope had led such an existence in his early days and knew the types he was describing. Yet it is the weakest part of the novel. In the course of this survey I have more than once made comparison between Trollope and Dickens, mostly to the detriment of the latter. While I maintain that as far as the portraiture of normal human beings goes Trollope wins hands down, I have in all justice to admit that when it comes to the seamier side, low-life, so called, boarding-house establishments and the vagaries of young hopefuls and middle-aged fools, Dickens is in his kingdom amd remains supreme, the incomparable, the unsurpassed. And he, one feels, would have given a lift, another dimension, to Ma Roper's establishment and its inmates and made them sublimely comic and the highlight of the novel. Trollope, one feels, misses a great potential here. But it is only fair to show the reverse of the coin and to add that Dickens could not have achieved anything like Lily, Crosbie, the clerics, the high life at either the castle or Guestwick Manor. From each according to his ability . . . .

As regards Johnny Eames, it is generally believed that he is a self-portrait. We know from the *Autobiography* something of the awkward, nervous, shy, grubby, unhappy schoolboy Trollope was and how it took him years to gain self-confidence and ability to move in society with any ease. Knowing this we have only to read the description of Eames at his first appearance on the scene to feel that Trollope was seeing himself in that awkward, ungainly, self-conscious young man who in his day-dreams is at his most eloquent in the society of beautiful women and 'without any of Don Juan's heartlessness, is able to conquer in all encounters through the force of his wit and the sweetness of his voice . . . ' Yet poor Johnny, for all his faithfulness and the sincerity of his love, even when he has outgrown his hobbledehoydom and become a man, cannot win the heart of Lily Dale. The scenes between them are among the highlights of the novel, and I shall have more to say of them when coming to deal with its sequel and the last of the series — *The Last Chronicle of Barchester*.

I cannot leave the book without a reference to a character who, though very minor, shows that Trollope could, without any Dickensian exaggeration, portray a genuine countryman. I mean, of course, Hopkins, the squire's old gardener and retainer who, like the cross-grained but well-meaning squire himself, is drawn to the life. Everyone — at least everyone who is country bred — knows the type — loyal, trustworthy, but crusty and a positive tyrant in his own particular domain and who will not be dictated to by anyone, be he squire or whatever, concerning his job. The little incident of his sword-crossing with the squire because of his high-handedness with Jolliffe the bailiff over the matter of stable manure is a delicious little piece of comedy. Moreover, Trollope uses him more importantly in a very subtle way to influence the course of the action. Mrs Dale and her daughters have fallen out with the squire and given him notice of their intention to leave the Small House and move into rooms in the village — a fact which, unknown to them, has cut him to the heart. This is the situation in chapter 53, 'Loquitur Hopkins', when Lily and her mother are discussing the matter.

'I think Hopkins will miss us more than any one else,' she said. 'Hopkins will have no one to scold.'

Just at that moment Hopkins appeared at the parlour window, and signified his desire for a conference.

'You must come round,' said Lily. 'It's too cold for the window to be opened. I always like to get him into the house, because he feels himself a little abashed by the chairs and tables; or, perhaps, it is the carpet that is too much for him. Out on the gravel-walks he is such a terrible tyrant, and in the greenhouse he almost tramples upon one!'

Hopkins, when he did appear at the parlour door, seemed by his manner to justify Lily's discretion. He was not at all masterful in his tone or bearing, and seemed to pay to the chairs and tables all the deference which they could have expected.

'So you be going in earnest, ma'am,' he said, looking down at Mrs. Dale's feet.

As Mrs. Dale did not answer him at once, Lily spoke: — 'Yes, Hopkins, we are going in a very few days, now. We shall see you sometimes, I hope, over at Guestwick.'

'Humph!' said Hopkins. 'So you be really going! I didn't think it'd ever come to that, miss; I didn't indeed, — and no more it oughtn't; but of course it ain't for me to say anything. But this I will say, I've lived here about t' squire's place, man and boy, jist all my life, seeing I was born here, as you knows, Mrs. Dale; and of all the bad things I ever see come about the place, this is a sight the worst.'

'Oh, Hopkins!'

'The worst of all, ma'am; the worst of all! It'll just kill t' squire! There's ne'ery doubt in the world about that. It'll be the very death of t' old man.'

'That's nonsense, Hopkins,' said Lily.

'Very well, miss. I don't say but what it is nonsense; only you'll see. There's Mr. Bernard, — he's gone away; — and by all accounts he never did care very much for the place. They all say he's a-going to the Hingies. And Miss Bell is going to be married, — which is all proper, in course; why should your mamma be all for going away? She ain't going to marry no one. Here's the house, and there's she, and there's t' squire; and why should she be for going away? So much going away all at once can't be for any good. It's just a breaking up of everything, as though nothing wasn't good enough for nobody. I never went away, and I can't abide it.'

'Well, Hopkins; it's settled now,' said Mrs. Dale, 'and I'm afraid it can't be unsettled.'

'Settled; — well. Tell me this: do you expect, Mrs. Dale, that he's to live there all alone by hisself without any one to say a cross word to, — unless it be me or Dingles, for Jolliffe's worse than nobody, he's so mortial cross hisself. Of course he can't stand it. If you goes away, Mrs. Dale, Mister Bernard, he'll be squire in less than twelve months. He'll come back from the Hinges, then, I suppose?'

'I don't think my brother-in-law will take it in that way, Hopkins.'

'Ah, ma'am, you don't know him, — not as I knows him; — all the ins and outs and crinks and crannies of him. I knows him as I does the old apple-trees that I've been a-handling for forty year. There's a deal o'f bad wood about them old cankered trees, and some folk say they ain't worth the ground they stand on; but I know where the sap runs, and when the fruit-blossom shows itself I know where the fruit will be the sweetest. It don't take much to kill one of them old trees, — but there's life in 'm yet if they be well handled.'

'I'm sure I hope my brother's life may be long spared to him,' said Mrs. Dale.

'Then don't be taking yourself away, ma'am, into them gashly lodgings at Guestwick. I says they are gashly for the likes of a Dale. It is not for me to speak, ma'am, of course. And I only came up now just to know what things you'd like with you out of the greenhouse.'

'Oh, nothing, Hopkins, thank you,' said Mrs. Dale.

'He told me to put up for you the best I could pick, and I means to do it;' and Hopkins, as he spoke, indicated by a motion of his head that he was making reference to the squire.

'We shan't have any place for them,' said Lily.

'I must send a few, miss, just to cheer you up a bit. I fear you'll be very dolesome there. And the doctor, — he ain't got what you can call a regular garden, but there is a bit of a place behind.'

'But we wouldn't rob the dear old place,' said Lily.

'For the matter of that what does it signify? T' squire'll be that wretched he'll turn sheep in here to destroy the place, or he'll have the garden ploughed. You see if he don't. As for the place, the place is clean done for if you leave it. You don't suppose he'll go and let the Small House to strangers. T' squire ain't one of that sort any ways.'

'Ah me!' exclaimed Mrs. Dale, as soon as Hopkins had taken himself off.

'What is it, mamma? He's a dear old man, but surely what he says cannot make you really unhappy.'

'It is so hard to know what one ought to do. I did not mean to be selfish, but it seems to me as though I were doing the most selfish thing in the world.'

'Nay, mamma; it has been anything but selfish. Besides, it is we that have done it; not you.'

'Do you know, Lily, that I also have that feeling as to breaking up one's old mode of life of which Hopkins spoke. I thought that I should be glad to escape from this place, but now that the time has come I dread it.'

'Do you mean that you repent?'

Mrs. Dale did not answer her daughter at once, fearing to commit herself by words which could not be retracted. But at last she said, 'Yes, Lily; I think I do repent. I think that it has not been well done.'

'Then let it be undone,' said Lily.

And so, thanks to Hopkins' protest and homely eloquence, their quarrel with the Squire is made up and the Dales stay on at the Small House.

Technically the novel may not be as perfect as *Barchester Towers* — it has its small Trollopian prolixities — but it goes deeper, and must be reckoned as one of his half-dozen greatest works.

RACHEL RAY

Every woman, every schoolgirl should read this novel if only to make her aware of how much she has to be thankful for in living at the present time rather than in the nineteenth century. For in Rachel Ray, Trollope gives us the first of his many portraits of the average middle-class Victorian girl or young unmarried woman, and to us an astonishing, incredibly spineless being we find her to be. But surrounded as she was by a cloud of taboos and 'proprieties' (the most overworked word in the vocabulary of both Jane Austen and Trollope, and indeed of most Victorian novelists), and brought up in conditions that seem appalling to us and which no young woman would tolerate today for an instant, we must not be too hasty in condemning and despising her. She was under the domination of her parents to an extent that parents today must regard with a mixture of aversion and wry envy, and her whole upbringing was aimed at teaching her explicit obedience to their wishes and commands, and to regard herself as a meek, submissive, inferior being without any ideas or ambition of her own, a mere shadow of her male counterpart, all clinging feminine weakness, leaning for support firstly on her parents then on her husband, unfit for education, votes or intelligent discussion, a purveyor of domestic comfort and bearer of children, yet at the same time taught by their virtuous strait-laced mammas to regard sex as sinful, a thing not to be mentioned and only indulged in for the purpose of marital procreation. Her social proprieties were stringent and manifold. To be seen alone with a man,* to go anywhere unaccompanied,** to accept a lover's proposal the first time or without any 'maidenly reserve and hesitation', to allow a man to call her by her Christian name, was to break a whole code of Victorian morals and lay herself open to the charge of gross 'impropriety'. If she received or wrote a letter to a possible boy-friend it was expected that it should be shown to her parents. In fact she had precious little life of her own and no independence.

Bearing all this in mind there is no cause for surprise to read in Sir William Hardman's *Letters and Memoirs* written pretty well in the middle of the century: 'Unmarried girls are a mistake. Set them down to sober conversation with men of the world and they are little better than idiots. The humanising influences of matrimony are required to fit a woman for the society of men'; or in poor Mr Bennet's rueful acknowledgement of the character of his daughters: ' "They have none of them much to recommend them . . . . they are all silly and ignorant like other girls." '; or in Jane Austen's own comment on Catherine Morland in *Northanger Abbey*: 'and her mind about as ignorant and uninformed as the female mind at seventeen usually is'; or in Byron's satiric comment on English girls as against Italians in *Beppo*:

> 'Tis true your budding Miss is very charming,
>   But shy and awkward at first coming out,
> And so alarm'd that she is quite alarming,
>   All giggle, blush, half pertness and half pout,
> And glancing at Mamma for fear there's harm in
>   What you, she, it or they may be about.
> The nursery still lisps out in all they utter —
> Besides, they always smell of bread and butter.

In view of their home life and upbringing is it any wonder that Victorian girls spent so much time, energy, ingenuity and in many cases downright hypocrisy in order to

---

* And this applied not only to unmarried girls but to elderly spinsters as well. In *Wives and Daughters* we find: 'But Miss Phoebe, who did not consider it quite maidenly to go and stand close to Mr Preston, and survey the shelves of books in such close proximity to a gentleman . . . .'

** Readers of *Pride and Prejudice* may recall that Elizabeth's unexpected appearance at Netherfield to enquire after her sister 'created a great deal of surprise. That she should have walked three miles . . . . and *by herself*, was almost incredible to Mrs Hurst and Miss Bingley; and Elizabeth was convinced that they held her in contempt for it.'

procure husbands at almost any price? — a fact brought home to us by Trollope in such characters as Lucinda Roanoke, Arabella Trefoil, Griselda Grantly, Alexandrina de Courcy and other lonely, trampled-on figures. But even when married their bondage was by no means over and their status still deplorable, expected as they were to be subservient to their husbands' 'authority' and to hand themselves, their fortune (if any) and their children to the man's control be he never so much a tyrant or debauchee.* These facts should be borne in mind by readers today when they tend to lose patience and sympathy with certain Victorian fictional females.

Rachel Ray, living with her widowed mother and widowed elder sister, Mrs Prime (Dorothea), is just such a one — with more spirit than her mindless vacillating mother and without the religious fanaticism of her sister, but a typical Victorian girl, pliant and obedient and with any sense of rebellion kept dutifully under control. With Dorothea Prime, Trollope has drawn a picture of a narrow-minded religious bigot taken (like her would-be wooer, the Revd Prong) to almost Dickensian lengths. To her, men are wolves who regard women as their natural prey, and to be kept at bay at all costs. So that when a rumour comes to her ears that her young sister has been seen alone, actually alone with a young man, she regards it as 'tidings which hardly admitted of being discussed with decency and which had to be spoken of below the breath.' But when timidly questioned by her mother, Rachel has the spirit to admit that she has indeed been "walking under the churchyard elms with — that young man from the brewery," and to maintain not only that there was nothing wrong about it but that she was prepared to meet him again. On hearing this, Dorothea regards her as a lost soul, and Mrs Ray, in a typical Victorian weepy scene, is brought near to the dreadful conclusion that her daughter is dead to all decency. But worse is to come. After giving her mother the assurance that Luke Rowan is away and will not be at the Tappitts where she is going to spend the afternoon with her friends the three Tappitt girls, that same evening the horrified Dorothea comes to her mother red hot with news.

"Rachel has not come home yet, of course?" said Mrs. Prime.

"No; not yet. She is with the Miss Tappitts."

"No, mother, she is not with the Miss Tappitts:" and her voice, as she said these words, was dreadful to the mother's ears.

"Isn't she? I thought she was. Do you know where she is?"

"Half an hour since I saw her alone with —"

"With whom? Not with that young man from the brewery, for he is at Exeter."

"Mother, he is here, — in Haslehurst! Half an hour since he and Rachel were standing alone together beneath the elms in the churchyard. I saw them with my own eyes."

So when she returns home poor Rachel finds an atmosphere of ice and gloom and she herself regarded as a brand to be plucked from the burning, and all because Luke had returned unexpectedly from Exeter and had escorted her most of the way home from the Tappitts. And so horrified is Dorothea at such immoral goings-on that she declares she

---

* One of the reasons why *The Tenant of Wildfell Hall* fell foul of some reviewers and many readers was because Anne Brontë not only allowed Helen Huntingdon to escape from her husband, but also to take their son with her against all the canons of Victorian law.

must leave home and live elsewhere. But Rachel succeeds in talking her mother round, in the course of which conversation we are given another (to us) scarcely credible Victorian social convention.

> Mrs. Ray was soon led into talking about Mr. Rowan as though he were not a wolf . . . . There was no word spoken of him as a lover; but Rachel told her mother that the man had called her by her Christian name, and Mrs. Ray had fully understood the sign. "My darling, you mustn't let him do that." "No, mamma, I won't. But he went on talking so fast that I had not time to stop him, and after that it was not worth while."

For a Victorian gentleman to address a lady by her first name was regarded as being too-too familiar; and in fact they went on calling one another Mr — and Miss — even when in love, if not actually engaged. The mind boggles trying to envisage their reaction if they could be placed in our society where everyone, regardless of familiarity, decorum or age, calls everyone else by their first name, and women smoke and drink and swear as openly as men.

But it is all the more a triumph of Trollope's art that he is able to make the love story of such a conventional, sat-on, timid, inexperienced, uneducated, law-abiding average Victorian girl a subject of unflagging interest and practically the whole theme of the novel. When Charlotte Brontë boasted that she created Jane Eyre as a challenge to contemporary fictional convention that a heroine must be beautiful and attracting many lovers, she was not in the same running as Trollope here. Jane Eyre may be plain, small and insignificant to look at, but she is well educated and can make a living as a governess. Rachel Ray has no such advantages: all that can be said of her was that she was 'well made, tall and straight, with great appearance of health and strength', with 'hair, not flaxen, but of light-brown tint, thick, and full, and glossy.' But without any of the melodrama of Charlotte Brontë's novel (no already-married masterful men as lovers or mad secret wives hidden away in rambling manor houses and gibbering about the passages at night) Trollope makes ordinary Rachel Ray and her love for Luke Rowan infinitely more convincing. She, along with her mother and Mrs Tappitt, is yet another example of Trollope's unrivalled genius for getting under the skin of everyday unattractive women and making them not only convincing but interesting — an ability quite beyond Dickens and Thackeray, or for that matter any other male novelist.

Shortly after the furore caused by the advent of Luke Rowan as her suitor, Rachel receives a written formal invitation to Mrs Tappitt's party — an affair regarded as one of the highlights of Haslehurst's social life. It is typical of Victorian prudery and Mrs Ray's weakmindedness that family reaction to the invitation should be negative, dancing being regarded by the more puritanically religious as sinful, and that Mrs Ray, with Rachel showing strong signs of desiring to go and being stubborn, and Dorothea condemning such an idea out of hand, should take herself off to consult her minister, the Revd Comfort, about it. When she finds that the reverend gentleman is surprisingly broad-minded and sees no harm either in Rachel's associating with Luke or in going to the party, she cannot of course carry her objections any further, and gives her her permission — to the horror of Dorothea who, declaring this to be the last straw, packs bag and baggage and leaves to share a home with her equally silly and bigoted friend, Miss Pucker.

The two chapters describing the ball are Trollope at his best, and in their own very different way compare with the famous description of Natasha's first grand ball in *War and Peace*. In both, the emotions of the young girls are marvellously caught: we can almost hear the beating of their hearts with the excitement of anticipation, fear of making mistakes, of being ignored, of a dozen things. But Natasha, for all her fears, is a Russian girl from an aristocratic home which has sensible views on the association of men and women and dancing and sexual matters, and knows nothing of that spirit-crushing damnable puritanism and inculcated sex inferiority that was the English girl's birthright. Trollope's task is therefore so much the more difficult than Tolstoy's; but he rises to it magnificently. Every emotion, every detail is made vivid: her ignorance of how to use her card; the anger of Mr Buckett when she forgets her engagement to dance with him; the annoyance of Walter Cornbury when Luke thwarts his attempt to flirt with her; the unconcealed frustration of Mr Griggs when she declares she is too tired to dance with him; her tremulous delight in, yet fear of, Luke's intimate remarks while dancing with her; the smothered anger of Mr Tippett on discovering that his wife has secretly run him to the expense of heaven knows how many bottles of champagne; the lip-biting anger of Mrs Tippett as she perceives that Luke Rowan (as indeed all the men) prefers Rachel to her own daughters, more particularly since the main object of the ball was to use them as hooks to bait him with; Rachel's alarm when Luke, warmed by the dancing and drinking, begins to say things which sound very like declarations of love and driving her into leaving the ball early — all this is superbly done.

The story runs its inevitable course. Luke, undeterred, and instinctively feeling Rachel does love him, calls on Mrs Ray, and wins her reluctant good will and permission to be accepted as Rachel's lover. But when he comes a second time and finds Rachel alone, we get this ultra-Victorian scene:

She had filled herself full of resolutions as to what she would do when this moment came, — as to how she would behave and what words she would utter. But all that was gone from her now. She could only stand still and tremble. Of course he might call her Rachel; — might call her what he pleased. To him, with his wider experience, that now became manifest enough.

"You must give me leave for more than that, Rachel, if you would not send me away wretched. You must let me call you my own." Then he moved round the table towards her; and as he moved, though she retreated from him, she did not retreat with a step as rapid as his own. "Rachel," — and he put out his hand to her — "I want you to be my wife." She allowed the tips of her fingers to turn themselves toward him, as though unable altogether to refuse the greeting which he offered her, but as she did so she turned away from him, and bent down her head. She had heard all she wanted to hear. Why did he not go away, and leave her to think of it? He had named to her the word so sacred between man and woman. He had said that he sought her for his wife. What need was there that he should stay longer?

He got her hand in his, and then passed his arm round her waist. "Say, love; say, Rachel; — shall it be so? Nay, but I will have an answer from you. You shall look it to me, if you will not speak it;" and he got his head round over her shoulder, as though to look into her eyes.

"Oh, Mr. Rowan; pray don't; — pray don't pull me."

"But, dearest, say a word to me. You must say some word. Can you learn to love me, Rachel?"

Learn to love him! The lesson had come to her very easily. How was it possible, she had once thought, not to love him.

"Say a word to me," said Rowan, still struggling to look into her face; "one word, and then I will let you go."

"What word?"

"Say to me, 'Dear Luke, I will be your wife.' "

She remained for a moment quite passive in his hands, trying to say it, but the words would not come. Of course she would be his wife. Why need he trouble her further?

"Nay, but, Rachel, you shall speak, or I will stay with you here till your mother comes, and she shall answer for you. If you had disliked me I think you would have said so."

"I don't dislike you," she whispered.

"And do you love me?" She slightly bowed her head. "And you will be my wife?" Again she went through the same little piece of acting. "And I may call you Rachel now?" In answer to this question she shook herself free from his slackened grasp, and escaped away across the room.

"You cannot forbid me now. Come and sit down by me, for of course I have got much to say to you. Come and sit down, and indeed I will not trouble you again."

Then she went to him very slowly, and sat with him, leaving her hand in his, listening to his words, and feeling in her heart the full delight of having such a lover.

To his contemporary readers, male and female, but especially female, such a scene would no doubt seem normal enough. Our reaction must be to marvel at the unresponsive timidity and hypocrisy of the Victorian female and to wonder that men ever bothered to persuade them to marry them. But that is nothing to what is to come in the way of female door-mattery; for after all the if-ing and but-ing and the counter-plot of Luke's mother and Mrs Tippett to sabotage his engagement to Rachel, when Luke writes her her first love letter with its mention of their being married 'after Christmas' Rachel, like the dutiful Victorian daughter she is, gives her mother the letter to read. And once more the mindless Mrs Ray, finding the problem too much for her, has to say to her daughter: ' "If you don't mind, my dear, I'll take the young man's letter out to Mr. Comfort, and consult him. I never felt myself so much in need of somebody to advise me. Mr. Comfort is an old man, and you won't mind his seeing the letter." '

> Rachel did mind it very much, but she had no means of saving herself from her fate. She did not like the idea of having her love-letter submitted to the clergyman of the parish. I do not know any young lady who would have liked it . . . .

Imagine a modern girl in the same position! Even this is not the end, for worse is to come. As a result of the Revd Comfort's perusal and advice, poor Rachel is given her orders: she is to answer Luke's letter herself, but she must not give rein to any expression of affection and must address him as 'Mr. Rowan' and end the letter with 'Yours truly'. And knowing in her heart that such a letter will almost certainly make her lover very indignant and angry and perhaps even drive him into no longer loving her — and it is this which must sink her most in the eyes of today's reader — she nevertheless meekly does as she is ordered. The same reader can be forgiven if he takes the line that it would serve her right if her lover threw her over there and then. Trollope's readers, presumably, would tell themselves what a good and obedient girl she was and pray that Luke would understand and forgive, and that all would come right in the end. Which it does, of course. After carrying umbrage a little way; after a late glimmer of sense from Mrs Ray, all misunderstandings are cleared up — but not in the usual way or by the expected characters. This is left to two women who are minor protagonists — Mrs Cornbury and Mrs Stuart. The former, as a friend of Rachel and the married daughter of the Revd Comfort, feels partly responsible for the dreadful letter, seeks out Luke and gives him a straight talking to. The latter, a blunt countrywoman and neighbour of the Rays, with no time for Mrs Ray's mindless shilly-shallying, arranges for the young couple to meet and be alone together in her cottage, where all misunderstandings are cleared away. Luke gets his Rachel and his delayed triumph over the Tippetts at the brewery.

I conclude by repeating my first words. The novel should be read by every man and woman — and especially every woman — who feels in these uneasy and difficult times that the nineteenth century was a better era for living in. Never have the humbug and cant of Victorian society been so exposed, and ironically by a novelist who had no axe to grind (unlike Gissing, for example), and who, we are constantly being told, simply accepted the social scene as it was and did no more than use its accepted codes and manners to describe them as he saw them, with unprotesting objectivity. As such it is a triumph.

CAN YOU FORGIVE HER?

Of all Trollope's novels this, the first of the Palliser or 'political' series, is *the* curate's egg among them. Those parts which are good must be counted as equalling anything he ever wrote; the bad ones are among the worst.

The novel is an amalgam of three separate narratives, each of which is concerned with a triangle of characters — two men and a woman: (1) George Vavasor, John Grey and Alice Vavasor (2) Lady Glencora, Plantagenet Palliser and Burgo Fitzgerald (3) Widow Greenow, Cheesacre and Bellfield. Let us get the bad third of the egg thrown out right away and say that the sections which have the widow and her rival suitors for theme are an artistic blemish which comes near to ruining the book. Not only are the episodes pathetic failures in themselves but, even if they had succeeded as comic relief — which is far from being the case — their blending with the rest of the story would have been as successful as the proverbial oil and water or salt put in the tea instead of sugar. As Edward Marsh succinctly expressed it in his Preface to the Crown Edition of The Oxford Trollope: 'Trollope's sense of social distinctions, usually so accurate, has deserted him here.' Or more concisely and bluntly, Trollope had no gift for low comedy. The flaw is to Trollope's novel very similar to the Jewish episodes in George Eliot's *Daniel Deronda* in that both mar what would otherwise have been a masterpiece. Fortunately in both novels the flaw is detachable, and as far as this novel is concerned the reader is advised to skip ruthlessly all the chapters dealing with Aunt Greenow and her rustic suitors.

For compensation the other themes are superbly done. Some critics have no time for Alice Vavasor and her indecisions — the *raison d'être* of the book's silly title. It would have served her right, they say, if she had lost both her lovers: John Grey who was too good for her, and her cousin George Vavasor who was not good enough, adding that in any case in modern eyes her dilemma is very much a storm in a tea cup since we no longer hold the Victorian view so trenchantly expressed by Lady Midlothian in her horrified letter to poor Alice that 'There are things in which a young lady has no right to change her mind . . . and when a young lady has accepted a gentleman, that is one of them. He cannot legally make you become his wife, but he has a right to claim you before God and man.' But here I think such critics tend to judge from a contemporary viewpoint and miss the subtlety of Trollope's portrait. It is precisely because she has a mind of her own that Alice falls between the stools and brings misery, anger and frustration not only to her lovers but to herself. Rachel Ray or Lucy Morris, for example, typical Victorian women in that they are single minded, passively meek and completely unenterprising, would never have found themselves in Alice's dilemma: they would have clung to the first lover to declare himself with no second thoughts or hesitations, quite prepared to accept their lot without questioning the will of their sovereign lord and master. But Alice is made of better stuff. Had she lived today she would have had no difficulty in resolving her problem which in essence was a desire to make something of her life; and her dilemma forcibly thrusts home to us the unenviable lot of the Victorian woman, more particularly if she were intelligent and well-educated. She could not hope to be a doctor, nurse, teacher, editor, journalist, welfare officer, solicitor — any of those things in fact which women take for granted today. Practically the only job open to her to make herself independent was that of governess (and then only if she was reasonably qualified) — and we know from the Brontës the miseries that could entail. For ninety per cent of them the only future open to them was marriage — marriage at all costs: hence all the Victorian female's tricks and wiles in order to catch her man.

Trollope shows us acutely and perhaps with a little gentle irony (he was no Women's Rights enthusiast) both Alice's vague aspirations and the varying attitudes they engender in her towards her two lovers.

> A woman's life is important to her, — as is that of a man to him, — not chiefly in regard to that which she shall do with it. The chief thing for her to look to is the manner in which that something shall be done. It is of moment to a young man when entering life to decide whether he shall make hats or shoes; but not of half the moment that will be that other decision, whether he shall make good shoes or bad. And so with a woman; — if she shall have recognised the necessity of truth and honesty for the purposes of her life, I do not know that she need ask herself many questions as to what she will do with it.
>
> Alice Vavasor was ever asking herself that question, and had by degrees filled herself with a vague idea that there was a something to be done; a something over and beyond, or perhaps altogether beside that of marrying and having two children; — if she only knew what it was. She had filled herself, or had been filled by her cousins, with an indefined ambition that made her restless without giving her any real food for her mind. When she told herself that she would have no scope for action in that life in Cambridgeshire which Mr. Grey was preparing for her, she did not herself know what she meant by action. When she did contrive to find any answer to that question as to what she should do with her life, — or rather what she would wish to do with it if she were a free agent, it was generally of a political nature. She was not so far advanced as to think that women should be lawyers and doctors, or to wish that she might have the privilege of the franchise for herself; but she had undoubtedly a hankering after some second-hand political manoeuvring. She would have liked, I think, to have been the wife of the leader of a Radical opposition, in the time when such men were put into prison, and to have kept up for him his seditious correspondence while he lay in the Tower. She would have carried the answers to him inside her stays, — and have made long journeys down into northern parts without any money, if the cause required it. She would have liked to have around her ardent spirits, male or female, who would have talked of 'the cause,' and have kept alive in her some flame of

political fire. As it was, she had no cause. Her father's political views were very mild. Lady Macleod's were deadly Conservative. Kate Vavasor was an aspiring Radical just now, because her brother was in the same line; but during the year of the love-passages between George and Alice, George Vavasor's politics had been as Conservative as you please. He did not become a Radical till he had quarrelled with his grandfather. Now, indeed, he was possessed of very advanced views, — views with which Alice felt that she could sympathise. But what would be the use of sympathising down in Cambridgeshire? John Grey had, so to speak, no politics. He had decided views as to the treatment which the Roman Senate received from Augustus, and had even discussed with Alice the conduct of the Girondists at the time of Robespierre's triumph; but for Manchester and its cares he had no apparent solicitude, and had declared to Alice that he would not accept a seat in the British House of Commons if it were offered to him free of expense. What political enthusiasm could she indulge with such a companion down in Cambridgeshire?

It is essential that we should understand and sympathize with this vague longing of Alice's, otherwise we can feel no sympathy for her vacillations and quandaries which, I have already stated, are the mainspring of the typically off-putting title.

The novel opens admirably with a first chapter which puts Alice and her not very paternal father before us, followed by a second revealing a situation which cannot fail to grip the reader by the sheer potentiality of its possibilities. Alice is engaged to John Grey after having been in love with her cousin George Vavasor, though not formally betrothed to him. But George is a spendthrift and complete egotist and had treated her badly and been unfaithful to her, forcing her to break off the affair. But she had done so with a sad heart, and still holds him in affection even against her will. Now, we learn, she is on the verge of taking a holiday in Switzerland with her cousin Kate, George's doting sister, and George himself as their guide and 'protector'. The news of this gets around, and a horrified Lady Macleod, a sort of aunt and guardian of the girl, descends on her to enquire into the matter. But she gets no change out of Alice who, we discover from the interview, is a refreshing variation from the Rachel Rays and Emily Whartons, knows her own mind and sticks to her guns. The only trouble is that it is this very independent spirit of Alice's that gets her into such deep waters. The average Victorian heroine would have been happy beyond belief with her present fiancé and regarded her affair with cousin George as a mental aberration to be put from her mind for ever. But Alice has doubts. And here Trollope yet again shows his knowledge of female nature as in the next two chapters he draws us portraits of the two lovers side by side: hero and villain, Hyperion and Satyr, the one so good, so understanding, so tolerant, so temperate, with his nature so under control as to be almost perfect; the other not without good qualities, but violent, selfish and egotistical, so brutally male. The choice, one might think, is obvious. But Alice's nature has that in it which is drawn to the more impulsive, volatile, even violent sexual opposite. In her mind she is continually comparing the two men, and she 'was tormented by a feeling that she had had a more full delight in that love than in this other that had sprung up subsequently'. And over and above this, the idea of being able to help her cousin by her money in his political ambitions appeals to her far more than merely retiring into the wilds of Cambridgeshire to vegetate as John Grey's wife. As she wrote to him, begging him to postpone their marriage: 'What if I should wake some morning after six months living with you, and tell you that the quiet of your home was making me mad?' And when he is forced to accept her decree and tells her it is driving him to despair, we are given this significant passage:

> She looked up into his face, but it was still serene in all its manly beauty. Her cousin George if he were moved to strong feeling, showed it at once in his eyes, — in his mouth, in the whole visage of his countenance. He glared in his anger, and was impassioned in his love. But Mr. Grey when speaking of the happiness of his entire life, when confessing that it was now at stake with a decision against him that would be ruinous to it, spoke without a quiver in his voice, and had no more sign of passion in his face than if he were telling his gardener to move a rose tree.

And now, with this acute dilemma facing her, she is planning to spend a holdiay abroad with her cousin Kate and this very same George. The situation is explosive, and explode it does.

' "And does Mr. Grey know that he is going?" ' Lady Macleod had demanded of Alice, suggesting pointedly that he would strongly disapprove, and that as a meek little wife-to-be she ought to be ruled by him and respect his wishes. John Grey did know, since Alice had written and told him, and although not entirely happy with the state of affairs, he had replied in a temperate, understanding, characteristic letter in the course of which he makes a statement, a sort of half prophecy, of particular interest to us today who see its fulfilment in the slips of girls who travel all over the world unattended and think nothing of it.

> Touching the tour, I quite agree with you that you and Kate would have been uncomfortable alone. It's a very fine theory, that of women being able to get along without men as well as with them; but, like other fine theories, it will be found very troublesome by those who first put it in practice. Gloved hands, petticoats, feminine softness, and the general homage paid to beauty, all stand in the way of success. These things may perhaps some day be got rid of, and possibly with advantage; but while young ladies are still encumbered with them a male companion will always be found to be a comfort.

The effect of the letter on Alice (and here Trollope gives us yet another instance of his profound understanding of the female heart) is to make her wish that he were less perfect. 'She knew that he was noble and a gentleman to the last drop of his blood. And yet — yet — yet there was almost a feeling of disappointment in that he had not written such a letter as Lady Macleod had anticipated.'

The two chapters devoted to the Swiss holiday are among the finest ever penned by Trollope. He has been criticized for the plodding prosaicness of his style. But then, apart from perhaps Thackeray (and this is the only superiority to which he can lay claim) which of the nineteenth century novelists can be said to have style? They were all too busy concentrating on plot, narrative and character to pay much attention to that. When it comes to description and plain statement Trollope can be very ordinary and flat, altogether lacking that cutting edge of memorableness which Dickens at his best can give. This admitted, let us go on to qualify it by adding that when the scene demands it he nearly always rises to the occasion. And since it is given to few novelists to be supreme in every branch of their art, one can surely be content with that and pass over their defects.

But to return to the two chapters I have singled out. In these ('The Balcony at Basle' and 'The Bridge over the Rhine') Trollope rises to memorableness, almost to poetry.

The young people's holiday is almost over, and the three are sitting on the balcony of their hotel overlooking the Rhine before turning in for the night. On the pretext of having to pack, Kate, whose greatest desire in life is to get Alice and George married, purposely leaves them together. Their dialogue, made to the romantic accompaniment of the river-noises and the deepening twilight, is hypnotic in its power of suggestion, in its very reticence. For the first time since their separation he refers to their past. "I am not going to make love to you," he says, nor does he; but he skilfully manoeuvres the conversation along intimate lines, pours scorn on her fiancé and his placid character and mode of life and tells her he can never be her friend if she marries him — all to her deep distress. Kate returns, and the three take a good-night stroll over the bridge, and after their return to the hotel there is a poignant scene between Alice and Kate. The next day they begin their journey home, and Trollope concludes the chapter in this superbly non-committal way:

> There is nothing further to be told of their tour. They were but two days and nights on the road from Basle to London; and during those two days and nights neither George nor Kate spoke a word to Alice of her marriage, nor was any allusion made to the balcony at the inn, or to the bridge over the river.

But the reader is made to feel that the affair is by no means over — as indeed it is far from being. Moreover — though we do not realize it at the time — we have been made to see for the one and only time George Vavasor at his best: a fact which, when we come to realize it, makes his future infamy and degradation all the more poignant. That renewed contact with George, and especially her conversation on the balcony with him, and the contrast he makes in her mind with John Grey, upset all Alice's calculations and open up old-new emotions. Torn by these, she becomes less and less assured that Grey can make her happy, and in spite of his arguments and remonstrations she puts off the date of their marriage to the Greek Kalends. This alone causes scandal among her relatives; but as though that were not enough, in answer to a letter from George telling her of his political ambitions and asking for her help and her hand in marriage, she accepts him, only stipulating that he should wait twelve months to give her time for her wounds to heal and her self-respect to be restored after her 'jilting' of Grey. And it is here that George, as any other man would have done, makes his vital error. Proud of his conquest of her and over his rival, instead of waiting and showing tact, having no tact he hurries round to her house. The scene beween them is one of the many highlights of the novel.

Chapter XXXV

PASSION VERSUS PRUDENCE

It had not occurred to Alice that her accepted lover would come to her so soon. She had not told him expressly of the day on which she would return, and had not reflected that Kate would certainly inform him. She had been thinking so much of the distant perils of this engagement, that this peril, so sure to come upon her before many days or hours could pass by, had been forgotten. When the name struck her ear, and George's step was heard outside on the landing-place, she felt the blood rush violently to her heart, and she jumped up from her seat panic-stricken and in utter dismay. How should she receive him? And then again, with what form of affection would she be accosted by him? But he was there in the room with her before she had had a moment allowed to her for thought.

She hardly ventured to look up at him; but, nevertheless, she became aware that there was something in his appearance and dress brighter, more lover-like, perhaps newer, than was usual with him. This in itself was an affliction to her. He ought to have understood that such an engagement as theirs not only did not require, but absolutely forbade, any such symptom of young love as this. Even when their marriage came, if it must come, it should come without any customary sign of smartness, without any outward mark of exaltation. It would have been very good in him to have remained away from her for weeks and months; but to come upon her thus, on the first morning of her return, was a cruelty not to be forgiven. These were the feelings with which Alice regarded her betrothed when he came to see her.

'Alice,' said he, coming up to her with his extended hand, — 'Dearest Alice!'

She gave him her hand, and muttered some word which was inaudible even to him; she gave him her hand, and immediately endeavoured to resume it, but he held it clenched within his own, and she felt that she was his prisoner. He was standing close to her now, and she could not escape from him. She was trembling with fear lest worse might betide her even than this. She had promised to marry him, and now she was covered with dismay as she felt rather than thought how very far she was from loving the man to whom she had given this promise.

'Alice,' he said, 'I am a man once again. It is only now that I can tell you what I have suffered during these last few years.' He still held her hand, but he had not as yet attempted any closer embrace. She knew that she was standing away from him awkwardly, almost showing a repugnance to him; but it was altogether beyond her power to assume an attitude of ordinary ease. 'Alice,' he continued, 'I feel that I am a strong man again, armed to meet the world at all points. Will you not let me thank you for what you have done for me?'

She must speak to him! Though the doing so should be ever so painful to her, she must say something . . . .

'You have come to me too quickly, George, and do not reflect how much there is that I must remember. You have said that bygones should be bygones. Let them be so, at any rate as far as words are concerned. Give me a few months in which I may learn, —not to forget them, for that will be impossible, — but to abstain from speaking of them.'

There was something in her look as she spoke, and in the tone of her voice, that was very sad. It struck him forcibly, but it struck him with anger rather than with sadness. Doubtless her money had been his chief object when he offered to renew his engagement with her. Doubtless he would have made no such offer had she been penniless, or even had his own need been less pressing. But, nevertheless, he desired something more than money. The triumph of being preferred to John Grey, — of having John Grey sent altogether adrift, in order that his old love might be recovered, would have been too costly a luxury for him to seek, had he not in seeking it been able to combine prudence with the luxury. But though his prudence had been undoubted, he desired the luxury also. It was on a calculation of the combined advantage that he had made his second offer to his cousin. As he would by no means have consented to proceed with the arrangement without the benefit of his cousin's money, so also did he feel unwilling to dispense with some expression of her love for him, which would be to him triumphant. Hitherto in their present interview there had certainly been no expression of her love.

'Alice,' he said, 'your greeting to me is hardly all that I had hoped.'

'Is it not?' said she. 'Indeed, George, I am sorry that you should be disappointed; but what can I say? You would not have me affect a lightness of spirit which I do not feel?'

'If you wish,' said he, very slowly, — 'If you wish to retract your letter to me, you now have my leave to do so.'

What an opportunity was this of escape! But she had not the courage to accept it. What girl, under such circumstances, would have had such courage? How often are offers made to us which we would almost give our eyes to accept, but dare not accept because we fear the countenance of the offerer? 'I do not wish to retract my letter,' said she, speaking as slowly as he had spoken; 'but I wish to be left awhile, that I may recover my strength of mind. Have you not heard doctors say, that muscles which have been strained, should be allowed rest, or they will never entirely renew their tension? It is so with me now; if I could be quiet for a few months, I think I could learn to face the future with a better courage.'

'And is that all that you can say to me, Alice?'

'What would you have me say?'

'I would fain hear one word of love from you; is that unreasonable? I would wish to know from your own lips that you have satisfaction in the renewed prospect of our union; is that too ambitious? It might have been that I was over-bold in pressing my suit upon you again; but as you accepted it, have I not a right to expect that you should show me that you have been happy in accepting it?'

But she had not been happy in accepting it. She was not happy now that she had accepted it. She could not show to him any sign of such joy as that which he desired to see. And now, at this moment, she feared with an excessive fear that there would come some demand for an outward demonstration of love, such as he in his position might have a right to make. She seemed to be aware that this might be prevented only by such demeanour on her part as that which she had practised, and she could not, therefore, be stirred to the expression of any word of affection. She listened to his appeal, and when it was finished she made no reply. If he chose to take her in dudgeon, he must do so. She would make for him any sacrifice that was possible to her, but this sacrifice was not possible.

'And you have not a word to say to me?' he asked. She looked up at him, and saw that the cicature on his face was becoming ominous; his eyes were bent upon her with all their forbidding brilliance, and he was assuming that look of angry audacity which was so peculiar to him, and which had so often cowed those with whom he was brought in contact.

'No other word, at present, George; I have told you that I am not at ease. Why do you press me now?'

He had her letter to him in the breast-pocket of his coat, and his hand was on it, that he might fling it back to her, and tell her that he would not hold her to be his promised wife under such circumstances as these. The anger which would have induced him to do so was the better part of his nature. Three or four years since, this better part would have prevailed, and he would have given way to his rage. But now, as his fingers played upon the paper, he remembered that her money was absolutely essential to him, — that some of it was needed by him almost instantly, — that on this very morning he was bound to go where money would be demanded from him, and that his hopes with regard to Chelsea could not be maintained unless he was able to make some substantial promise of providing funds. His sister Kate's fortune was just two thousand pounds. That, and no more, was now the capital at his command, if he should abandon this other source of aid. Even that must go, if all other sources should fail him; but he would fain have that untouched, if it were possible. Oh, that that old man in Westmoreland would die and be gathered to his fathers, now that he was full of years and ripe for the sickle! But there was no sign of death about the old man. So his fingers released their hold on the letter, and he stood looking at her in his anger.

'You wish me then to go from you?' he said.

'Do not be angry with me, George!'

'Angry! I have no right to be angry. But, by heaven, I am wrong there. I have the right, and I am angry. I think you owed it me to give me some warmer welcome. Is it to be thus with us always for the next accursed year?'

'Oh, George!'

'To me it will be accursed. But is it to be thus between us always? Alice, I have loved you above all women. I may say that I have never loved any woman but you; and yet I am sometimes driven to doubt whether you have a heart in you capable of love. After all that has passed, all your old protestations, all my repentance, and your proffer of forgiveness, you should have received me with open arms. I suppose I may go now, and feel that I have been kicked out of your house like a dog.'

'If you speak to me like that, and look at me like that, how can I answer you?'

'I want no answer. I wanted you to put your hand in mine, to kiss me, and to tell me that you are once more my own. Alice, think better of it; kiss me, and let me feel my arm once more round your waist.'

She shuddered as she sat, still silent, on her seat, and he saw that she shuddered. With all his desire for her money, — his instant need of it, — this was too much for him; and he turned upon his heel, and left the room without another word. She heard his quick step as he hurried down the stairs, but she did not rise to arrest him. She heard the door slam as he left the house, but still she did not move from her seat. Her immediate desire had been that he should go, — and now he was gone. There was in that a relief which almost comforted her. And this was the man from whom, within the last few days, she had accepted an offer of marriage.

In the midst of these emotional fluxes we enter the aristocratic world of the Pallisers. Lady Glencora Palliser is a cousin of Alice's, though their only previous contact had been when Glencora, in love with Burgo Fitzgerald, had appealed to her to allow them the use of her rooms as a meeting place, and Alice had refused. Despite this, Glencora writes to Alice, inviting her to stay with them at Matching Priory, and after some hesitation, and urged by George, who sees in her association with the Palliser wealth, influence and possible political advantages for himself, she accepts and goes. In the episodes which follow we meet the two characters Trollope always believed to be, along with the Revd Crawley, his greatest creative triumph. I have no wish to dispute that belief, though personally I do not think they overtop Lizzie Eustace, George Vavasor, Dr Grantly, or Mrs Proudie. Still, they are triumph enough, and as living as any characters in fiction: he the typical English aristocrat absorbed in his political ambitions, knowing nothing of passionate love, jealousy, desire, or passionate anything, reticent in his emotions and speech, feeling himself very comfortably and happily married and fully believing Glencora to feel the same. (In parenthesis it must be recalled that we had already made his acquaintance in *The Small House at Allington* where he appears in a ridiculous light as a bachelor and makes feeble passes at the dim already-married Lady Dumbello only to be dismissed with his tail between his legs and a sense of relief that he has failed in his pretensions. The episode is completely out of character. Clearly Trollope then had no thought of the future status he was to give to Palliser, and we simply have, like Palliser himself, to forget the incident.) But unknown to the noble duke his wife is anything but comfortably married. She had been married to the duke by her family almost by force to prevent her making a disgraceful match with the handsome, poverty-stricken, completely irresponsible scapegrace Burgo Fitzgerald, and she carries a chip on her shoulder about it and retains romantic visions of her first love. Thus in her Alice finds, as it were, a double to herself: both being bound morally to one man while in love with another.

Trollope is at his sparkling best whenever the Pallisers — especially Cora — take the stage or he has their marital relationships in review.

If he was dull as a statesman he was more dull in private life, and it may be imagined that such a woman as his wife would find some difficulty in making his society the source of her happiness. Their marriage, in a point of view regarding business, had been a complete success, — and a success, too, when on the one side, that of Lady Glencora, there had been terrible dangers of shipwreck, and when on his side also there had been some little fears of a mishap. As regards her it has been told how near she went to throwing herself, with all her vast wealth, into the arms of a young man whom no father, no guardian, could have regarded as a well-chosen husband for any girl; — one who as yet had shown no good qualities, who had been a spendthrift, unprincipled, and debauched. Alas, she had loved him! It is possible that her love and her wealth might have turned him from evil to good. But who would have ventured to risk her, — I will not say her and her vast inheritances, — on such a chance? That evil, however, had been prevented, and those about her had managed to marry her to a young man, very steady by nature, with worldly prospects as brilliant as her own, and with a station than which the world offers nothing higher. His little threatened mischance, — a passing fancy for a married lady who was too wise to receive vows which were proffered not in the most ardent manner, — had, from special reasons, given some little alarm to his uncle, which had just sufficed at the time to make so very judicious a marriage doubly pleasant to that noble duke. So that all things and all people had conspired to shower substantial comforts on the heads of this couple, when they were joined together, and men and women had not yet ceased to declare how happy were both in the accumulated gifts of fortune.

And as regards Mr. Palliser, I think that his married life, and the wife, whom he certainly had not chosen, but who had dropped upon him, suited him admirably. He wanted great wealth for that position at which he aimed. He had been rich before his marriage with his own wealth, — so rich that he could throw thousands away if he wished it; but for him and his career was needed that colossal wealth which would make men talk about it, — which would necessitate an expansive expenditure, reaching far and wide, doing nothing, or less than nothing, for his own personal comfort, but giving to him at once that rock-like solidity which is so necessary to our great aristocratic politicians. And his wife was, as far as he knew, all that he desired. And since his marriage he had thought that things matrimonial had gone well with him, and with her too. He gave her almost unlimited power of enjoying her money, and interfered but little in her way of life. Sometimes he would say a word of caution to her with reference to those childish ways which hardly became the dull dignity of his position; and his words then would have in them something of unintentional severity, — whether instigated or not by the red-haired Radical Member of Parliament, I will not pretend to say; — but on the whole he was contented and loved his wife, as he thought, very heartily, and at least better than he loved any one else. One cause of unhappiness, or rather one doubt as to his entire good fortune, was beginning to make itself felt, as his wife had to her sorrow already discovered. He had hoped that before this he might have heard that she would give him a child. But the days were young yet for that trouble, and the care had not become a sorrow.

But this judicious arrangement as to properties, this well-ordered alliance between families, had not perhaps suited her as well as it had suited him. I think that she might have learned to forget her early lover, or to look back upon him with a soft melancholy hardly amounting to regret, had her new lord been more tender in his ways with her. I do not know that Lady Glencora's heart was made of that stern stuff which refuses to change its impressions; but it was a heart, and it required food. To love and fondle some one, — to be loved and fondled, were absolutely necessary to her happiness. She wanted the little daily assurance of her supremacy in the man's feelings, the constant touch of love, half accidental half contrived, the passing glance of the eye telling perhaps of some little joke understood only between them two rather than of love, the softness of an occasional kiss given here and there when chance might bring them together, some half-pretended interest in her little doings, a nod, a wink, a shake of the head, or even a pout. It should have been given to her to feed upon such food as this daily, and then she would have forgotten Burgo Fitzgerald. But Mr. Palliser understood none of these things; and therefore the image of Burgo Fitzgerald in all his beauty was ever before her eyes.

But not the less was Mr. Palliser a prosperous man, as to the success of whose career few who knew him had much doubt. It might be written in the book of his destiny that he would have to pass through some violent domestic trouble, some ruin in the hopes of his home, of a nature to destroy then and for ever the worldly prospects of other men. But he was one who would pass through such violence, should it come upon him, without much scathe. To lose his influence with his party would be worse to him than to lose his wife, and public disgrace would hit him harder than private dishonour.

And the present was the very moment in which success was, as was said, coming to him. He had already held laborious office under the Crown, but had never sat in the Cabinet. He had worked much harder than Cabinet Ministers generally work, — but hitherto had worked without any reward that was worth his having. For the stipend which he had received had been nothing to him, — as the great stipend which he would receive, if his hopes were true, would also be nothing to him. To have ascendancy over other men, to be known by his countrymen as one of their real rulers, to have an actual and acknowledged voice in the management of nations, — those were the rewards for which he looked; and now in truth it seemed as though they were coming to him. It was all but known that the existing Chancellor of the Exchequer would separate himself from the Government, carrying various others with him, either before or immediately consequent on the meeting of Parliament; — and it was all but known, also, that Mr. Palliser would fill his place, taking that high office at once, although he had never hitherto sat in that august assembly which men call the Cabinet. He could thus afford to put up with the small everyday calamity of having a wife who loved another man better than she loved him.

That quiet mordant irony is more telling than any emotional indulgence. Glencora comes alive from the moment we meet her as she drives Alice from the station to Matching Priory. Confidences pour from her, half merry but with sad undertones, as she tells the tale of her love for Burgo to the scandalized Alice, keeping nothing back and describing the various personages she will have to meet with schoolgirl venomous glee. She is so young, so naïve, so spirited, so unhappy with such a brave face to the world that we love her instantly.

The story of her final break with Burgo at Lady Monk's party is yet another superb piece of writing. The scene is completely representative of Trollope. All his art is in it. If the reader cannot appreciate this then Trollope is not for him. The episode deals with the supreme crisis in Glencora's life. Will she run away with Burgo, leave her husband and sacrifice name, wealth and position for love? Or will prudence prevail? Had Dickens or Charlotte Brontë given us the same situation, how much more 'drama' they would have extracted from it, with panic stations everywhere for everyone, spies and tell-tales rushing to and fro, interceptions, hysteria, the lot. Trollope keeps it all low key. Everything happens that would happen in life in such a situation. Burgo, vague and shiftless as ever, has made no real plans apart from sponging on his complaisant aunt for £200 and having a post-chaise in possible readiness near by; Glencora herself has not been able to make up her mind. Warned by the detestable duenna, Mrs Marsham, Palliser returns to the party and quietly and without fuss takes his wife home from the very arms of her would-be lover. Burgo is checkmated. Furthermore — and this is the ultimate glory of the episode — when Palliser and his wife eventually get down to explanations (chapter LVIII 'The Pallisers at Breakfast') the whole situation bursts open like an abscess brought to a head. She accuses him of setting spies on her; he denies it and she is forced to believe him as being utterly sincere in his denial.

There was something of feeling in his voice as he said this, — something that almost approached to passion which touched his wife's heart. Whether or not spies would be of any avail, she knew that she had in truth done that of which he had declared that he had never suspected her. She had listened to words of love from her former lover. She had received, and now carried about with her a letter from this man, in which he asked her to elope with him. She had by no means resolved that she would not do this thing. She had been false to her husband; and as her husband spoke of his confidence in her, her own spirit rebelled against the deceit which she herself was practising.

'I know that I have never made you happy,' she said. 'I know that I never can make you happy.'

He looked at her, struck by her altered tone, and saw that her whole manner and demeanour were changed. 'I do not understand what you mean,' he said. 'I have never complained. You have not made me unhappy.' He was one of those men to whom this was enough. If his wife caused him no uneasiness, what more was he to expect from her? No doubt she might have done much more for him. She might have given him an heir. But he was a just man, and knew that the blank he had drawn was his misfortune, and not her fault.

But now her heart was loosed and she spoke out, at first slowly, but after a while with all the quietness of strong passion. 'No, Plantagenet; I shall never make you happy. You have never loved me, nor I you. We have never loved each other for a single moment. I have been wrong to talk to you about spies; I was wrong to go to Lady Monk's; I have been wrong in everything that I have done; but never so wrong as when I let them persuade me to be your wife!'

'Glencora!'

'Let me speak now, Plantagenet. It is better that I should tell you everything; and I will. I will tell you everything; — everything! I do love Burgo Fitzgerald. I do! I do! I do! How can I help loving him? Have I not loved him from the first, — before I had seen you? Did you not know that it was so? I do love Burgo Fitzgerald, and when I went to Lady Monk's last night, I had almost made up my mind that I must tell him so, and that I must go away with him and hide myself. But when he came to speak to me —'

'He has asked you to go with him, then?' said the husband, in whose bosom the poison was beginning to take effect, thereby showing that he was neither above nor below humanity.

Glencora was immediately reminded that though she might, if she pleased, tell her own secrets, she ought not, in accordance with her ideas of honour, tell those of her lover. 'What need is there of asking, do you think, when people have loved each other as we have done?'

'You wanted to go with him, then?'

'Would it not have been the best for you? Plantagenet, I do not love you; — not as women love their husbands when they do love them. But, before God, my first wish is to free you from the misfortune that I have brought on you.' As she made this attestation she started up from her chair, and coming close to him, took him by the coat. He was startled, and stepped back a pace, but did not speak; and then stood looking at her as she went on.

'What matters it whether I drown myself, or throw myself away by going with such a one as him, so that you might marry again, and have a child? I'd die; — I'd die willingly. How I wish I could die! Plantagenet, I would kill myself if I dared.'

He was a tall man and she was short of stature, so that he stood over her and looked upon her, and now she was looking up into his face with all her eyes. 'I would,' she said. 'I would — I would! What is there left for me that I should wish to live?'

Softly, slowly, very gradually, as though he were afraid of what he was doing, he put his arm round her waist. 'You are wrong in one thing,' he said. 'I do love you.'

She shook her head, touching his breast with her hair as she did so.

'I do love you,' he repeated. 'If you mean that I am not apt at telling you so, it is true, I know. My mind is running on other things.'

'Yes,' she said, 'your mind is running on other things.'

'But I do love you. If you cannot love me, it is a great misfortune to us both. But we need not therefore be disgraced. As for that other thing of which you spoke, — of our having, as yet, no child' — and in saying this he pressed her somewhat closer with his arm — 'you allow yourself to think too much of it; — much more of it than I do. I have made no complaints on that head, even within my own breast.'

'I know what your thoughts are, Plantagenet.'

'Believe me that you wrong my thoughts. Of course I have been anxious, and have, perhaps, shown my anxiety by the struggle I have made to hide it. I have never told you what is false, Glencora.'

'No; you are not false!'

'I would rather have you for my wife, childless, — if you will try to love me, — than any other woman, though another might give me an heir. Will you try to love me?'

She was silent. At this moment, after the confession that she had made, she could not bring herself to say that she would even try. Had she said so, she would have seemed to have accepted his forgiveness too easily.

'I think, dear,' he said, still holding her by her waist, 'that we had better leave England for a while. I will give up politics for this season. Should you like to go to Switzerland for the summer, or perhaps to some of the German baths, and then on to Italy when the weather is cold enough?' Still she was silent 'Perhaps your friend, Miss Vavasor, would go with us?'

He was killing her by his goodness. She could not speak to him yet; but now, as he mentioned Alice's name, she gently put up her hand and rested it on the back of his.

From now on Burgo's is a lost cause and he is a lost man. Palliser keeps his word. Resisting the invitation to become Chancellor of the Exchequor, his life's ambition, he turns his back on the political scene and takes his wife, together with Alice for feminine company, to Switzerland. The narration of their travels in the course of which all three attain their ultimate happiness — Glencora by finding herself pregnant, Palliser by the long-deferred hope that he will have a son and heir to his dukedom and wealth, and Alice by the unexpected turning up of the persevering and faithful John Grey — satisfactorily rounds off the story. (Parenthesis: the reader will find the hush-hush marital method of breaking the news of possible pregnancy, and the impossibility of the husband to pass the great news on to a female friend, irresistibly comic.) Burgo Fitzgerald and George Vavasor are, so to speak, cast into the outer darkness of their own useless and malevolent selves. This is not just a sop to the Victorian reader as so many of Dickens's and Thackeray's endings are. Their several ends are just as they would in all probability turn out to be in life.

A word in conclusion. The title is listed as the first of the 'political' novels, but the description should be in inverted commas. Neither in this novel nor in its sequels is there anything that can be called strictly political; some of the main characters happen to be ministers of the crown, that is all. The Palliser novels are no more political than the Barchester novels are religious. In them Trollope very wisely treads only on the fringe of political matters, treating them in terms of social manners and of repercussions in the conduct of his characters. At the same time, by small but astute, knowledgeable means he makes us feel the shadow of the Mother of Parliaments falling over the pages. In such scenes, for example, as that in which George Vavasor takes his seat in the House for the first time; by his constant and usually ironic references to Palliser and his frustrated attempts to rationalize and decimalize the antediluvian British currency (a true case, this, of coming events casting shadows before.) Trollope does indeed give some political flavour to the novel. But flavour is as far as the thing goes in the first three novels of the series at least. When, as in the later ones, he tries to go further and fills his pages with speeches from the House and political names and titles, then the stories sag and the interest flags.* But I shall have more to say on this head when dealing with those novels.

MISS MACKENZIE

Some idea of the range of Trollope's creative powers can be gauged from the fact that between *Can You Forgive Her?* and *The Belton Estate* he wrote so disparate a work as this: a comparatively short novel whose main character is a middle-aged spinster who, unexpectedly left by will enough money to enable her to live in careful independence, is trailed by three money-greedy impecunious predatory males. Margaret Mackenzie is very ignorant of the world and its ways, particularly the male world, having spent the best part of her young life cooped up nursing first her father then her younger brother Walter, an invalid. At the age of thirty-five, following the death of her brother, she finds he has left her the whole of his estate, which brings her in an income of some £800 a year — a fact incidentally which brings down on her head the bitter recrimination of the rest of the Mackenzie family.

Margaret decides to put London behind her and begin a fresh life on her own in Littlebath, where she takes furnished lodgings. At once she finds herself in a cross-fire between her neighbour Miss Todd ('a stout jolly-looking dame with a capacious bonnet', who plays cards and enjoys life generally, doesn't go to church and snaps her fingers at religious fuddy-duddies) and the Revd and Mrs Stumfold and their small circle. Being religious and given to church-going like all Victorian ladies, she joins the Stumfold lot, but has eventually to confess that she prefers Miss Todd with all her 'iniquities' on her head. Trollope's description of an evening with the Stumfold group is reminiscent of that of Dickens's description of the one graced by Tony Weller in *The Pickwick Papers*. If the former lacks the latter's punch and outrageous humour, it has its satirical bite none the less.

> The prayer was begun immediately, Mr. Stumfold taking this duty himself. Then Mr. Maguire read half a chapter in the Bible, and after that Mr. Stumfold explained it. Two ladies asked Mr. Stumfold questions with great pertinacity, and these questions Mr. Stumfold answered very freely, walking about the room the while, and laughing often as he submitted himself to their interrogations. And Miss Mackenzie was much astonished at the special freedom of his manner — how he spoke of St. Paul as Paul, declaring the saint to have been a good fellow; how he said he liked Luke better than Matthew, and how he named even a holier name than these with infinite ease and an accustomed familiarity which seemed to delight the other ladies; but which at first shocked her in her ignorance.
>
> "But I'm not going to have anything more to say to Peter and Paul at present," he

---

* Or as Henry James observed in his essay on Trollope in *The House of Fiction*: 'His political novels are distinctly dull, and I confess I have not been able to read them.'

declared at last.

"You'd keep me here all night, and the tea will be spoilt."

Then they all laughed again at the absurd idea of this great and good man preferring his food — his food of this world — to that other food which it was his special business to dispense. There is nothing which the Stumfoldian ladies of Littlebath liked so much as these little jokes which bordered on the profanity of the outer world, which made them feel themselves to be almost as funny as the sinners, and gave them a slight taste, as it were, of the pleasures of iniquity.

"Wine maketh glad the heart of woman, Mrs. Jones," Mr. Stumfold would say as he filled for the second time the glass of some old lady of his set; and the old lady would chirrup and wink, and feel that things were going almost as jollily with her as they did with that wicked Mrs. Smith, who spent every night of her life playing cards, or as they had done with that horrid Mrs. Brown, of whom such terrible things were occasionally whispered when two or three ladies found themselves sufficiently private to whisper them; that things were going almost as pleasant here in this world, although accompanied by so much safety as to the future in her own case, and so much danger in those other cases! I think it was this aptitude for feminine rakishness which, more than any of his great virtues, more even than his indomitable industry, made Mr. Stumfold the most popular man in Littlebath. A dozen ladies on the present occasion skipped away to the tea-table in the back drawing-room with a delighted alacrity, which was all owing to the unceremonious treatment which St. Peter and St. Paul had received from their pastor.

Miss Mackenzie had just found time to cast an eye round the room and examine the scene of Mr. Stumfold's pleasantries while Mr. Maguire was reading. She saw that there were only three gentlemen there besides the two clergymen. There was a very old man who sat close wedged in between Mrs. Stumfold and another lady, by whose joint dresses he was almost obliterated. This was Mr. Peters, a retired attorney. He was Mrs. Stumfold's father, and from his coffers had come the superfluities of comfort which Miss Mackenzie saw around her. Rumour, even among the saintly people of Littlebath, said that Mr. Peters had been a sharp practitioner in his early days — that he had been successful in his labours was admitted by all.

"No doubt he has repented," Miss Baker said one day to Miss Todd.

"And if he has not, he has forgotten all about it, which generally means the same thing," Miss Todd had answered.

Mr. Peters was now very old, and I am disposed to think he had forgotten all about it.

And it is here that she meets the Revd Maguire — a meeting fraught with consequences for the future. Trollope's descriptive powers, whether of places or persons, are not usually notable for vividness or originality, but Mr. Maguire is an exception.

Miss Mackenzie found him to be the possessor of a good figure, of a fine head of jet black hair, of a perfect set of white teeth, of whiskers which were also black and very fine, but streaked here and there with a grey hair — and of the most terrible squint in his right eye which ever disfigured a face that in all other respects was fitted for an Apollo. So egregious was the squint that Miss Mackenzie could not keep herself from regarding it, even while Mr. Stumfold was expounding. Had she looked Mr. Maguire full in the face at the beginning, I do not think it would so much have mattered to her; but she had seen first the back of his head, and then his profile, and had unfortunately formed a strong opinion as to his almost perfect beauty. When, therefore, the defective eye was disclosed to her, her feelings were moved in a more than ordinary manner. How was it that a man graced with such a head, with such a mouth and chin and forehead, nay, with such a left eye, could be cursed with such a right eye! She was still thinking of this when the frisky movement into the tea-room took place around her.

And later:

And now Miss Mackenzie found herself seated next to Mr. Maguire. She had been carried away in the crowd to a further corner, in which there were two chairs, and before she had been able to consider the merits or demerits of the position, Mr. Maguire was seated close beside her. He was seated close beside her in such a way as to make the two specially separated from all the world beyond, for in front of them stood a wall of crinoline — a wall of crinoline divided between four or five owners, among whom was shared the eloquence of Mr. Startup, who was carrying on an evangelical flirtation with the whole of them in a manner that was greatly pleasing to them, and enthusiastically delightful to him. Miss Mackenzie, when she found herself thus entrapped, looked into Mr. Maguire's eye with dismay. Had that look been sure to bring down upon her the hatred of that reverend gentleman, she could not have helped it. The eye fascinated her, as much as it frightened her. But Mr. Maguire was used to have his eye inspected, and did not hate her. He fixed it apparently on the corners of the wall, but in truth upon her, and then he began:

"I am so glad that you have come among us, Miss Mackenzie."

"I'm sure that I'm very much obliged."

"Well; you ought to be. You must not be surprised at my saying so that it sounds uncivil. You ought to feel obliged, and the obligation should be mutual. I am not sure, that when all things are considered, you could find yourself in any better place in England, than in the drawing-room of my friend Stumfold; and, if you will allow me to say so, my friend Stumfold could hardly use his drawing-room better, than by entertaining you."

His purpose is clear from the outset. He soon learns that she is a single lady with independent means, and intends to make himself the possessor of both. So too does Samuel Rubb, junior, of the oilcloth firm of Rubb and Mackenzie (the latter being her elder brother, Tom), who cadges capital from her for the firm without legal guarantee of return. He is a prepossessing, specious man of forty, and she almost falls for him. Finally, there is a distant relative, John Ball, a barrister, in his forties, and 'a widower with a large family and small means'; but he lives at the Cedars, a comparative mansion, with his grumbling testy father and class-snob mother, Sir John and Lady Ball, and will be able to put 'Bart.' after his name some day. When Miss Mackenzie pays them a visit in order to try to put herself on friendly terms with that hitherto unfriendly and unrecognizant branch of the family, Lady Ball instantly sees in her a prospective wife for her widowed impecunious son and a convenient stepmother for his children, and urges him to ingratiate himself with her. Nothing loath, at the end of her three-weeks stay he proposes to her. She likes him very much, but not quite enough, and prevaricates by promising to think it over and give him his answer from Littlebath, and leaving him in suspense and his mother in the highest state of dudgeon.

Back in Littlebath she reflects on her strange position. A not particularly attractive woman in her mid-thirties, she has already had a definite proposal from one man, with two other proposals, she senses, in the offing. She recalls one of Lady Ball's more offensive remarks to her after she had refused to accept her son's proposal there and then. "It is not as if you two were young people, and wanted to be billing and cooing," she had said. And here we are given her reflections and a notable little scene which must have startled and probably shocked Victorian readers.

Miss Mackenzie, as she thought of this, was not so sure that Lady Ball was right. Why should she not want billing and cooing as well as another? It was natural that a woman should want some of it in her life, and she had had none of it yet. She had had a lover, certainly, but there had been no billing and cooing with him. Nothing of that kind had been possible in her brother Walter's house.

And then the question naturally arose to her whether her aunt had treated her justly in bracketing her with John Ball in that matter of age. John Ball was ten years her senior; and ten years, she knew, was a very proper difference between a man and his wife. She was by no means inclined to plead, even to herself, that she was too young to marry her cousin; there was nothing in their ages to interfere, if the match was in other respects suitable. But still, was not he old for his age, and was not she young for hers? And if she should ultimately resolve to devote herself and what she had left of youth to his children and his welfare, should not the sacrifice be recognised? Had Lady Ball done well to speak of her as she certainly might well speak of him? Was she beyond all aptitude for billing and cooing, if billing and cooing might chance to come in her way?

Thinking of this during the long afternoon, when Susanna was at school, she got up and looked at herself in the mirror. She moved up her hair from off her ears, knowing where she would find a few that were grey, and shaking her head, as though owning to herself that she was old; but as her fingers ran almost involuntarily across her locks, her touch told her that they were soft and silken; and she looked into her own eyes, and saw that they were bright; and her hand touched the outline of her cheek, and she knew that something of the fresh bloom of youth was still there; and her lips parted, and there were her white teeth; and there came a smile and a dimple, and a slight purpose of laughter in her eye, and then a tear. She pulled her scarf tighter across her bosom, feeling her own form, and then she leaned forward and kissed herself in the glass.*

After which she writes the promised letter to John Ball, regretting she is unable to accept the honour he has done her.

That she is only too right in her surmise about the Revd Maguire is soon revealed. Again, flattered, she almost gives in to his eloquent suit, but saves herself by agreeing to consider his proposal and to allow him to return in a fortnight for his answer.

How she organizes herself among her three would-be lovers the reader may learn for himself; also how, through a startlingly unpleasant legal discovery, she finds that the money on which she has been living so comfortably turns out not to be hers at all but John Ball's — the very cousin she has turned down. Trollope's timing is superb here, and the reader is kept in doubt almost to the end.

If the novel is not quite worthy of a two star recommendation, it certainly deserves one, exemplifying as it does Trollope's multigenerous genius.

---

* The incident has a startling affinity with that in Dumas's *The Queen's Necklace* written six years before this of Trollope's, in which Jeanne de la Motte admires herself erotically in her mirror.

THE CLAVERINGS

The novel is one of the five singled out by Michael Sadleir as the most perfectly constructed — without 'a loose end or a patch of drowsiness.' His assessment is reasonably valid, though not entirely so: and in addition I consider it to be the most 'realistic' of them all. The term needs explaining in as much as all Trollope's best work is realistic. He has neither the inclination nor the talent for the exaggeration, the melodrama or the comic sublime of Dickens. His characters are almost always people we know in everyday life, or, if unusual, with no more than the quirks and oddities of the common run of humanity. His squires, clerics, solicitors, doctors, politicians, spinsters, mothers and so on are as human as the types we know ourselves. To whatever depths of misery they may be brought either by their own conduct or that of others, however nefarious their machinations, they do not indulge in crime. (The murder of Bontine in *Phineas Redux*, the suicide of Harcourt in *The Bertrams* and Melmotte in *The Way We Live Now* are the only exceptions.) Nor do they undergo violent changes in character under different circumstances. None is completely black or oppressively white. In short there are no Quilps, Heeps, Carkers, Agneses, Amelias, Dobbins or Jonas Chuzzlewits.

If I were asked to choose one novel as being most representative of Trollope I think this would be the one. If it has none of the highlights of his greatest novels, with a minor exception it maintains a consistently high level of achievement, and moves unhurriedly but relentlessly along to its — I was about to say climax; but in fact, unless we are to regard the conclusion as such, it really has no climax, and simply tapers off as such situations in real life do. Hence its realism.

The theme is one which became a favourite with Trollope: that of a woman who deliberately sacrifices love to wealth, and of a man torn between his love for two women. In this it is a more mature relation of *The Bertrams*. Julia Brabazon is another Caroline Waddington, Harry Clavering another George Bertram. The novel too is a perfect example of Trollope's love of involving a family, in this case the Claverings. To him the appeal was like that of chess, and in the literary sense he was a superb chess player, knowing the exact potential of each piece, seeing the game through from the opening gambits to the final checkmate. In this case, indeed, the family relationships are so complicated and interwoven that the reader can be exasperatedly confused. So for anyone who is about to tackle the book for the first time the following lay-out of the dramatis personae may be found helpful.

Hermione (Lady Clavering) elder daughter of Lord Brabazon, m. to Sir Hugh Clavering.
Julia, younger daughter of Lord Brabazon, m. to Lord Ongar.
Revd Henry Clavering, rector of Clavering.
Mrs. Clavering, his wife.
Mary Clavering, their elder daughter, m. to the Revd Edward Fielding.
Fanny, their younger daughter.
Harry Clavering, their only son.

Sir Hugh Clavering, nephew of the Revd Henry Clavering and cousin to Mary, Fanny and Harry Clavering.

Captain Archibald Clavering, his younger brother.

Mr and Mrs Burton, of Stratton.

Florence, their youngest daughter.

Theodore Burton of Onslow Crescent, brother of Florence.

Cecilia, his wife.

Revd Samuel Saul, the Revd Henry Clavering's curate.

The novel begins piquantly and without any of the tedious background building which mars some of the novels. In fact the opening scene, set in the garden of the aristocratic Clavering Park, is a masterly exposition — masterly not only as a piece of writing in itself, but as a significant pointer to the climax of the narrative, showing us that Trollope was not just a weaver of episodic events as some critics have maintained. Indeed, the novel is a supreme example of his constructive skill. The fact that many of his novels, like those of Dickens and Thackeray, were first published as magazine serials, did not conduce him to make his episodes finish with a dramatic 'curtain' in order to titillate readers and make them want to buy the next number of the magazine. As he asserted in his *Autobiography*:

> It had already been a principle with me in my art, that no part of a novel should be published until the entire story was completed. I knew, from what I read from month to month, that this hurried publication of incompleted work was frequently, I might perhaps say always, adopted by the leading novelists of the day . . . . I was aware that an artist should keep in his hand the power of fitting the beginning of his work to the end.

The Claverings is arguably the outstanding proof of his claim. Just as the opening gambits in a game of chess lead to the final result, so here the first scene anticipates the denouement enacted in the same place by the same pair — a masterly touch of irony.

We learn at once from the dialogue between Julia Brabazon and Harry Clavering, that she is deliberately throwing him over for the sake of the wealth and social status that Lord Ongar can give her. Trollope certainly knew the type of woman who coldly and calculatingly chooses security without love rather than insecurity with it, but in each instance he makes her pay the price of it. In this case who is she 'jilting' him for? — a man who, though only thirty-six, is twelve years older than herself and known by everyone to be a 'worn-out debauché'. So the lovers part. But Trollope keeps the pieces moving. In spite of his father's wishes (the Revd Henry Clavering is yet another of Trollope's aimiable but weak-minded, easy-going clerics with too little work) Harry decides against following in his father's footsteps, and after gaining a fellowship at Cambridge and working for a time as a schoolmaster, he throws everything up to begin an apprenticeship with a London firm of civil engineers. He lodges with Mr Burton, of the firm, and his wife, and eventually falls in love with their daughter, Florence. Trollope stresses her lack of beauty in comparison with the face and figure of Julia (the latter's sexual allure is deliberately emphasized) but conveys to the reader the fact that, in becoming engaged to her he has, in her own words, "learned to love her", and that she is one of those girls who grows on one rather than makes an instant impression, and so engenders a love which is likely to be deeper and more lasting than one blazed by sheer beauty at first sight. Her brother,

Theodore, and Harry, work in the same office, and although Harry 'could not bring himself to take a liking to him, because he wore cotton gloves and had an odious habit of dusting his shoes with his pocket handkerchief', after accepting an invitation to dinner with him and his family at Onslow Crescent he was instantly accepted by them as a welcome addition to the family, and eventually became greatly attached to all of them.

Still the pieces are kept moving. In the midst of these happy domestic scenes Lord Ongar has died in Florence and Julia, braving the scandalous rumours now surging around her name, has decided to leave Italy and return to England; and as Sir Hugh Clavering, her brother-in-law and nearest relative refuses to meet her, Harry goes instead. In passing it may be said that Hugh Clavering is, with the exception of the Marquis of Brotherton in *Is He Popenjoy?*, the nastiest piece of work Trollope ever saw fit to give us. There is no evil about him in a sinister sense, but there is no good either; he is simply despicable and revolting, cantankerous, morose and sour with his own relatives and treating his wife as though she was dirt. In fact a pathological case. When he learns from her of Julia's plans to return, he informs her he will have nothing to do with her and forbids her to bring her sister to the house. Harry not only meets Julia at Victoria station but goes to the trouble of finding a suite of rooms for her, where he proceeds to visit her more frequently than is wise as a former lover now engaged to someone else. The inevitable occurs. Her sexual appeal along with the memories they share begin to work on him, and he falls in love with her all over again. Too ashamed to confess he has plighted himself to Florence, yet too conscience-bitten to act as a free man, he hesitates to accept the love she has let him see she still has for him; and so, not understanding his reticence and half-hearted waverings, but knowing herself to be rich, independent, still young and beautiful, and above all, lonely, in defiance of all the Victorian codes she offers herself to him. Cornered, driven to making his decision, he takes her in his arms. He has thus promised himself to two women.

Then of course, since such facts cannot remain hidden, she hears of his engagment to Florence. This leads to a long and touching scene between them ending in her ordering him to go back to his fiancée. She has only herself to blame, she tells him. She had jilted him in the first place, and the situation has become a quid pro quo. But Harry is still reluctant to give her up, convinced he still loves her. One of the two women he is pledged to, then, must be made to suffer. From then on the story is a struggle between conscience and desire. How it ends the reader must discover for himself. But a point worth noting is this: while no doubt all the female readers of Trollope's day and probably those of our own would and will condemn Harry Clavering as weak-minded and double-faced, men will have some sympathy for him, and this is not just because of male fellow-feeling which will forbid them to throw the first stone, but because too they cannot have failed to remark that Florence is one of those simple-minded women who seem to enjoy prolonging their engagement and putting off the wedding date: or in blunt otherwords — consummation. When first he became engaged to her, and before Julia had returned, Harry had pressed her to marry him as soon as possible, only to be told they couldn't afford it; and when during a slight tiff over the matter he accuses her of not being in a hurry to be married, all he gets is:

> "What a goose you are! Do you know, I'm not sure that if you really love a person, and are quite confident about him — as I am of you — that having to look forward to being married is not the best part of it all. . . . "

And later, in chapter 9 entitled significantly 'Too Prudent By Half', she writes to her impatient lover:

> 'You are impatient about things, are you not? . . . . Dear Harry, you must not be angry, but I am sure that we ought to wait. We are both of us young, and why should we be in a hurry? I know what you will say, and of course I love you the more because you love me so well; but I fancy that I can be quite happy if I can see you two or three times in the year, and hear from you constantly . . . . '

Now a woman who can be as naïve as that must be either abysmally ignorant of masculine psychology and physiology or indifferent to them, and Trollope perfectly reads the difference between male and female nature when he writes immediately after Florence's letter:

> 'Harry Clavering was very angry when he got this letter. The primary cause of his anger was the fact that Florence should pretend to know what was better for him than he knew himself . . . . '

Had she shown more understanding, taken her lover at his word and risked life with him on his four hundred pounds a year, the return of Julia would have led to none of the disastrous results which followed. Her attitude must make her bear a part of the responsibility for what happened.

As I observed earlier, the story does not have an emotional climax, does not end happily for both women. How could it? One of the two so deeply involved must suffer. Trollope scores a triumph here. Having begun the novel by showing Julia in the act of jilting a man who loves her (a fearful sin in Victorian eyes) and so prejudicing us against her, by her resignation at the end, and by her acceptance of the fact that she had brought her grief and uncertain future on her own head, he brings her right back into our hearts. Her Nemesis is just, but tragic, and moves us as being such. Trollope will have no sentimentality, but he makes us have compassion. It is a true-to-life ending.

Brief mention should be made of two minor characters, namely, the rector's younger daughter and his curate. The serious, dedicated, unprepossessing Samuel Saul is in some ways an anticipation of Josiah Crawley of *The last Chronicle of Barset* destined to be born only two years later. Despised by the Claverings who, if they are his social superiors, are his inferiors in everything else, he proves to be one of the few genuine Christians among the several clerics Trollope has depicted, and as such stands in contrast to his lackadaisical rector. The forthright way in which he declares his love to Fanny and confesses it to her family is beautifully told by Trollope, and wins not only the reader's regard but, much more importantly, that of the reluctant Fanny herself.

It is a pity the novel cannot be left on the note of absolute encomium, but it would be uncritical not to mention its flaws, though they may be only minor ones. The mystery and rumours of divorce and misconduct surrounding Julia during her brief married life with Lord Ongar are never explained, and the intrusion of the supposedly sinister Count Paterhoff and his sister is quite unnecessary, as too are the characters of Archibald Clavering and his horsey friend Doodles, brought in as an attempt at mystery and humour. They merely pad the story and blemish what would otherwise have been perfect.

But taking the novel as a whole, if we continue with the chess metaphor I think it may be described as a superb game played by a Master. Let us be satisfied with that.

THE BELTON ESTATE

This uninteresting title covers one of Trollope's most flawless novels, arguably the equal in craftsmanship and characterization to the perfection of Jane Austen. There are no longueurs, no padding, no sub-plots, nothing to bore the reader or to detract from the centrepiece of the story, namely, the wooing of Clara Amedroz by her two suitors, Will Belton and Frederic Aylmer. The story is unfolded from the first page as simply and inevitably as the first moves in a game of chess.

Clara Amedroz lives with her father in Belton Castle, 'a pretty country seat, standing in a small but beautifully wooded park, close under the Quantock hills.' Her mother is dead, and her brother, after being expelled from Harrow, rusticated from Cambridge and living a life of dissipation in London, in a fit of despair has done away with himself: which means in terms of entail that on the death of old Mr Amedroz the estate will pass to a distant and unknown relative, Will Belton, a yeoman farmer living in the wilds of Norfolk.

When the story opens Clara is twenty-five, mature and of a serious nature as might be expected after the tragic events in her family and her far from rosy prospects in the future. Her father is a weak, complaining old man, and apart from a neighbour, Mrs Askerton, she has no one else to talk to or visit. To make matters worse she has been brought up by a widowed aunt, Mrs Winterfield.

> When a girl has a mother, her aunt may be little or nothing to her. But when the mother is gone, if there be an aunt unimpeded with other family duties, then the family duties of that aunt begin — and are assumed sometimes with great vigour. Such had been the case with Mrs. Winterfield. No woman ever lived, perhaps, with more conscientious ideas of her duty as a woman than Mrs. Winterfield of Prospect Place, Perivale. And this, as I say it, is intended to convey no scoff against that excellent lady. She was an excellent lady — unselfish, given to self-restraint, generous, pious, looking to find in her religion a safe path through life — a path as safe as the facts of Adam's fall would allow her feet to find. She was a woman fearing much for others, but fearing also much for herself, striving to maintain her house in godliness, hating sin, and struggling with the weakness of her humanity so that she might not allow herself to hate the sinners. But her hatred for the sin she found herself bound at all time to pronounce — to show it by some act at all seasons. To fight the devil was her work — was the appointed work of every living soul, if only living souls could be made to acknowledge the necessity of the task. Now an aunt of that kind, when she assumed her duties towards a motherless niece, is apt to make life serious.

In other words, she is another of Trollope's religious bigots. Moreover she has money of her own, and as Mr Amedroz has very little of that commodity it is his hope that Mrs Winterfield will leave something to his daughter. But she destroys all his hopes by telling Clara one day that she intends to leave everything to her nephew, Frederic Aylmer, though it is her dearest wish that he and Clara will come together in marriage.

Such is the situation when there arrives a letter for Mr Amedroz from this same distant cousin in Norfolk who is the heir to his estate; and in his letter he has the effrontery to invite himself to visit him and Clara with the ostensible purpose of getting to know them. The old man, after venting his favourite anathema of "Heartless! quite heartless!" is finally persuaded by Clara to send a brief curt letter of acceptance, in response to which Will Belton duly arrives. Will is one of the triumphs of the novel. From the moment he enters the door he brings a breath of fresh air into the dull, stuffy place. With his big hands, massive body and wind-tanned face, his blunt country way of speaking his mind and sound practical common sense, he lives in every word and action as one of the most natural and lovable characters in fiction. Even Mr Amedroz, predetermined to dislike him and to take umbrage at everything he says and does, becomes quite won over. As for Clara, she too is quite bowled over — though not to the point of falling in love with him. In fact she feels for him as a solitary sister for an elder brother who suddenly turns up out of the blue and by his practical sense and warm affection brings unexpected comfort and happiness into what has so far been a sad and lonely life. But this does not satisfy Will, who with characteristic impetuosity falls in love with her and sees no reason why, after falling in love with her, he should not make his feelings known forthwith. He does not realize that a woman needs more time! She is not ready to think of him as a lover. As a 'brother' and a loving family helper — yes. The first love scene between them is beautifully done.

Will has to return to his farm in Norfolk disappointed, and Clara goes to stay with her aunt at Perivale, meeting Captain Frederic Aylmer MP *en route*. Their conversation in the train is highly significant. With a woman's typical lack of tact and understanding in such matters she sets up an antogonism in his mind against Will by praising the latter enthusiastically, though of course she doesn't go so far as to tell him that Will had proposed to her. Also in her conversation she reveals her firmness of character and strength of mind (for a Victorian woman at least) by twitting Aylmer on his masculine prerogative of eluding his aunt's dreary Sabbaths by inventing business calls on his time while she has to accept her enforced feminine dependence. The colloquy ends with her assertion:

> "You know very well that you could remain over Sunday without doing any harm to anybody; — only you don't like going to church three times, and you don't like hearing my aunt read a sermon afterwards. Why shouldn't you stay, and I go to the club?"
> "With all my heart, if you can manage it."
> "But I can't; we ain't allowed to have clubs, or shooting, or to have our own way in anything, putting forward pretences about lawyers."
> "Come, I'll stay if you'll ask me."
> "I'm sure I won't do that. In the first place you'd go to sleep, and then she would be offended; and I don't know that your sufferings would make mine any lighter. I'm not prepared to alter the ways of the world, but I feel myself entitled to grumble at them sometimes."

In that last sentence of Clara's Trollope spoke for all thoughtful women of his era. He also spoke for himself: it sums up his own attitude to society.

Now Mrs Winterfield, being old and pious, was on the contrary 'one of those women who have always believed that their own sex is in every respect inferior to the other.' Consequently when she informs Frederic she is leaving everything to him in her will and nothing to Clara and he tells her she ought to add a codicil to her benefit to the amount of some £1,500, she promptly agrees. This is important, and a great deal of the action to come hinges on it. For Clara is a little bit in love with Captain Aylmer, and he has twice seemed to be on the point of declaring himself to her but has shuffled it off. Thus her reaction to her aunt's information about her intended codicil and Frederic's 'generosity' is very different from what that lady had expected.

But Clara, in her heart, did not at all thank Captain Aylmer for his generosity. She would have had everything from him, or nothing. It was grievous to her to think that she should owe to him a bare pittance to keep her out of the workhouse, — to him who had twice seemed to be on the point of asking her to share everything with him. She did not love her cousin Will as she loved him; but her cousin Will's assurance to her that he would treat her with a brother's care was sweeter to her by far than Frederic Aylmer's well-balanced counsel to his aunt on her behalf. In her present mood, too, she wanted no one to have forethought for her; she desired no provision; for her, in the discomfiture of heart, there was consolation in the feeling that when she should find herself alone in the world, she would have been ill-treated by her friends all round her. There was a charm in the prospect of her desolation of which she did not wish to be robbed by the assurance of some seventy pounds a year, to be given to her by Captain Frederic Aylmer. To be robbed of one's grievance is the last and foulest wrong, — a wrong under which the most enduring temper will at last yield and become soured, — by which the strongest back will be broken. 'Well, my dear,' continued Mrs. Winterfield, when Clara made no response to this appeal for praise.

'It is so hard for me to say anything about it, aunt. What can I say but that I don't want to be a burden to any one?'

'That is a position which very few women can attain, that is, very few single women.'

'I think it would be well if all single women were strangled by the time they are thirty,' said Clara with a fierce energy which absolutely frightened her aunt.*

'Clara! how can you say anything so wicked, — so abominably wicked?'

'Anything would be better than being twitted in this way. How can I help it that I am not a man and able to work for my bread? But I am not above being a housemaid, and so Captain Aylmer shall find. I'd sooner be a housemaid, with nothing but my wages, then take the money which you say he is to give me. It will be of no use, aunt, for I shall not take it.'

'It is I that am to leave it to you. It is not to be a present from Frederic.'

'It is the same thing, aunt. He says you are to do it; and you told me just now that it was to come out of his pocket.'

'I should have done it myself long ago, had you told me all the truth about your father's affairs.'

'How was I to tell you? I would sooner have bitten my tongue out. But I will tell you the truth now. If I had known that all this was to be said to me about money, and that our poverty was to be talked over between you and Captain Aylmer, I would not have come to Perivale. I would rather that you should be angry with me and think that I had forgotten you.'

'You would not say that, Clara, if you remembered that this will probably be your last visit to me.'

'No, no; it will not be the last. But do not talk about these things. And it will be so much better that I should be here when he is not here.'

'I had hoped that when I died you might both be with me together, — as husband and wife.'

'Such hopes never come to anything.'

'I still think that he would wish it.'

'That is nonsense, aunt. It is indeed, for neither of us wish it.' A lie on such a subject from a woman under such circumstances is hardly to be considered a lie at all. It is spoken with no mean object, and is the only bulwark which the woman has ready at her need to cover her own weakness.

---

* This outburst of Clara's may serve as a vivid reminder to the reader of my remarks on the plight of the Victorian spinster in the review of *Rachel Ray* and *Ayala's Angel*.

But Mrs Winterfield dies before she can add the controversial codicil; nevertheless Captain Aylmer determines to honour his aunt's last wishes which were not only to see Clara provided for but, unknown to her, to marry her. In spite of his being an MP and used to making public announcements, he is at the same time (and Trollope underscores the fact) in his private life diffident and uncertain of himself, not to say cold-blooded and calculating. By this very human contrast Trollope clearly intends portraying a trenchant comparison between him and Will Belton — a comparison which is to make its impression on Clara more and more decisively as time passes. The reader may find it difficult to believe that any man can be quite as cold sexually and tactless as Frederic is made out to be, and may consider him to be overdrawn simply as a contrast with Will. The criticism is possibly valid. On the other hand a novelist may surely be allowed some 'poetic licence', and on the whole Aylmer is quite credible, and certainly no more overdrawn than, say, Jane Austen's Mr Collins, whose pompous fatuity gives us such delight. Trollope sums him up beautifully with ' . . . he was a man somewhat diffident of himself, though sufficiently conscious of the value of the worldly advantages he possessed; — and he was, perhaps, a little afraid of Clara, giving her credit for an intellect superior to his own.'

Eventually, however, after a lot of dithering he does bring himself to the point of asking her to become his wife; and here Clara in her forthright honesty and joy makes her mistake. Instead of keeping him temporarily dangling in suspense, she confesses her love at once and ardently, with the result that Frederic, who in his diffidence had anticipated a dubious reply if not a downright refusal, is taken aback by a sense of too-easy triumph. Trollope's analysis of his feelings is acutely pointed.

As regarded herself, she was quite equal to the occasion; but had she known more of the inner feelings of men and women in general, she would have been slower to show her own. What is there that any man desires, — any man or any woman, — that does not lose half its value when it is found to be easy of access and easy of possession? Wine is valued by its price, not its flavour. Open your doors freely to Jones and Smith, and Jones and Smith will not care to enter them. Shut your doors obdurately against the same gentlemen, and they will use all their little diplomacy to effect an entrance. Captain Aylmer, when he heard the hearty tone of the girl's answer, already began almost to doubt whether it was wise on his part to devote the innermost bin of his cellar to wine that was so cheap.

Not that he had any idea of receding. Principle, if not love, prevented that. 'Then the question about the house is decided,' he said, giving his hand to Clara as he spoke.

'I don't care a bit about the house now,' she answered.

'That's unkind.'

'I am thinking so much more of you, — of you and of myself. What does an old house matter?'

'It's in very good repair,' said Captain Aylmer.

'You must not laugh at me,' she said; and in truth he was not laughing at her. 'What I mean is that anything about a house is indifferent to me now. It is as though I had got all that I want in the world. Is it wrong of me to say so?'

'Oh, dear, no; — not wrong at all. How can it be wrong?' He did not tell her that he also had got all he wanted; but his lack of enthusiasm in this respect did not surprise her, or at first even vex her. She had always known him to be a man careful of his words, — knowing their value, — not speaking with hurried rashness as would her dear cousin Will. And she doubted whether, after all, such hurried words mean as much as words which are slower and calmer. After all his heat in love and consequent disappointment, Will Belton had left her apparently well contented. His fervour had been short-lived. She loved her cousin dearly, and was so very glad that his fervour had been short-lived!

'When you asked me, I could but tell you the truth,' she said, smiling at him.

The truth is very well, but he would have liked it better had the truth come to him by slower degrees. When his aunt had told him to marry Clara Amedroz, he had been at once reconciled to the order by a feeling on his own part that the conquest of Clara would not be too facile. She was a woman of value, not to be snapped up easily, — or by any one. So he had thought then; but he began to fancy now that he had been wrong in that opinion.

The walk back to the house was not of itself very exciting, though to Clara it was a short period of unalloyed bliss. No doubt had then come upon her to cloud her happiness, and she was 'wrapped up in measureless content.' It was well that they should both be silent at such a moment. Only yesterday had been buried their dear old friend, — the friend who had brought them together, and been so anxious for their future happiness! And Clara Amedroz was not a young girl, prone to jump out of her shoes with elation because she had got a lover. She could be steadily happy without many immediate words about her happiness. When they reached the house, and were once more together in the drawing-room, she again gave him her hand, and was the first to speak. 'And you; are you contented?' she asked. Who does not know the smile of triumph with which a girl asks such a question at such a moment as that?

'Contented? — well, — yes; I think I am,' he said.

But even those words did not move her to doubt.

'If you are,' she said, 'I am. And now I will leave you till dinner, that you may think over what you have done.'

'I had thought about it before, you know,' he replied. Then he stooped over her and kissed her. It was the first time he had done so; but his kiss was as cold and proper as though they had been man and wife for years! But if sufficed for her, and she went to her room as happy as a queen.

Clara now has ample time for reflection, and she begins to feel something of his cold-bloodedness and lack of warmth and to wish she had been less on-coming and self-revealing with him. And when next day he carelessly lets fall that their marriage is according to his aunt's last wishes, she really takes fire, and the scene ends with her insisting that their engagement is broken off. He is forced to accept her terms, and she leaves Perivale. Then after she has gone his feelings undergo a change — and here yet again Trollope shows his psychological penetration. Might it not be for the best were his first thoughts, if she chose to be so stubbornly indifferent to her own welfare?

But as the day wore on with him, something more generous in his nature came to his aid, and something also that was akin to real love. Now that she was no longer his own, he again felt a desire to have her. Now that there would be again something to be done in winning her, he was again stirred by a man's desire to do that something . . . .

Hard on these events Will Belton, true to his word, and deeply in love with Clara, makes a return visit. In the meantime Frederic has written to her a (for him) warm letter of repentant explanation asking for her hand again, and she has accepted him for the second time. When they learn of her engagement both her father and Will are shattered: the former much prefers Will! But Mrs Askerton is delighted. She has never liked Will, and hearing that he has been making enquiries about her in London she and her husband ask Clara not to bring him to their house any more. This contretemps is important in view of what is to come. So now poor Clara is between the devil and the deep sea with the Askertons for her, her father against her and Will telling her he loves her more than ever and will take no nonsense about being a 'brother' to her. In the midst of all this she receives another letter from Frederic and reproduced in full by Trollope 'in the hope that it may be taken by gentlemen about to marry as a fair specimen of the sort of letter they ought not to write to the girls of their hearts.' It is in fact a letter so crass, so tactless, that it is hard to credit that any man supposedly in love could write it. But clearly Trollope has the ultimate breakdown in view, likewise the intervention of the Askerton mystery which is to clinch the rupture.

With Clara's visit to Aylmer Park and her confrontation with the dreaded mother-in-law-to-be the novel attains its peak. Even the bare description of the residence, so often in Trollope over-long and flat, sparkles in its irony.

CHAPTER XVII
AYLMER PARK

Aylmer Park and the great house of the Aylmers together formed an important and, as regarded in some minds, an imposing country residence. The park was large, including some three or four hundred acres, and was peopled, rather thinly, by aristocratic deer. It was surrounded by an aristocratic paling, and was entered, at three different points, by aristocratic lodges. The sheep were more numerous than the deer, because Sir Anthony, though he had a large income, was not in very easy circumstances. The ground was quite flat; and though there were thin belts of trees, and some ornamental timber here and there, it was not well wooded. It had no special beauty of its own, and depended for its imposing qualities chiefly on its size, on its three sets of double lodges, and on its old established character as an important family place in the county. The house was of stone, with a portico of Ionic columns which looked as though it hardly belonged of right to the edifice, and stretched itself out grandly, with two pretentious wings, which certainly gave it a just claim to be called a mansion. It required a great many servants to keep it in order, and the numerous servants required an experienced duenna, almost as grand in appearance as Lady Aylmer herself, to keep them in order. There was an open carriage and a close carriage, and a butler, and two footmen, and three gamekeepers, and four gardeners, and there was a coachman, and there were grooms, and sundry inferior men and boys about the place to do the work which the gardeners and gamekeepers and grooms did not choose to do themselves. And they all became fat, and lazy, and stupid, and respectable together; so that, as the reader will at once perceive, Aylmer Park was kept up in the proper English style.

And in the description of the inmates — the flabby-minded, heavy-bodied Sir Anthony, his domineering dragon of a wife and their mindless daughter — we are treated to some Austen-like acidity of observation. The whole narration of Clara's unhappy stay there is nineteenth century fiction at its best. From the first meeting of Clara and Lady Aylmer it is daggers drawn between them and a fight to the death.

CHAPTER XXV
MISS AMEDROZ HAS SOME HASHED CHICKEN

Clara felt herself to be a coward as the Aylmer Park carriage, which had been sent to meet her at the station, was drawn up at Sir Anthony Aylmer's door. She had made up her mind that she would not bow down to Lady Aylmer, and yet she was afraid of the woman. As she got out of the carriage, she looked up, expecting to see her in the hall; but Lady Aylmer was too accurately acquainted with the weights and measures of society for any such movement as that. Had her son brought Lady Emily to the house as his future bride, Lady Aylmer would probably have been in the hall when the arrival took place; and had Clara possessed ten thousand pounds of her own, she would probably have been met at the drawing-room door; but as she had neither money nor title, — as she in fact brought with her no advantages of any sort, — Lady Aylmer was found stitching a bit of worsted, as though she had expected no one to come to her. And Belinda Aylmer was stitching also, — by special order from her mother. The reader will remember that Lady Aylmer was not without strong hope that the engagement might even yet be broken off. Snubbing, she thought, might probably be efficacious to this purpose, and so Clara was to be snubbed.

Clara, who had just promised to do her best to gain Lady Aylmer's opinion, and who desired to be in some way true to her promise, though she thoroughly believed that her labour would be in vain, put on her pleasantest smile as she entered the room. Belinda, under the pressure of the circumstances, forgetting somewhat of her mother's injunctions, hurried to the door to welcome the stranger. Lady Aylmer kept her chair, and even maintained her stitch, till Clara was half across the room. Then she got up, and with great mastery over her voice, made her little speech.

'We are delighted to see you, Miss Amedroz,' she said, putting out her hand, — of which Clara, however, felt no more than the finger.

'Quite delighted,' said Belinda, yielding a fuller grasp. Then there were affectionate greetings between Frederic and his mother and Frederic and his sister, during which Clara stood by, ill at ease. Captain Aylmer said not a word as to the footing on which his future wife had come to his father's house. He did not ask his mother to receive her as another daughter, or his sister to take his Clara to her heart as a sister. There had been no word spoken of recognized intimacy. Clara knew that the Aylmers were cold people. She had learned as much as that from Captain Aylmer's words to herself, and from his own manner. But she had not expected to be so frozen by them as was the case with her now. In ten minutes she was sitting down with her bonnet still on, and Lady Aylmer was again at her stitches.

'Shall I show you your room?' said Belinda.

'Wait a moment, my dear,' said Lady Aylmer. 'Fredric has gone to see if Sir Anthony is in his study.'

Sir Anthony was found in his study, and now made his appearance.

'So this is Clara Amedroz,' he said. 'My dear, you are welcome to Aylmer Park.' This was so much better, that the kindness expressed — though there was nothing special in it — brought a tear into Clara's eye, and almost made her love Sir Anthony.

'By the by, Sir Anthony, have you seen Darvel? Darvel was wanting to see you especially about Nuggins. Nuggins says that he'll take the bullocks now.' This was said by Lady Aylmer, and was skilfully arranged by her to put a stop to anything like enthusiasm on the part of Sir Anthony. Clara Amedroz had been invited to Aylmer Park, and was to be entertained there, but it would not be expedient that she should be made to think that anybody was particularly glad to see her, or that the family was at all proud of the proposed connexion.

The feminine war with feminine weapons is narrated with a detailed realism unapproached by any other male novelist. The climax comes when Lady Aylmer deliberately brings up the Askerton affair. It is to be the acid test of Clara's fitness to become an Aylmer. Is she (Lady Aylmer) to believe that the woman her son is proposing to marry can contemplate continuing her known association with a woman who was so debased as to leave her husband to become the mistress of another man, even though that man has eventually married her? But at the mention of Mrs

Askerton's name Clara is roused.

'You must excuse me, Lady Aylmer, but what I know of Mrs. Askerton, I know altogether in confidence; so that I cannot speak to you of her past life.'

'But, Miss Amedroz, pray excuse me if I say that I must speak of it. When I remember the position in which you do us the honour of being our visitor here, how can I help speaking of it?' Belinda was stitching very hard, and would not even raise her eyes. Clara, who still held her needle in her hand, resumed her work, and for a moment or two made no further answer. But Lady Aylmer had by no means completed her task. 'Miss Amedroz,' she said, 'you must allow me to judge for myself in this matter. The subject is one on which I feel myself obliged to speak to you.'

'But I have got nothing to say about it.'

'You have, I believe, admitted the truth of the allegations made by us as to this woman.' Clara was becoming very angry. A red spot showed itself on each cheek, and a frown settled upon her brow. She did not as yet know what she would say or how she would conduct herself. She was striving to consider how best she might assert her own independence. But she was fully determined that in this matter she would not bend an inch to Lady Aylmer. 'I believe we may take that as admitted?' said her ladyship.

'I am not aware that I have admitted anything to you, Lady Aylmer, or said anything that can justify you in questioning me on the subject.'

'Justify me in questioning a young woman who tells me that she is to be my future daughter-in-law!'

'I have not told you so. I have never told you anything of the kind.'

'Then on what footing, Miss Amedroz, do you do us the honour of being with us here at Aylmer Park?'

'On a very foolish footing.'

'On a foolish footing! What does that mean?'

'It means that I have been foolish in coming to a house in which I am subjected to such questioning.'

'Belinda, did you ever hear anything like this? Miss Amedroz, I must persevere, however much you may dislike it. The story of this woman's life, — whether she be Mrs. Askerton or not, I don't know — '

'She is Mrs. Askerton,' said Clara.

'As to that I do not profess to know, and I dare say that you are no wiser than myself. But what she has been we do know.' Here Lady Aylmer raised her voice and continued to speak with all the eloquence which assumed indignation could give her. 'What she has been we do know, and I ask you, as a duty which I own to my son, whether you have put an end to your acquaintance with so very disreputable a person, — a person whom even to have known is a disgrace?'

'I know her, and — '

'Stop one minute, if you please. My questions are these — Have you put an end to that acquaintance? Are you ready to give a promise that it shall never be resumed?'

'I have not put an end to that acquaintance, — or rather that affectionate friendship as I should call it, and I am ready to promise that it shall be maintained with all my heart.'

'Belinda, do you hear her?'

'Yes, mamma.' And Belinda slowly shook her head, which was now bowed lower than ever over her lap.

'And that is your resolution?'

'Yes, Lady Aylmer; that is my resolution.'

'And you think that becoming to you, as a young woman?'

'Just so; I think that becoming to me, — as a young woman.'

'Then let me tell you, Miss Amedroz, that I differ from you altogether, — altogether.' Lady Aylmer, as she repeated the last word, raised her folded hands as though she were calling upon heaven to witness how thoroughly she differed from the young woman!

'I don't see how I am to help that, Lady Aylmer. I dare say we may differ on many subjects.'

'I dare say we do. I dare say we do. And I need not point out to you how very little that would be a matter of regret to me but for the hold you have upon my unfortunate son.'

'Hold upon him, Lady Aylmer! How dare you insult me by such language?' Hereupon Belinda again jumped in her chair; but Lady Aylmer looked as though she enjoyed the storm.

'You undoubtedly have a hold upon him, Miss Amedroz, and I think that it is a great misfortune. Of course, when he hears what your conduct is with reference to this — person, he will release himself from his entanglement.'

'He can release himself from his entanglement whenever he chooses,' said Clara, rising from her chair. 'Indeed, he is released. I shall let Captain Aylmer know that our engagement must be at an end, unless he will promise that I shall never in future be subjected to the unwarrantable insolence of his mother.' Then she walked off to the door, not regarding, and indeed not hearing, the parting shot that was fired at her.

This, added to Frederic's spineless apologies for his mother's treatment of her, is the last straw for Clara, and she leaves Aylmer Park without saying goodbye and with her fiancé weakly saying something about writing to and following her. He does both, and her determination to break the engagement once and for all is made difficult by the fact that for the first time, now that he is on the verge of losing her for good, he appeals to her with something like real sincerity and feeling. For a moment she hesitates.

She found that the task before her was very difficult, — so difficult that she almost broke down in performing it. It would have been so easy and, for the moment, so pleasant to have yielded. He had his hand upon her arm, having attempted to take her hand. In preventing that she had succeeded, but she could not altogether make herself free from him without rising. For a moment she had paused, — paused as though she were about to yield. For a moment, as he looked into her eyes, he had thought that he would again be victorious. Perhaps there was something in his glance, some too visible return of triumph to his eyes, which warned her of her danger. 'No!' she said, getting up and walking away from him; 'no!'

Thereafter the story takes its inevitable turn — the turn for which the reader has been long waiting. Will Belton gets the reward his single-mindedness and perseverance deserve; and Captain Aylmer gets his: he marries Lady Emily Tagmaggert, 'the youngest daughter of the Earl of Mull'.

I can only end my review of the novel as I began it, by reiterating that it is one of the best, and a must for any Trollope admirer or would-be reader.

NINA BALATKA
LINDA TRESSEL
THE GOLDEN LION OF GRANPÈRE

In 1867, 68 and 71 Trollope tried his hand at something different. This something different was the trio of tales named above, all with one thing in common — a foreign setting. Their awkward length presents a problem to anyone wishing to cover only the novels since the stories in question fall between the stools of short story and novel, being in fact examples of what has since come to be known as the *nouvelle*. To avoid mention of them altogether would not, I feel, be playing fair to Trollope, who certainly intended them to be considered as short novels. On the other hand, to allow them the full and separate treatment accorded to his full-scale fiction would be to give them a face value above their deserts. I have therefore decided on the compromise of discussing them as a group.

The *casus belli* of the stories was two-fold and more interesting than the tales themselves. In 1861 and 62 Trollope had had published two volumes of short stories — *Tales of All Countries*. These, as their title suggests, were the part result of his many travels abroad and had foreign settings. Though of no great merit — he simply did not have the touch of the short story writer — they had given him a liking for the genre. Then round about 1865, at the height of his fame, he had been assailed by a spasm of despondent quixotism which took the form of a conviction (for Trollope was one of those men whom success makes determinedly pessimistic and failure determinedly optimistic) that his status as a novelist with the critics and the public was due to the label of his name on the cover of his books rather than to their intrinsic merit. So when towards the end of 1865 he finished *Nina Balatka*, to put his theory to the test, on handing the MS over to George Smith he tried to persuade him to publish it anonymously. On Smith's turning down the suggestion Trollope approached Blackwood who, only too delighted to publish anything by the most successful author of the day, accepted the story on Trollope's terms and published it anonymously, first in *Blackwood's Magazine*, and then in two volumes. *Linda Tressel* followed close on its heels, similarly published.

It was unfortunate that Trollope should have made these stories the test cases for his theory. Both are far from being vintage Trollope, with the result that neither was a success, causing their author the pangs of deepest disappointment and forcing him into the conviction that his supposition was right and that it was indeed his name and not his novels themselves that made him popular. Recalling the matter in his *Autobiography* he wrote:

> Both stories were written with a considerable amount of labour and after visits to the towns in which the scenes are laid — Prague and Nuremburg . . . . There was more of romance proper than had been usual with me, and I made an attempt at local colouring . . . . In all this I am confident that I was in a measure successful. In the loves and fears and hatreds, both of Nina and Linda, there is much that is pathetic . . . . I know that the stories are good, but they missed the object with which they had been written. Of course there is not in this any evidence that I might not have succeeded a second time as I succeeded before, had I gone on with the same dogged perseverance. Another ten years of unpaid, unflagging labour might have built up a second

reputation. But this at any rate did seem clear to me, that with all the increased advantages which practice in my art must have given me, I could not at once induce English readers to read what I gave to them unless I gave it with my name.

Ignoring Trollope's own opinion, one may say that *Nina Balatka* is the mediocre better of the two 'anonymous' stories. This tale of a Czech Christian girl, Nina, and her love for the Jewish Anton Trendellsohn, both caught in the toils of a horrific but historical feud between Jews and Christians, has a compulsion about it altogether lacking in the other. The style is so strangely spare, for Trollope, the narrative so taut, that one could almost believe the story to be a translation from some Eastern European writer. Its weakness, it seems to me, is that instead of ending happily it should have been seen through to the bitter end as tragedy. Nina's despairing loitering on the famous bridge over the Moldau with the intention of throwing herself into the river — a powerful piece of writing,* should, one feels, have had a different ending than the slick last-minute intervention of Souchy and Rebecca. But Trollope shrank from the tragic but more consistent and compatible issue and allows it to end with the lovers leaving Prague to start a new life in 'one of the great cities of the west.'

Linda Tressel, written in six weeks, has Nuremburg for its scene, and for its theme the tyranny of a bigotedly religious Calvinist aunt, Charlotte Staubach, over her niece, Linda, whose guardian she is. To her horror Linda refuses to become betrothed to a highly respectable middle-aged Peter Steinmarc whom her aunt favours as being the most suitable husband for her, preferring the 'dissolute' and 'revolutionary' young Ludovic Valcarm as a lover. The aunt makes it her mission in life to crush the very soul of her niece by religious domination, and she succeeds. Linda, after running away from home, dies from exposure, weakness and sheer despairing soul-weariness. This is the reverse error of *Nina Balatka*: the tragic ending is given to the wrong story. The characters too, and the narrative, are inferior to the earlier book.

The two *nouvelles* have one thing in common, and one is forced to ask oneself whether Trollope had in mind something more than just a wish to try his hand at something different. This common factor is — hatred and intolerance engendered by religion. With this in mind, a brief discussion of Trollope's attitude towards religion and clerics becomes a subject of more than academic interest. There is no question of considering him an 'unbeliever'. Like ninety per cent of his contemporaries he regarded himself as a professing Christian of the respectable Church of England. In moments of crisis he makes more than one of his characters declare with a conviction leaving no room for doubt that they place their trust in an all-seeing God. But it is difficult not to believe, reading — not between the lines but the lines themselves — that his opinion of the generality of the purveyors of religion was anything but low, and that Victorian concession to piety in the form of constant church-going and family prayers, a sham. The Warden, the Revd Frank Fenwick and the Revd Crawley apart, not one of the many clerics who fill his pages is portrayed as being genuine from a religious and spiritual point of view. Again and again, too often for

---

* Some idea of the effect it had on one reader at least may be gauged by a letter from Mrs Oliphant to Blackwood following the appearance of the tale in his magazine. Writing from Prague she says: 'I am here for three-quarters of a day and am just going to look for Nina Balatka's bridge.'

the fact not to strike us forcibly, clerics and such characters as make religion and good works a dominant factor in their lives (in *Rachel Ray, Miss Mackenzie, The Belton Estate, Marion Fay, John Caldigate, He Knew He Was Right,* for example) are made to appear either unsympathetic, ridiculous, nauseous or even downright evil. A clue is given us by Michael Sadleir in the chapter 'The Portrait of Anthony' of his *Trollope: A Commentary,* where he observes:

> To some extent Trollope deliberately veiled his spiritual self . . . . He was a Christian and (though without great conviction) a conforming member of the Anglican Church. But, as one who knew him well observes, 'he was something of a *frondeur* in these matters.' His dislike of caste-supremacy, his instinctive reaction against an imposed code, whether of belief or morals or social deportment, disposed him to be exceptionally critical of Church dogma and Church discipline. Once in a letter to a young friend, he declared that taking Orders was crippling to a man's mentality. The novels are full of the sense of contrast between the practice and profession of those clergymen and ministers who think more of their Order than of their faith . . . . Conversely, he was convinced that unhappiness must inevitably come from unbelief. By 'unbelief' he meant denial of God, and not refusal to subscribe to any one religious creed.

As he wrote in his marginalia to Bacon's essay on Atheisme: 'Conviction of the existence and of the goodness of God is compatible with the absence of all Religion so-called.'

The truth is that Trollope detested exaggeration in any shape or form, whether social, religious or literary (which is one reason why he could never take to Dickens). He realized only too well that all the virtues, taken to excess, become failings, sometimes even vices. Modesty can become prudery, religion bigotry, humility cowardice, frankness effrontery, independence selfishness and aggressiveness, kind-heartedness sentimentality, and so on. Thus religion taken to excess becomes a drug no less than any other indulgence, and induces fanaticism, narrow-mindedness, bigotry. Hence his savage portraiture of such in Mrs Bolton, Robert Kennedy, Mrs Winterfield, Dorothea Ray — all of them well-intentioned people whose natures have been warped by the very intensity of their beliefs and who in the name of religion bully or dominate some poor soul to the utter misery of both. The true Christian, he believed, did not carry his convictions to the point of thrusting his belief down people's throats or condemning unbelief or different belief out of hand. Intolerance in any shape or form was anathema to him, whether between Jew and Christian, Catholic and Protestant, believer or unbeliever.

These two stories are, I believe, a fictionalized attempt to show the disastrous consequences of such intolerance. The Christian Nina is ostracized by her family and friends who are prepared to go to any lengths to prevent her marriage to a Jew. For a girl to enjoy the delight of having a young impetuous boy for a lover is repugnant to the Calvinistic, sex-hating, joy-killing widowed aunt, and a thing to put an end to at any price. That price is the death of Linda Tressel.

The Golden Lion of Granpère was written (in his own words to Blackwell) as 'a third story after the manner of "Linda" and "Nina".' But Blackwell, much as he admired Trollope, refused the offer — justifiably, one feels. The story, set in the Vosges, of a young couple's misunderstandings and final reunion, might have made a reasonably good short story. Spun out to the length it is it becomes far too tenuous. As for being French in atmosphere, it is as much the genuine article as the average south country version of Yorkshire pudding: it is so in name only. One cannot help thinking that Trollope would have been better advised if he had published them as a third volume of his series *Tales of All Countries*. As they stand, *Nina Balatka* dubiously excepted, they are dispensable.

THE LAST CHRONICLE OF BARSET

It is to be remarked that each novel of the Barsetshire series is longer than its predecessor. It is as though Trollope had become obsessed with his creations and had to purge his system of them. This, the last of them, is by far the longest. In his *Autobiography* he comments on it: 'Taking it as a whole, I regard this as the best novel I have written.' As I have already observed, Trollope's assessments of his own work as of that of others is generally suspect. A man who places *Ivanhoe* and *Henry Esmond* above *Pride and Prejudice* can hardly be accepted as an ideal of literary criticism. Nevertheless in this instance we can so far agree with him if we slightly alter his own words and claim it as 'one of the best novels I have written.' It would even have been his best but for the almost invariable prolixity, that passion for variation and 'entertaining the reader' by dragging in *ex abundati* episodes and personages which are out of character with the main story and merely succeed in padding it — in this case the Dobbs Broughton/Dalrymple/Demolines/Musselboro sections which are not so much incredible (human nature and London society being what it is) as completely out of key with the rest. Had Trollope not indulged himself by these excrescences he could with greater truth have claimed it as his greatest. No doubt he told himself that something more dramatic, more violent, was needed to mix with the humdrum everyday life that was his main preoccupation; a splash of colour to brighten the sombre clerical black of his main characters. But in this he miscalculated: the colours clash, and the London arty-cum-business episodes, unconvincing anyway, unbalance the otherwise perfect proportions of the story.

This criticism apart, the novel is a masterpiece with all the virtues of *The Small House*, and is, in fact, a true sequel to that novel, with further appearances of Lily Dale, Johnny Eames, Mr Crawley, the archdeacon, Mrs Proudie and others. Putting aside the London matter, the story basically runs in two strands: the narration of Mr Crawley's supposed theft of a cheque and his final vindication, and the wooing of Major Henry Grantly, son of the archdeacon, and Grace Crawley, Mr Crawley's daughter. This second strand is yet another replica of the situations in the novel's two predecessors, viz. the courtship of two young people in the teeth of parental opposition on account of the girl's lack of fortune, or social position, or both. The theme was becoming almost an obsession with Trollope. Was this merely because he thought it made a good subject for a novel? Or did he have a bee in his bonnet about this particular aspect of Victorian social ethics? Probably there was something of both reasons in his choice, but he does give us clues that he saw no good in and held no brief for the generally accepted dictatorship of parents over children and husbands over wives. In every case the parents are made to look silly, and the husbands are morally defeated; and to come back to the clues: in the second chapter of this novel he makes Mrs Crawley, the archdeacon's wife, observe to their son Henry in the course of encouraging him to marry again (he is a widower with a small daughter) but at the same time to take his eyes off Grace Crawley who is poor and with no social position — "My dear Henry . . . Do you know those two girls at Chaldicotes?"

"What, Mrs Thorne's nieces?"

"No, they are not her nieces, but her cousins. Emily Dunstable is very handsome; and as for money . . ."

"But what about birth, mother?"

"One can't have everything, my dear." And she goes on to reflect that it was too bad that Henry refused to look at Emily Dunstable rather than Grace Crawley when 'Nothing had been wanting to Emily Dunstable's education, and it was calculated that she would have at least twenty thousand pounds on the day of her marriage.' Mrs Grantly, although wife of a dignitary of the Church, had the Victorian passion for knowing all the possible brides' dowries and naming them in round figures. Later Trollope has a still more revealing passage. The archdeacon, furious with his son for being prepared to sacrifice his future for the sake of Grace Crawley and for refusing to give way to his pleas and even threats, decides to go to the heart of the matter and appeal to Grace herself. The scene is one of the many highlights of the novel, but at the moment I am concerned only with the archdeacon's thoughts as he meditates over his project.

The archdeacon, as he walked across from the Court to the parsonage, was very thoughtful and his steps were very slow. This idea of seeing Miss Crawley herself had been suggested to him suddenly, and he had to determine how he would bear himself towards her, and what he would say to her. Lady Lufton had beseeched him to be gentle with her. Was the mission one in which gentleness would be possible? Must it not be his object to make this young lady understand that she could not be right in desiring to come into his family and share in all his good things when she had got no good things of her own, — nothing but evil things to bring with her? And how could this be properly explained to the young lady in gentle terms? Must he not be round with her, and give her to understand in plain words, — the plainest which he could use, — that she would not get his good things, though she would most certainly impose the burden of all her evil things on the man whom she was proposing to herself as a husband. He remembered very well as he went, that he had been told that Miss Crawley had herself refused the offer, feeling herself to be unfit for the honour tendered to her; but he suspected the sincerity of such a refusal. Calculating in his own mind the unreasonably great advantages which would be conferred on such a young lady as Miss Crawley by a marriage with his son, he declared to himself that any girl must be very wicked indeed who should expect, or even accept, so much more than was her due; — but nevertheless he could not bring himself to believe that any girl, when so tempted, would, in sincerity, decline to commit this great wickedness. If he was to do any good by seeing Miss Crawley, must it not consist in a proper explanation to her of the selfishness, abomination, and altogether damnable blackness of such wickedness as this on the part of a young woman in her circumstances? 'Heaven and earth!' he must say, 'here are you, without a penny in your pocket, with hardly decent raiment on your back, with a thief for your father, and you think that you are to come and share in all the wealth that the Grantlys have amassed, that you are to have a husband with broad acres, a big house, and game preserves, and become one of a family whose name has never been touched by a single accusation, — no, not by a suspicion? No; — injustice such as that shall never be done betwixt you and me. You may wring my heart, and you may ruin my son; but the broad acres and the big house, and the game preserves, and the rest of it, shall never be your reward for doing so.' How was all that to be told effectively to a young woman in gentle words? And then how was a man in the archdeacon's position to be desirous of gentle words, — gentle words which would not be efficient, — when he knew well in his heart of hearts that he had nothing but his threats on which to depend. He had no more power of disinheriting his own son for such an offence as that contemplated than he had of blowing out his own brains, and he knew that it was so. He was a man incapable of such persistency of wrath against one whom he loved. He was neither cruel enough nor strong enough to do such a thing. He could only threaten to do it, and make what best use he might of threats, whilst threats might be of avail. In spite of all that he had said to his wife, to Lady Lufton, and to himself, he knew very well that if his son did sin in this way he, the father, would forgive the sin of the son.

Yet the man who harbours these thoughts and intentions is an archdeacon, a pillar of the Church. Christians and non-Christians alike, reading this passage, must surely ask themselves whether the supposedly Christian principles of Dr Grantly should not have been just the reverse, and whether he should not have gone to the girl of his son's choice and made her welcome to the good things of life which he was able to offer her and of which she had been unjustly deprived. The reader who misses Trollope's line of thought here misses the half of him.

The centrepiece of the novel, however, is the Revd Crawley. Trollope considered him to be his best-drawn character, and he may well have been right. Trollope loved contrasting characters, and Crawley is the antithesis of the archdeacon — the one worldly, prosperous, militant and social, fundamentally a good man but letting his religion sit lightly on his broad shoulders; the other unworldly, poor, a social misfit who thinks, talks and acts like an Old Testament minor prophet. The only characteristic the two have in common is pride, and even that is of a very different quality. The archdeacon is proud of his position in the church hierarchy and his worldly position; the poor curate is so ashamed of his poverty and lack of advancement that he is driven to covering it up with a pride that is almost vicious — a pride which makes him refuse all offers of help, makes him ostentatious in his poverty and all but costs him the friendship of his close friend and former college companion, Arabin. Two characters sum him up perfectly (and note Trollope's art in this) — Mark Robarts, the worldly 'sporty parson' of *Framley Parsonage*, and Mr Walker, the lawyer. The former visits him at his Hogglestock home to try to persuade him to employ a barrister in his defence in the forthcoming trial. Crawley, knowing him to be worldly, sporty and, above all, successful, is antagonistic to him on principle.

"I crave your pardon, Mr. Robarts," he said, "that I should keep you waiting."
Now Mr. Robarts had not been there ten minutes, and any such asking of pardon was hardly necessary. And, even in his own house, Mr. Crawley affected a mock humility, as though, either through his own debasement, or because of the superior station of the other clergyman, he were not entitled to put himself on equal footing with his visitor. He would not have shaken hands with Mr. Robarts — intending to indicate that he did not presume to do so while the present accusation was hanging over him — had not the action been forced upon him . . . . Mr. Robarts, without analysing it, understood it all, and knew that behind the humility there was a crushing pride . . . . It was, perhaps, after all, a question whether the man was not served rightly by the extremities to which he was reduced. There was something radically wrong with him which had put him into antagonism with all the world, and which produced these never-dying grievances.

The lawyer, a shrewd judge of men, comments on him to Mr Toogood: "The worst of your cousin is that he has an aptitude to quarrel with everybody. He is one of those men who always think themselves to be ill-used."

Not an attractive personality, the Revd Crawley: so burningly single-minded in his religion and Greek scholarship as to be scarcely fit for mortal consumption. But at least he is, what few of Trollope's clerics are, a practising Christian. Would Mark Robarts or the archdeacon or any of the Barchester clerics have gone among the poverty-stricken Hogglestock brick-workers to instruct their children, or, when their wives were ill, read the Bible to them or turned their washing mangles for them? The reader knows he could never have stolen the cheque: he would not have known how to do it. So, in spite of his pride, obstinacy, over-done religiosity and masochism, his sheer goodness and unworldly innocence shine through to us. And then, let us not forget, was he not the only cleric in the diocese who could not only stand up to Mrs Proudie (Dr Tempest later was to do as much) but to crush her and the bishop at one and the same time? We are almost prepared to forgive him everything for the sake of that momentous interview at the palace. And we cannot leave him without drawing attention to the fact that he has given us one of the great moments in British fiction. It occurs in chapter 62 where, in view of his impending trial, he has decided to resign his living. The family fortunes are at their lowest ebb. His wife, though loyal to him in all his miseries and never doubting his innocence, is being driven almost out of her mind by their poverty and the public shame surrounding them. The knowledge of possible imprisonment for her husband and the workhouse for herself and her two daughters stares her in the face. He returns home after a visit to his Hogglestock brick-workers with the intention of writing his letter of resignation to the bishop.

> But before he commenced his task, he sat down with his youngest daughter, and read, — or made her read to him, — a passage out of a Greek poem, in which are described the troubles and agonies of a blind giant. No giant would have been more powerful, — only that he was blind, and could not see to avenge himself on those who had injured him. 'The same story is always coming up,' he said, stopping the girl in her reading. 'We have it in various versions, because it is so true to life.
>   Ask for this great deliverer now, and find him
>   Eyeless in Gaza, at the mill with slaves.
> It is the same story. Great power reduced to impotence, great glory to misery, by the hand of Fate, — Necessity, as the Greeks called her; the goddess that will not be shunned! At the mill with slaves! People, when they read it, do not appreciate the horror of the picture. Go on, my dear. It may be a question whether Polyphemus had mind enough to suffer; but, from the description of his power, I should think that he had. "At the mill with slaves!" Can any picture be more dreadful than that? Go on, my dear. Of course you remember Milton's Samson Agonistes. Agonistes indeed!' His wife was sitting stitching at the other side of the room; but she heard his words, — heard and understood them; and before Jane could again get herself into the swing of the Greek verse, she was over at her husband's side, with her arms round his neck. 'My love!' she said. 'My love!'
>   He turned to her, and smiled as he spoke to her. 'These are old thoughts with me. Polyphemus and Belisarius, and Samson and Milton, have always been pets of mine. The mind of the strong blind creature must be so sensible of the injury that has been done to him! The impotency, combined with his strength, or rather the impotency with the memory of former strength and former aspirations, is so essentially tragic!'
>   She looked into his eyes as she spoke, and there was something of the flash of old days, when

the world was young to them, and when he would tell her of his hopes, and repeat to her long passages of poetry, and would criticize for her advantage the works of old writers. 'Thank God,' she said, 'that you are not blind. It may yet be all right with you.'

'Yes, — it may be,' he said.

'And you shall not be at the mill with slaves.'

'Or, at any rate, not eyeless in Gaza, if the Lord is good to me. Come, Jane, we will go on.'

The scene is only brief — a tiny vignette, but its impact is terrific. It has in little all the power of Greek tragedy. No other English novelist has given us a passage more moving in its nobility, poetry and pathos.

Crosbie, Johnny Eames and the Dales also make reappearances, Lily in all her pristine beauty. The crux of her life comes when Crosbie, now widowed and desperate in his unhappiness, writes to Mrs Dale confessing his love for Lily and hoping she might forgive him. But Lily, after long and uncertain reflection, refuses to go back to him. Why? the reader asks, when she still loves him and both are free. She gives us the reason in answer to her mother's "He has nothing at least, for which to condemn you."

'But he would have, were I to marry him now. He would condemn me because I had forgiven him. He would condemn me because I had borne what he had done to me, and had still loved him — loved him through it all. He would feel and know the weakness; — and there is weakness. I have been weak in not being able to rid myself of him altogether. He would recognize this after a while, and would despise me for it. But he would not see what there is of devotion to him in my being able to bear the taunts of the world in going back to him, and your taunts, and my own taunts. I should have to bear his also, — not spoken aloud, but to be seen in his face and heard in his voice, — and that I could not endure. If he despised me, and he would, that would make us both unhappy. Therefore, mamma, tell him not to come; tell him that he can never come; but, if it be possible, tell him this tenderly.' Then she got up and walked away, as though she were going out of the room; but her mother had caught her before the door was opened.

'Lily,' she said, 'if you think you can be happy with him, he shall come.'

'No, mamma, no. I have been looking for the light ever since I read his letter, and I think I see it. And now, mamma, I will make a clean breast of it. From the moment in which I heard that that poor woman was dead, I have been in a state of flutter. It has been weak of me, and silly, and contemptible. But I could not help it. I kept on asking myself whether he would ever think of me now. Well; he has answered the question; and has so done it that he has forced upon me the necessity of a resolution. I have resolved, and I believe that I shall be the better for it.'

The letter which Mrs Dale wrote to Mr Crosbie, was as follows:-

'Mrs Dale presents her compliments to Mr Crosbie, and begs to assure him that it will not now be possible that he should renew the relations which were broken off three years ago, between him and Mrs Dale's family.'

The reader is further perplexed, and perhaps even a little vexed with her when, after turning down Crosbie's offer, she goes on refusing to give her hand to the ever-constant Johnny Eames, who over all makes four unsuccessful attempts to win her. His third effort (chapter 35, 'Lily Dale writes two words in her book') is so beautifully done and moreover makes clear her state of mind so perceptively that it must be quoted. In the course of their little walk together Johnny has just helped her over what she has told him is "the worst stile of all."

'Let me help you always,' he said, keeping her hands in his after he had aided her to jump from the stile to the ground.

'Yes, as my brother.'

'That is nonsense, Lily.'

'Is it nonsense? Nonsense is a hard word.'

'It is nonsense as coming from you to me. Lily, I sometimes think that I am persecuting you, writing to you, coming after you, as I am doing now, — telling the same whining story, — asking, asking and asking for that which you say you will never give me. And then I feel ashamed of myself, and swear that I will do it no more.'

'Do not be ashamed of yourself; but yet do it no more.'

'And then,' he continued, without minding her words, 'at other times I feel that it must be my own fault; that if I only persevered with sufficient energy I must be successful. At such times I swear that I will never give it up.'

'Oh, John, if you could only know how little worthy of such pursuit it is.'

'Leave me to judge of that, dear. When a man has taken a month, or perhaps only a week, or perhaps not more than half an hour, to make up his mind, it may be very well to tell him that he doesn't know what he is about. I've been in the office now for over seven years, and the first day I went I put on oath into a book that I would come back and get you for my wife when I had got enough to live upon.'

'Did you, John?'

'Yes. I can show it you. I used to come and hover about the place in the old days, before I went to London, when I was such a fool that I couldn't speak to you if I met you. I am speaking of a time long before, — before that man came down here.'

'Do not speak of him, Johnny.'

'I must speak of him. A man isn't to hold his tongue when everything he has in the world is at stake. I suppose he loved you after a fashion, once,'

'Pray, pray do not speak ill of him.'

'I am not going to abuse him. You can judge of him by his deeds. I cannot say anything worse of him than what they say. I suppose he loved you; but he certainly did not love you as I have done. I have at any rate been true to you. Yes, Lily, I have been true to you. I am true to you. He did not know what he was about. I do. I am justified in saying that I do. I want you to be my wife. It is no use your talking about it as though I only half wanted it.'

'I did not say that.'

'Is not a man to have any reward? Of course if you had married him there would have been an end of it. He had come in between me and my happiness, and I must have borne it, as other men bear such sorrows. But you have not married him; and, of course, I cannot feel that I may yet have a chance. Lily, answer me this. Do you believe that I love you?' But she did not answer him. 'You can at any rate tell me that. Do you think that I am in earnest?'

'Yes, I think you are in earnest.'

'And do you believe that I love you with all my heart and all my strength and all my soul?'

'Oh, John!'

'But do you?'

'I think you love me.'

'Think! what I am to say or to do to make you understand that my only idea of happiness is the idea that sooner or later I may get you to be my wife? Lily, will you say that it shall be so? Speak, Lily. There is no one that will not be glad. Your uncle will consent, — has consented. Your mother wishes it. Bell wishes it. My mother wishes it. Lady Julia wishes it. You would be doing what everybody about you wants you to do. And why should you not do it? It isn't that you dislike me. You wouldn't talk about being my sister, if you had not some sort of regard for me.'

'I have a regard for you.'

'Then why will you not be my wife? Oh, Lily, say the word now, here, at once. Say the word, and you'll make me the happiest fellow in all England.' As he spoke he took her by both arms, and held her fast. She did not struggle to get away from him, but stood quite still, looking into his face, while the first sparkle of a salt tear formed itself in each eye. 'Lily, one little word will do it, — half a word, a nod, a smile. Just touch my arm with your hand and I will take it for a yes.' I think that she almost tried to touch him; that the word was in her throat, and that she almost strove to speak it. But there was no syllable spoken, and her fingers did not loose themselves to fall upon his sleeve. 'Lily, Lily, what can I say to you?'

'I wish I could,' she whispered; — but the whisper was so hoarse that he hardly recognized the voice.

'And why can you not? What is there to hinder you? There is nothing to hinder you, Lily.'

'Yes, John; there is that which must hinder me.'

'And what is it?'

'I will tell you. You are so good and so true, and so excellent, — such a dear, dear, dear friend, that I will tell you everything, so that you may read my heart. I will tell you as I tell mamma, — you and her and no one else; — for you are the choice friend of my heart. I cannot be your wife because of the love I bear for another man.'

'And that man is he, — he who came here?'

'Of course it is he. I think, Johnny, you and I are alike in this, that when we have loved we cannot bring ourselves to change. You will not change, though it would be so much better you should do so.'

'No; I will never change.'

'Nor can I. When I sleep I dream of him. When I am alone I cannot banish him from my thoughts. I cannot define what it is to love him. I want nothing from him, — nothing, nothing. But I move about through my little world thinking of him, and I shall do so to the end. I used to feel proud of my love, though it made me so wretched that I thought it would kill me. I am not proud of it any longer. It is a foolish poor-spirited weakness, — as though my heart had been only half formed in the making. Do you be stronger, John. A man should be stronger than a woman.'

'I have none of that sort of strength.'

'Nor have I. What can we do but pity each other, and swear that we will be friends, — dear friends. There is the oak-tree and I have got to turn back. We have said everything that we can say, — unless you will tell me that you will be my brother.'

'No; I will not tell you that.'

'Good-by, then, Johnny,'

He paused, holding her by the hand and thinking of another question which he longed to put to her, — considering whether he would ask her that question or not. He hardly knew whether he were entitled to ask it; — whether or no the asking of it would be ungenerous. She had said that she would tell him everything, — as she had told everything to her mother. 'Of course,' he said, 'I have no right to expect to know anything of your future intentions?'

'You may know them all, — as far as I know them myself. I have said that you should read my heart.'

'If this man, whose name I cannot bear to mention, should come again — '

'If he were to come again he would come in vain, John.' She did not say that he had come again. She could tell her own secret, but not that of another person.

'You would not marry him, now that he is free?!

She stood and thought a while before she answered him. 'No, I should not marry him now. I think not.' Then she paused again. 'Nay, I am sure I would not. After what has passed I could not trust myself to do it. There is my hand on it. I will not.'

'No, Lily, I do not want that.'

'But I insist. I will not marry Mr Crosbie. But you must not misunderstand me, John. There; — all that is over for me now. All those dreams about love, and marriage, and of a house of my own, and children, — and a cross husband, and a wedding-ring growing always tighter as I grow fatter and older. I have dreamed of such things as other girls do, — more perhaps than other girls, more than I should have done. And now I accept the thing as finished. You wrote something in your book, you dear John, — something that could not be made to come true. Dear John, I wish for your sake it was otherwise. I will go home and I will write in my book, this very day, Lilian Dale, Old Maid. If ever I make that false, do you come and ask me for the page.'

'Let it remain there till I am allowed to tear it out.'

'I will write it, and it shall never be torn out. You I cannot marry. Him I will not marry. You may believe me, Johnny, when I say there can never be a third?'

'And is that to be the end of it?'

'Yes; — that is to be the end of it. Not the end of our friendship. Old maids have friends.'

'It shall not be the end of it. There shall be no end of it with me.'

'But, John — '

'Do not suppose that I will trouble you again, — at any rate not for a while. In five years' time perhaps, — '

'Now, Johnny, you are laughing at me. And of course it is the best way. If there is not Grace, and she has caught me before I have turned back. Good-by, dear, dear John. God bless you. I think you the finest fellow there is in the world. I do, and so does mamma. Remember always that there is a temple at Allington in which your worship is never forgotten.' Then she pressed his hand and turned away from him to meet Grace Crawley. John did not stop to speak a word to his cousin, but pursued his way alone.

Johnny makes a fourth attempt, a final one, but has to leave her defeated yet again, and the novel ends with both of them unmarried. Why, demanded irate readers, couldn't Trollope have relented and let the wedding bells ring in the approved Victorian manner? Some critic — I forget whom — suggested that her creator couldn't bear to let her be married because he was in love with her himself. Only a novelist, perhaps, can appreciate this passion of a creator for his creations; but I do believe there is more than a grain of truth in the contention. Lily Dale was his favourite heroine. In his own words as he introduces her to us in *The Small House*: 'Lilian Dale, dear Lily Dale — for my reader must know that she is to be very dear, and that my story will be nothing to him if he do not love Lily Dale . . . . ' He must be a poor man indeed, and she a poor woman too, if they do not love her.

I cannot leave the book without mentioning two characters who have given us so much pleasure in the course of the Barchester series: the archdeacon and his irrevocable antagonist, the bishop's wife, Mrs Proudie. We may not consider either of them to be model Christians, but the scene is never dull when they are about, and we take leave of both with a softened regard.

To take the archdeacon first. I referred earlier to his intended visit of denunciation to Grace Crawley. He goes: but what happens? Their interview takes a very different line from the one he had envisaged. She cuts the ground from under his feet by telling him firmly that so long as her father is under suspicion as a thief she will not injure her lover or his family marrying him, although her promise has been given. Touched by this, and influenced by her beauty which seems to grow under his eyes (as Mrs Grantly knew, her husband, in Trollope's carefully chosen words — was 'keenly susceptible to the influences of feminine charm') — he melts and relents. 'And as he looked down upon her face two tears formed themselves in his eyes, and gradually trickled down his old nose. "My dear," he said, "if this cloud passes away from you, you shall come to us and be my daughter." And thus he also pledged himself.'

He was often — too often — angry with people who crossed him in his desires, and his quarrel with his son is a piece of heavy father business which for the moment alienates him from our sympathies. But Trollope summed him up when he observed of him: 'And indeed it was the nature of the man that when he had been very angry with those he loved, he should be unhappy until he had found some escape from his anger. He could not endure to have to own himself to have been in the wrong, but he could be content with a very incomplete recognition of his having been in the right.' Trollope was proud of the archdeacon as a piece of characterization, and he had every reason to be so.

Finally, Mrs Proudie. Like her creator most of us must confess to a love-hate involvement with that large-looming figure, and Trollope has been condemned for taking notice of those babbling clerics he overheard in the Athenaeum complaining of her reappearances in the Barchester series, and whose criticism decided him to kill her off; for surely a novelist should be above the comments of amateur readers. He was to have second thoughts about the matter, and confesses in his *Autobiography* 'It was with many misgivings that I killed my old friend Mrs Proudie . . . . I have sometimes regretted the deed, so great was my delight in writing about Mrs Proudie . . . . ' And let us say in passing that she did indeed have 'shades' in her character. She is no caricature, no unfeeling tyrannical she-monster. We are made to feel that she is not at heart a bad woman; that despite her complete domination of her mouse of a husband she loves him and wants to rouse him so that she can be proud of him; and that, as is proved by her reaction to the pitiful appeal of poor Mrs Quiverful, under her forbidding exterior she has a heart and is human.

To return to her demise. There are two schools of thought on the subject, one condemning it as out of key with her character and the story, the other of reluctant acceptance. A first reading, I think, pushes one into the former camp. Such an end, one feels, comes too suddenly, and in any case should be reserved for tragic figures, and Mrs Proudie is hardly that. But a careful re-reading can change, or at least modify that opinion. One becomes more aware of the skill with which Trollope has prepared his ground. Following the quarrel with Dr Tempest the bishop has at last been driven to rounding on his wife for her constant interference in his affairs, telling her that she has "disgraced him," and had been "wrong — very wrong" — and had "broken his heart." Further, he has refused her peace offering to forget "as Christians." Already, then, a serious rift looms, and what was once comedy is taking on a look of something very different. All her efforts at reconciliation, 'to bring him back to something like life,' fail:

and when she failed, as she did fail day after day, she would go slowly to her own room, and lock her door, and look back in her solitude at all the days of her life. She had agonies in these minutes of which no one near her knew anything. She would seize with her arm the part of the bed near which she would stand, and hold by it, grasping it, as though she were afraid to fall; and then, when it was at the worst with her, she would go to her closet — a closet that no eyes ever saw unlocked but her own — and fill for herself and swallow some draught; and then she would sit down with her Bible before her, and read it sedulously . . . . '

Now when we learn that someone we lack sympathy with, or even dislike, has had to live with a secret mortal illness, the knowledge immediately mitigates our hostility, turns it to sympathy. So with Mrs Proudie. She had kept her illness and pain hidden from the world, and at once she becomes more than a figure of comedy. And observe, with the above passage in mind, how Trollope prepares us for and anticipates the tragic finale. In his last recriminations her husband, speaking with words more full of meaning than he was aware of, had exclaimed, "There will be an end of all this very soon — very soon:" on which she had left him 'without uttering another word', to ruminate sadly on her sudden overwhelming knowledge that her husband now no longer loved her. Later that same day she was found dead in her room.

> The body was still resting on its legs, leaning against the end of the side of the bed, while one of the arms was clasped round the bed-post. The mouth was rigidly closed, but the eyes were open as though staring at him . . . .

This unforeseen and abrupt death of a being so full of vitality comes as a shock; but I do not think it to be artistically wrong. Indeed, one might go so far as to suggest that Trollope was subtler than he realized when he decided to kill her off. The character of a bully, a dominating figure, a would-be controller of weaker personalities, can be a flimsy thing. The first show of contest can expose its weakness. So here. When, driven beyond himself, the bishop turns on her, her spirit shrinks, her world collapses, subtly revealing that she needed him as much as, if not more than, he needed her. Unrealized by all, she is in fact the weaker vessel, and her driving force being frustrated and made useless, she fades to a shadow of herself, without the will to live.

In any event, her creator's final words on her must be our own. 'I have never dissevered myself from Mrs Proudie, and still live much in company with her ghost,' he confessed in his *Autobiography*. And for the last paragraph of the 'Conclusion' to *The Last Chronicle* he was moved to write:

> And now, if the reader will allow me to seize him affectionately by the arm, we will together take our last farewell of Barset and of the towers of Barchester. I may not venture to say to him that, in this country, he and I together have wandered often through the country lanes, and have ridden together over the too-well wooded fields, or have stood together in the cathedral nave listening to the peals of the organ, or have together sat at good men's tables, or have confronted together the angry pride of men who were not good. I may not boast that any beside myself have so realized the place, and the people, and the facts, so to make such reminiscences possible as those which I should attempt to evoke by an appeal to perfect fellowship. But to me Barset has been a real county, and its city a real city, and the spires and towers have been before my eyes, and the voices of the people are known to my ears, and the pavement of the city ways are familiar to my footsteps. To them all I now say farewell. That I have been induced to wander among them too long by my love of old friendships, and by the sweetness of old faces, is a fault for which I may perhaps be more readily forgiven, when I repeat, with some solemnity of assurance, the promise made in my title, that this shall be the last chronicle of Barset.

PHINEAS FINN

The fact that Trollope was paid the highest sum he was ever to receive for his next novel (£3,200) together with the feeling that he could now be confident of his ability to keep himself and his family on his literary earnings decided him to take a crucial and irreversible step, namely, that of giving in his resignation to the Post Office. This was in the September of 1867. He was fifty-two. He did not know it, but he was now at the height of his powers and his popularity. Slowly, from now on, as with all prolific writers, he was to know the bitterness of waning powers, waning popularity and falling sales: the penalty, in fact, for flooding the market.

It was typical that following the flops of *Nina Balatka* and *Linda Tressel* Trollope should follow them with one of his best. Perhaps the failure of his two anonymous ventures stirred him to show the British reading public what he could really do, and that the Barsetshire novels were not the be-all-and-end-all of his genius. Perhaps too the fact that one month after resigning from his job, at James Vertue's insistent pleas he accepted with some reluctance the editorship of a new literary journal, *Saint Paul's Magazine*, at a salary of £1,000 a year. In addition Vertue paid him £3,500 for the serial rights of his new novel, *Phineas Finn*.

So, securely and newly launched, Trollope set to work on the second of what has come to be known as the 'Palliser' or 'political' series of novels of which *Can You Forgive Her?* had been the first, finishing it in six months.

Some critics, including Hugh Walpole,* have castigated the titular hero as being 'tame' and 'a hollow drum' — a criticism clearly stemming from the fact that Phineas, like Tom Jones, like Byron's Don Juan, like David Copperfield, like so many titular heroes, in fact, belonged (to quote J.P. Hennessy) 'to that gigantic category of passive persons with little volition to whom things merely happen.' This in turn came to breed the other criticism that Trollope was creating characters who were 'too like real life for literature' — clearly a case of you pays your money and you takes your choice.

Certainly I think one must concede that for a 'handsome' (Trollope makes much of the epithet) and virile Irishman full of the blarney, Phineas hardly comes up to expectation; and one must own that his fatal charm for the fair sex is difficult to understand. If the novel is one of Trollope's best this is due more to the characters of Madame Max Goesler, Laura Standish, Violet Effingham and Lord Chiltern, who compensate us for the absence of the Pallisers, rather than to the theoretical charm of Phineas himself.

The story is simple in outline but complex politically and socially. Phineas, son of an Irish country doctor in County Clare, comes to London to read law with an English barrister, and after three years was called to the Bar. A member of the Reform Club, he mixes with men of high political reputation, and to his surprise, on the dissolution of Parliament he is advised to stand as candidate for the Irish borough of Loughshane. He becomes elected and an MP. A bright career has begun for him; but as with everything in

* See his *Anthony Trollope* in the 'English Men of Letters' series, 1929.

this world, the bitters run along with it. As some wise person once observed, life would be delightfully simple if there were no women in it. Women were to be the making and unmaking, the sweet and the sour of his career. With all an Irishman's blarney, good-looking, pleasing, modest, naïve, attracted by and attractive to women, he goes from one crisis to another in one affair after another. In this he makes the ideal 'hero' because his susceptible heart is always getting him into entanglements, and we never know what is going to happen next. He is perennially interesting, so much so that he makes even the duller political parts of the narrative relatively interesting.

The first of his lady loves (unless we count his youthful flame, Mary Flood) is Lady Laura Standish. From his first status as MP to his final rise to the post of Under-Secretary of State, she is the big influence behind him. She is unusual for her time, being a politically-minded, highly intelligent woman of the sort who later made themselves suffragettes. Without being beautiful she is attractive and moreover is related to or knows all and everyone of importance in the political scene. She schemes in a quasi-sisterly way for Phineas's advancement, and all goes well until the inevitable happens, and the relationship passes out of the bounds of the platonic into that of the emotional. This comes to its climax when Mr Kennedy, Liberal MP for a Scottish group of boroughs, 'an unmarried man, with an immense fortune, a magnificent place, a seat in Parliament and not perhaps above forty years of age,' but dour, unattractive and lymphatic, invites a covey of Parliamentary bigwigs (including, to his surprise, Finn), to his country seat at Loughlinter for hunting, shooting, fishing, riding — all the usual sport and relaxations, in fact, of the upper classes. Lady Laura is also to be there — a fact which suddenly takes on significance for Finn, though he cannot believe she could bring herself to accept such a boring man as Kennedy despite his position and wealth. Nevertheless, he realizes that time is of the essence, and so on the last day of his stay he decides he must propose to Lady Laura at all costs, despite the difference in their social positions and his poverty (and such differences, the reader must bear in mind, meant something in the times when Trollope was writing). He hurries back from the shoot, finds her alone and asks her to walk with him up the glen.

> "After all that climbing," he said, "will you not sit down for a moment?" As he spoke to her she looked at him and told herself that he was as handsome as a god. "Do sit down for a moment," he said. "I have something that I desire to say to you, and to say it here."
> "I will," she said; "but I also have something to tell you, and will say it while I am yet standing. Yesterday I accepted an offer of marriage from Mr. Kennedy."
> "Then I am too late," said Phineas, and putting his hands into the pockets of his coat, he turned his back upon her, and walked away across the mountain.

By accepting Kennedy she seals her doom: she is to find no love in the sort of existence the puritanical sabbatarian husband forces on her and, too late, that she does love Phineas and has thrown all her life's happiness away. From now on she becomes a bewildered heroine of high tragedy.

Phineas, although feeling that 'his back was broken,' pursues his political and social way, finds that time heals his wound and prepares for his next love affair, this time with Violet Effingham. Now Violet is 'a very dear friend of Lady Laura's . . . an orphan, an heiress and a beauty; with a terrible aunt, one Lady Baldock.' Like Glencora Palliser, she is a 'character', and her dragon of an aunt has a terrible time trying to control her.

Trollope's first introduction of her to the reader makes its immediate impact.

> Violet Effingham was certainly no puppet. She was great at dancing, — as perhaps might be a puppet, — but she was great also at archery, great at skating, — and great, too, at hunting. With reference to that last accomplishment, she and Lady Baldock had had more than one terrible tussle, not always with advantage to the dragon. 'My dear aunt,' she had said once during the last winter, 'I am going to the meet with George,' — George was her cousin, Lord Baldock, and was the dragon's son, — 'and there, let there be an end of it.' 'And you will promise me that you will not go further,' said the dragon. 'I will promise nothing to-day to any man or to any woman,' said Violet. What was to be said to a young lady who spoke in this way, and who had become of age only a fortnight since? She rode that day the famous run from Bagnall's Gorse to Foulsham Common, and was in at the death.

Being great friends, she and Lady Laura are frequently found together, and their dialogues sparkle. Both women come alive through the mere action of their tongues. No comparable understanding of female language and character has been achieved by any other male novelist. It is as though Trollope had listened invisibly to dozens of women's conversations. If the reader thinks I exaggerate, let him read the chapter 'Violet Effingham' which is one long dialogue and a perfect example. Then too her courtship by Lady Laura's brother, Lord Oswald Chiltern, is absorbingly vivid too. Chiltern is a slightly milder, more civilized version of George Vavasor. He is a drinking, betting man and generally considered unfit for marriage. This is his introduction to the reader.

> At that moment the door of the room was opened, and a man entered with quick steps, came a few yards in, and then retreated, slamming the door after him. He was a man with thick short red hair, and an abundance of very red beard. And his face was red, and, as it seemed to Phineas, his very eyes. There was something in the countenance of the man which struck him almost with dread — something approaching to ferocity.
>
> There was a pause a moment after the door was closed, and then Lady Laura spoke. "It was my brother Chiltern. I do not think that you have ever met him."

Phineas is to know him first as a friend and then as a rival for the hand of Violet Effingham and to fight a duel with him. Which of the two men does she really love? She cannot make up her mind, and so the reader is kept guessing. But since Chiltern has known her for most of their lives, and it is his sister's dearest wish to pair them off, the odds seem to be in favour of the savage red-head. But Chiltern has strange notions of proposing to a woman. His first attempt is made in the presence of his sister. The three have been reminiscing about old times, contrasting then and now, and Violet remarks, "And so you see everything is changed as well as my name."

> 'Everything is not changed,' said Lord Chiltern, getting up from his seat. 'I am not changed, — at least not in this, that as I loved you better than any being in the world, — better even than Laura there, — so do I love you now infinitely the best of all. Do not look so surprised at me. You knew it before as well as you do now; — and Laura knows it. There is no secret to be kept in the matter among us three.'
>
> 'But, Lord Chiltern, — ' said Miss Effingham, rising also to her feet, and then pausing, not knowing how to answer him. There had been a suddenness in his mode of addressing her which had, so to say, almost taken away her breath; and then to be told by a man of his love before his sister was in itself, to her, a matter so surprising, that none of those words came at her command

which will come, as though by instinct, to young ladies on such occasions.

'You have known it always,' said he, as though he were angry with her.

'Lord Chiltern,' she replied, 'you must excuse me if I say that you are, at the least, very abrupt. I did not think when I was going back so joyfully to our childish days that you would turn the tables on me in this way.'

'He has said nothing that ought to make you angry,' said Lady Laura.

'Only because he has driven me to say that which will make me appear to be uncivil to himself. Lord Chiltern, I do not love you with that love of which you are speaking now. As an old friend I have always regarded you, and I hope that I may always do so.' Then she got up and left the room.

'Why were you so sudden with her, — so abrupt, — so loud?' said his sister, coming up to him and taking him by the arm almost in anger.

'It would make no difference,' said he. 'She does not care for me.'

Meeting Violet frequently, and hearing that she has twice turned Chiltern down, Phineas begins to come under her spell. They have long conversations together in which (with great dramatic irony in view of what is to come) they discuss Chiltern's character; and in the chapter 'Phineas returns to London' there occur two notable examples of Trollope's uncanny knowledge of the human heart, male and female. Finn and Lady Laura have been talking about her brother and Violet, and despite the two refusals Lady Laura declares:

'I believe she loves him in her heart; but she is afraid of him. As she says herself, a girl is bound to be so careful of herself. With all her seeming frolic, Violet Effingham is very wise.'

Phineas, though not conscious of anything akin to jealousy, was annoyed at the revelation made to him. Since he had heard that Lord Chiltern was in love with Miss Effingham, he did not like Lord Chiltern quite as well as he had done before. He himself had simply admired Miss Effingham, and had taken pleasure in her society; but, though this had been all, he did not like to hear of another man wanting to marry her, and he was almost angry with Lady Laura for saying that she believed Miss Effingham loved her brother. If Miss Effingham had twice refused Lord Chiltern, that ought to have been sufficient. It was not that Phineas was in love with Miss Effingham himself. As he was still violently in love with Lady Laura, any other love was of course impossible; but, nevertheless, there was something offensive to him in the story as it had been told. 'If it be wisdom on her part,' said he, answering Lady Laura's last words, 'you cannot find fault with her for her decision.'

'I find no fault; — but I think my brother would make her happy.'

Lady Laura, when she was left alone, at once reverted to the tone in which Phineas Finn had answered her remarks about Miss Effingham. Phineas was very ill able to conceal his thoughts, and wore his heart almost upon his sleeve. 'Can it be possible that he cares for her himself?' That was the nature of Lady Laura's first question to herself upon the matter. And in asking herself that question, she thought nothing of the disparity in rank or fortune between Phineas Finn and Violet Effingham. Nor did it occur to her as at all improbable that Violet might accept the love of him who had so lately been her own lover. But the idea grated against her wishes on two sides. She was most anxious that Violet should ultimately become her brother's wife, — and she could not be pleased that Phineas should be able to love any woman.

Driven to desperation by his feelings, Phineas, during a ride with Violet, confesses his love; but she abruptly cuts him short, leaving him without hope. In his misery he then determines to carry out a despairing piece of audacity, namely, to confess his passion to

Lady Laura and beg her help! He even prepares to carry his plan out at Loughlinter on the very spot where he had first spoken of his feelings for her twelve months before. But yet again, as she had done on that occasion, she forestalls him, this time by a confession a woman can make only to someone near and dear to her and whom she can trust — a confession that her marriage has been a tragic mistake on her part and a half-hidden avowal of her love for him. The whole chapter — 'Lady Laura Kennedy's Headache' is a masterpiece of narrative and character study. Even Phineas, blind and naïve as he is, understands that the moment is not propitious. But it is only delayed. Soon after his duel with Chiltern, who is still in love with Violet — despite two refusals on her part, he seeks her out and in the chapter 'Lady Laura is told' he takes the plunge. Her reaction is what anyone not as naïve as Phineas nor so blinded by his present passion would have anticipated. But Trollope sees further than her immediate outraged feelings. When he had left her:

> She rose from her chair as he left the room, and waited till she heard the sound of the great door closing behind him before she again sat down. Then, when he was gone, — when she was sure that he was no longer there with her in the same house, — she laid her head down upon the arm of the sofa, and burst into a flood of tears. She was no longer angry with Phineas. There was no further longing in her heart for revenge. She did not now desire to injure him, though she had done so as long as he was with her. Nay, — she resolved instantly, almost instinctively, that Lord Brentford must know nothing of all this, lest the political prospects of the young member for Loughton should be injured. To have rebuked him, to rebuke him again and again, would be only fair, — would at least be womanly; but she would protect him from all material injury as far as her power of protection might avail. And why was she weeping now so bitterly? Of course she asked herself, as she rubbed away the tears with her hands, — Why should she weep? She was not weak enough to tell herself that she was weeping for any injury that had been done to Oswald. She got up suddenly from the sofa, and pushed away her hair from her face, and pushed away the tears from her cheeks, and then clenched her fists as she held them out at full length from her body, and stood, looking up with her eyes fixed upon the wall. 'Ass!' she exclaimed. 'Fool! Idiot! That I should not be able to crush it into nothing and have done with it! Why should he not have her? After all, he is better than Oswald.'

But Phineas is not to get Violet, who after three proposals from Chiltern and states of being 'off' and 'on', finally accepts him. (The scene of his final triumph is beautifully done.) Phineas, now left desolate and forlorn, turns more and more for consolation to his third love, the young, attractive, wealthy Austrian widow, Madame Max Goesler, who becomes the third outstanding character of the book. He confides his sorrows and ambitions to her and she pities him, and as we know from Shakespeare, pity is akin to love. But things are not to be as simple as that. While on a political visit to his own country Finn's conscience has been caught up in the iniquitous Irish tenantry problem. It has also been caught up by his conduct to his first love, Mary Flood, and in a mood of revulsion against politics and political ambitions, and embittered by his unfortunate love affairs with English society women, he becomes engaged to her. Back in London once more and among his old friends he cannot bring himself to speak of his engagement, especially to Madame Max. But the situation gets out of hand. When Phineas informs her (he has meantime lost his seat owing to his recalcitrant and insubordinate attitude to the Irish question) of his intention to resign from politics and to try to live as a lawyer in Dublin, she tells him not to be such a fool, and freely and nobly offers him her money so that he can fight again in the next election. The scene is inexpressibly moving.

'But, Madame Goesler, you who offer it would yourself despise me if I took it.'

'No; — I do deny it.' As she said this, — not loudly but with much emphasis, — she came and stood before him where he was sitting. And as he looked at her he could perceive that there was a strength about her of which he had not been aware. She was stronger, larger, more robust physically than he had hitherto conceived. 'I do deny it,' she said. 'Money is neither god nor devil, that it should make one noble and another vile. It is an accident, and, if honestly possessed, may pass from you to me, or from me to you, without a stain. You may take my dinner from me if I give it you, my flowers, my friendship, my, — my, — my everything, but my money! Explain to me the cause of the phenomenon. If I give to you a thousand pounds, now this moment, and you take it, you are base; — but if I leave it you in my will, — and die, — you take it, and are not base. Explain to me the cause of that.'

'You have not said it quite all,' said Phineas hoarsely.

'What have I left unsaid? If I have left anything unsaid, do you say the rest.'

'It is because you are a woman, and young, and beautiful, that no man may take wealth from your hands.'

'Oh, it is that!'

'It is that partly.'

'If I were a man you might take it, though I were young and beautiful as the morning?'

'No; — presents of money are always bad. They stain and load the spirit, and break the heart.'

'And specially when given by a woman's hand?'

'It seems so to me. But I cannot argue of it. Do not let us talk of it any more.'

'Nor can I argue. I cannot argue, but I can be generous, — very generous. I can deny myself for my friend, — can even lower myself in my own esteem for my friend. I can do more than a man can do for a friend. You will not take money from my hand?'

'No, Madame Goesler; — I cannot do that.'

'Take the hand then first. When it and all that it holds are your own, you can help yourself as you list.' So saying, she stood before him with her right hand stretched out towards him.

What man will say that he would not have been tempted? Or what woman will declare that such temptation should have had no force? The very air of the room in which she dwelt was sweet in his nostrils, and there hovered around her an halo of grace and beauty which greeted all his senses. She invited him to join his lot to hers, in order that she might give to him all that was needed to make his life rich and glorious. How would the Ratlers and the Bonteens envy him when they heard of the prize which had become his! The Cantrips and the Greshams would feel that he was a friend doubly valuable, if he could be won back; and Mr. Monk would greet him as a fitting ally, — an ally strong with the strength which he had before wanted. With whom would he not be equal? Whom need he fear? Who would not praise him? The story of his poor Mary would be known only in a small village, out beyond the Channel. The temptation certainly was very strong.

But he had not a moment in which to doubt. She was standing there with her face turned from him, but with her hand still stretched towards him. Of course he took it. What man so placed could do other than take a woman's hand?

'My friend,' he said.

'I will be called friend by you no more,' she said. 'You must call me Marie, your own Marie, or you must never call me by any name again. Which shall it be, sir?' He paused a moment, holding her hand, and she let it lie there for an instant while she listened. But still she did not look at him. 'Speak to me! Tell me! Which shall it be?' Still he paused. 'Speak to me. Tell me!' she said again.

'It cannot be as you have hinted to me,' he said at last. His words did not come louder than a low whisper; but they were plainly heard, and instantly the hand was withdrawn.

'Cannot be!' she exclaimed. 'Then I have betrayed myself.'

'No; — Madame Goesler.'

'Sir; I say yes! If you will allow me I will leave you. You will, I know, excuse me if I am abrupt to you.' Then she strode out of the room, and was no more seen of the eyes of Phineas Finn.

He never afterwards knew how he escaped out of that room and found his way into Park Lane. In after days he had some memory that he remained there, he knew not how long, standing on the very spot on which she had left him; and that at last there grew upon him almost a fear of moving, a dread lest he should be heard, an inordinate desire to escape without the sound of a footfall, without the clicking of a lock. Everything in that house had been offered to him. He had refused it all, and then felt that of all human beings under the sun none had so little right to be standing there as he. His very presence in that drawing-room was an insult to the woman whom he had driven from it.

But at length he was in the street, and had found his way across Piccadilly into the Green Park. Then, as soon as he could find a spot apart from the Sunday world, he threw himself upon the turf, and tried to fix his thoughts upon the thing that he had done. His first feeling, I think, was one of pure and unmixed disappointment; — of disappointment so bitter, that even the vision of his own Mary did not tend to comfort him. How great might have been his success, and how terrible was his failure! Had he taken the woman's hand and her money, had he clenched his grasp on the great prize offered to him, his misery would have been ten times worse the first moment that he would have been away from her. Then, indeed, — it being so that he was a man with a heart within his breast, — there would have been no comfort for him, in his outlooks on any side. But even now, when he had done right, — knowing well that he had done right, — he found that comfort did not come readily within his reach.

One wonders what Trollope's readers made of such a declaration of love from a woman. One wonders too how many of them realized that the scene is one of the 'greats' of fiction.

So Phineas, shorn of office and the love and encouragement of Madame Max, returns to Ireland to try to find solace in the arms of his Irish Mary. With true Finn luck, thanks to friends who still have his welfare at heart, he is offered a £1,000 a year job as Irish Inspector of Poor Houses in Dublin. And there we leave him — at least temporarily.

Although the novel received the approval of the generality of critics, it did not become one of his great successes. In Trollope's own words:

It was not a brilliant success, — because men and women not conversant with political matters could not care much for a hero who spent so much time either in the House of Commons or in a public office. But the men who would have lived with Phineas Finn read the book, and the women who would have lived with Laura Standish read it also. As this was what I had intended, I was contented.*

---

* *Autobiography*

HE KNEW HE WAS RIGHT

Written between *Phineas Finn* and *The Vicar of Bullhampton* and at the height of his popularity, the novel must have come as a jolt to Trollope's devotees. It still does. Here is something far removed from anything he had tried before. The main theme is no longer domestic comedy but domestic tragedy. Of course we remember *The Small House at Allington* and its unforgettable Lily Dale and her tragedy. But even that is different. This story is not just a tragedy: it is a psychological study of a monomania, years ahead of its time. And it can all be summed up in Hugh Stanbury's thoughts as he knocks on the self-outcast Trevelyan's door at Casalunga: 'Oh God, to what misery had a little folly brought two human beings who had had every blessing that the world could give within their reach!'

Told in brief outline, the tragedy of the Trevelyans is brought about by the clash of wills between husband and wife — he the typically dominant Victorian male driven first to jealousy and bewildered anger, and through fury and frustration to madness and death. Artistically the novel satisfies the Aristotlean concept that such a series of events should begin in happiness and harmony, with the opening chapter presenting us with a brief and satisfying account of the background of both Louis Trevelyan and the woman he chose as his wife — Emily Rowley, eldest daughter of Sir Marmaduke Rowley, governor of the Mandarin Island. Trevelyan is rich, handsome and intelligent, and Emily is tall, dark and attractive, so that there would seem to be no reason why their marriage should not be a happy one. But Trollope ominously entitles the chapter 'Showing How Wrath Began', and obliquely throws out a hint of trouble to come in the course of conversation between Sir Marmaduke and his wife. After giving a list of Trevelyan's many virtues Trollope adds the rider: 'Only, as Lady Rowley was the first to find out, he liked to have his own way. "But his way is such a good way," said Sir Marmaduke . . . . "But Emily likes her way too," said Lady Rowley.' She was only too observantly right, and the whole of the future catastrophe hinges on this clash of wills. Emily is no Rachel Ray, Dorothy Stanbury or any other typical Victorian mouse of a 'heroine' worshipping at her husband's feet; and it only required Colonel Osborne to come along for the fireworks to begin. Now Trollope is skilfully foreseeing in his delineation of Osborne. Had he been a young gallant with a roving eye for Emily, Trevelyan would have had every justification for his reaction. But far from being that, Colonel Osborne is almost the same age as Emily's father and an old family friend. He has every excuse for playing the 'uncle' and keeping an eye on a girl he had known from childhood. Why, then, should Trevelyan detest him and become jealous of him? The answer lies in Osborne's character. Although aged fifty, he is a bachelor and one of those men who pride themselves on keeping their looks and figures and liveliness, and is still a womanizer at heart. He has no intention of even trying to seduce the young wife, but he enjoys her company and likes to feast his eyes on this 'very handsome young woman, tall, with a bust rather full for her age.' Moreover, unknown to Emily, his reputation in these matters was far from good, and he had forced one young husband to take his wife abroad rather than let her have the man in his house. Colonel Osborne meant no harm, but he did rather enjoy a husband's jealousy: it flattered his ego. He was no melodramatic villain: simply what we would call today a respectable Victorian version of a dirty old man. Trevelyan was right to be suspicious of him and to hate him; but he went the wrong way about it with Emily. Using the common ploy of the Victorian husband he forbade her to invite him to their home. *He knew he was right*, and was determined to be 'master in his own house.' But he miscalculated Emily's reaction. Knowing herself to be completely innocent of any reflection on her own or her husband's honour, and ignorant of the man's reputation, she feels herself insulted, and refuses to obey. From this fact the path runs its inevitable course — arguments, bitter words, refusal to speak or eat together. Although he still loves her and their young son, Louey, he leaves the house and lives almost entirely at his club in gloomy, lonely misery, wearying his friends by calling on them and relating his grievances and demanding their sympathy. His loneliness drives him more and more into himself. She will not recant, and he feels himself a martyr. Driven desperate by his desire to vindicate himself he sinks to the degradation of employing Bozzle, a private detective, to shadow her and report back to him. From him he learns that Osborne has been to visit her while she is living with the Stanburys at Nuncombe Putney. No guilt is proved, nor is there any, but the knowledge drives him wild. He travels, goes abroad, visits Paris, Venice — anywhere, to try to forget. But he can't. His loneliness and misery only eat deeper and deeper into his heart until it becomes a seething bitterness charged with hate and a desire for revenge. The Victorian father's rights over his children were inviolable. He writes his wife letters threatening to have the boy taken from her custody if she does not acknowledge her wrong and ask his forgiveness. Terrified, she attempts to take the child to a place where he will be safe, but through the wiles of Bozzle little Louey is snatched from her from under her eyes, leaving her screaming hysterically.

For a time the Rowley family lose sight of them, but at last they learn that the two are living in poor health and solitude at Casalunga, a village in Italy. They follow. English friends take it on themselves to beard Trevelyan in his primitive house. They find the once fine, strong, handsome man ill, a shadow of himself, on the brink of insanity, and the boy listless and lonely. After arduous negotiating they manage to persuade him by degrees firstly to allow her to come and see the boy; secondly, after she has seen him (and even he can see that she needs him and he her above his own claim) to allow him to go back with her; and finally to agree to return to England *en famille* — this last because he knows he is too ill mentally and physically to look after himself. But still he will not forgive her or regard her as his wife until she has confessed her 'sin' and asked for forgiveness. And still she will not recant. The little of life left him they spend in a cottage at Twickenham where she nurses him through his last days. Still, when he feels strong enough to speak, he taxes her with infidelity, and all the old arguments are gone through. Though they still love, neither will recant. The final scene is harrowing.

'Emily,' he said, in the lowest whisper.
'Darling!' she answered, turning round and touching him with her hand.
'My feet are cold. There are no clothes on them.'
She took a thick shawl and spread it double across the bottom of the bed, and put her hand upon his arm. Though it was clammy with perspiration, it was chill, and she brought the warm clothes up close round his shoulders. 'I can't sleep,' he said. 'If I could sleep, I shouldn't mind.' Then he was silent again, and her thoughts went harping on, still on the same subject. She told

herself that if ever that act of justice were to be done for her, it must be done that night. After a while she turned round over him ever so gently, and saw that his large eyes were open and fixed upon the wall.

She was kneeling now on the chair close by the bed-head, and her hand was on the rail of the bedstead supporting her. 'Louis,' she said, ever so softly.

'Well.'

'Can you say one word for your wife, dear, dear, dearest husband?'

'What word?'

'I have not been a harlot to you; — have I?'

'What name is that?'

'But what a thing, Louis! Kiss my hand, Louis, if you believe me.' And very gently she laid the tips of her fingers on his lips. For a moment or two she waited, and the kiss did not come. Would he spare her in this the last moment left to him either for justice or for mercy? For a moment or two the bitterness of her despair was almost unendurable. She had time to think that were she once to withdraw her hand, she would be condemned for ever; — and that it must be withdrawn. But at length the lips moved, and with struggling ear she could hear the sound of the tongue within, and the verdict of the dying man had been given in her favour. He never spoke a word more either to annul it or to enforce it.

Such a prolonged and tragic study in a monomania, original and startling for its time as it was, would on its own be far too perdurable and stagnant in action to carry the interest over three volumes. More fortunate than with *Can You Forgive Her?* (q.v.) Trollope was inspired to weave into the main theme two other stories and groups of characters which are not only good in their own right, but skilfully blended into it, so that the reader passes from one to the other with no sense of irritation but rather of amusement, relief and delight. The second 'theme' centres round Jemima Stanbury, a well-to-do spinster who lives with her maid, Martha, in the Close in Exeter. She is one of Trollope's outstanding female characters. 'Aunt Stanbury', who in her antediluvian younger days had had a love affair that came to nothing, is, when we meet her, a crotchety, cantankerous, opinionated, ultra-conservative, religious, shrewish and astute old spinster; but while it would be straying from the truth to go so far as to say that under her crusty manners and exterior she had a heart of gold (unlike Dickens, Trollope did not believe in hearts of gold), she had purely feminine and natural longings for affection, for someone to share in her life and loneliness. True to type again, she thinks she can achieve her end by buying it or at least by putting people under some kind of obligation to her by means of her wealth. The first object of her favour is her nephew Hugh Stanbury, who (let the reader note the connection) had been Louis Trevelyan's friend when they were at Oxford together. Hugh's own family (his mother was a poor widow with two daughters) could not have done anything for him, and it was due entirely to Aunt Stanbury that he was able to go to Oxford and leave with the intention of becoming a barrister. It came as a dreadful shock to her, therefore, to learn that after four years of the silk, finding himself as impecunious as when he began, he had thrown his gown to the nettles to become first contributor to and then a correspondent for, the *Daily Record* — a paper doubly pernicious in the eyes of all respectable conservative people in that (1) it was revoltingly 'progressive', modern and 'liberal' in its views (2) it was cheap, costing only the disgustingly low price of one penny. A 'penny dreadful' indeed! Now his aunt:

Was a thorough Tory of the old school. Had Hugh taken to writing for a newspaper that had cost sixpence, or even three pence, for its copies, she might perhaps have forgiven him. At any rate the offence would not have been so flagrant. And had the paper been conservative instead of liberal, she would have had some qualms of conscience before she gave him up. But to live by writing for a newspaper! and for a penny newspaper!! and for a penny radical newspaper!!! It was more than she could endure. Of what nature were the articles which he contributed it was impossible that she should have any idea, for no consideration would have induced her to look at a penny newspaper, or to admit it within her doors. She herself took in the John Bull and the Herald, and daily groaned deeply at the way in which those once great organs of true British public feeling were becoming demoralised and perverted. Had any reduction been made in the price of either of them, she would at once have stopped her subscription. In the matter of politics she had long since come to think that every thing good was over. She hated the name of Reform so much that she could not bring herself to believe in Mr. Disraeli and his bill. For many years she had believed in Lord Derby. She would fain believe in him still if she could. It was the great desire of her heart to have some one in whom she believed.

She at once, therefore, wrote her errant nephew a tough typical brief letter to the effect that she wished it to be clearly understood that she would have no truck with 'radical scribblers and incendiaries', and that he must choose between giving up his present job and returning to legal respectability, or forfeiting her £100 allowance. Since Hugh had to live, and could do so only through his connection with the objectionable paper, he had no choice, and much against his will was forced to tell his aunt as much. 'He might as well have spared himself the trouble,' Trollope comments. 'She simply wrote across his own letter in red ink:- "The bread of unworthiness should never be earned or eaten," then sent the letter back under a blank envelope to her nephew.'

Bitterly disappointed in her nephew, and still yearning secretly for a young person's company and affection, after a week's anxious deliberation with both herself and her old servant, Martha, she came to a decision. This decision is clarified for the reader by a letter to her sister-in-law, a letter which, though short, is masterly in its characterization.

The Close, Exeter, 22nd April,
186—

My Dear Sister Stanbury,
    Your son, Hugh, has taken to courses of which I do not approve, and therefore I have put an end to my connection with him. I shall be happy to entertain your daughter Dorothy in my house if you and she approve of such a plan. Should you agree to this, she will be welcome to receive you or her sister, — *not her brother,* — in my house any Wednesday morning between half-past nine and half-past twelve. I will endeavour to make my house pleasant to her and useful, and will make her an allowance of £25 per annum for her clothes as long as she may remain with me. I shall expect her to be regular at meals, to be constant in going to church, and not to read modern novels.
    I intend the arrangement to be permanent, but of course I must retain the power of closing it if, and when, I shall see fit. Its permanence must be contingent on my life. I have no power of providing for any one *after my death.*

Yours truly,
JEMIMA STANBURY.

I hope the young lady does not have any false hair about her.

For the benefit of the reader it should be explained that the postscript was a reference to her particular detestation of the latest fashionable hair style of young women known as the 'chignon', described by her as "those band boxes which the sluts wear behind their noddles;"* for Miss Stanbury allowed herself the use of much strong language. Whether she chose Dorothy, the young sister, rather than Priscilla because she was aware of their very different natures, Trollope does not say, but she was wise in her choice. Dorothy is what is seemingly the typical Victorian young female and daughter — in fact another Fanny Price, humble, submissive, stickily sweet and, like her prototype, unfailingly conscious of her obligation to her aunt; whereas Priscilla is a prickly, speak-your-mind, tactless, independent young woman who stood for no reprimands from anyone, be they maiden aunts or otherwise. The perverse strength of her nature emerges, for example, in her conversation with Emily Trevelyan who is staying with the Dartmoor Stanburys. In answer to Emily's, "Why should not you get married, as well as Dorothy?" she says: "I am not fit to marry. I am often cross, and I like my own way, and I have a distaste for men. I never in my life saw a man whom I wished even to make my intimate friend. I should think any man an idiot who began to make soft speeches to me, and I should tell him so." One is almost driven to regretting that Trollope did not give her the more important role of the two sisters: but then on reflection one has to tell oneself that Priscilla would not have endured Aunt Stanley for a week, let alone a long stay, whereas 'Dolly', as her brother Hugh righly says, 'hardly knows that she has a self belonging to herself' . . . . and 'is a dear, loving, sweet-tempered creature who is only too ready to yield in all things.' She needed to be in order to live with her Aunt Stanbury!

But even a worm will turn; and when her aunt encourages the Reverend Gibson to visit her house and almost commands her niece to accept his advances, not liking him in the least she does have the spirit to tell her aunt (though she weeps most of the time while rebelling) that nothing will make her accept that gentleman's 'overtures', which she endures 'with abject submission'. However, the storm blows over, chiefly because that reverend gentleman is in the process of making a complete fool of himself. And it is here more than anywhere that Trollope gives us a rare measure of comedy which helps to dilute the somewhat oppressive acidity of the Trevelyan-Emily episodes, and forms a smaller third 'theme'.

The Revd Gibson had been a friend of Mrs French and her two daughters, Arabella and Camilla, for years, and in fact had seen the two sisters grow up together. But now they are nubile — so nubile that both have set their caps at him and are determined to have him. The weak-minded Mr Gibson, coming at last to realize the fact, is flattered but made to feel awkward since neither of the girls is particularly attractive, and he is not really in love with either. In the midst of his quandary Dorothy Stanbury appears on his horizon, with the effect already told. Rejected by her, he returns, rebuffed and disgruntled, to the Frenches' fold where, though his heinous sin has been discovered, he is forgiven and petted, since both girls are determined to 'make him their prey.' Arabella, as the elder, is the first to set about him. In a delectable scene (chapter 47: 'About Fishing, and Navigation, and Head-dresses') she corners him, making it so obvious to him that he is expected to propose, that he is driven to desperate measures. These measures reveal the eye of the born novelist. Trollope knew that when not blinded by

---

* Which helps to explain what I had always hitherto found puzzling in the well-known Irish song, namely, 'Nor did she wear a chignon, I'd have you all to know. And I met her in the garden where the praties grow.'

love, a man or a woman, even on the verge of half-reluctant consent, can become only too conscious of some physical defect in his/her opposite number which, though in itself trivial, can act as an irritant and enforce strong second thoughts. Trollope brings out this fact in the long scene between Gibson and Arabella.

Arabella French was painfully alive to the fact that she must do something. She had her fish on the hook; but of what use is a fish on your hook, if you cannot land him? When could she have a better opportunity than this of landing the scaly darling out of the fresh and free waters of his bachelor stream, and sousing him into the pool of domestic life, to be ready there for her own household purposes? 'I had known you so long, Mr. Gibson,' she said, 'and had valued your friendship so — so deeply.' As he looked at her, he could see nothing but the shapeless excrescence to which his eyes had been so painfully called by Miss Stanbury's satire. It is true that he had formerly been very tender with her, but she had not then carried about with her that distorted monster. He did not believe himself to be at all bound by anything which had passed between them in circumstances so very different. But yet he ought to say something. He ought to have said something; but he said nothing. She was patient, however, very patient; and she went on playing him with her hook. 'I am so glad that I did not go out to-night with mamma. It has been such a pleasure to me to have this conversation with you. Camilla, perhaps, would say that I am — unmaidenly.'

'I don't think so.'

'That is all that I care for, Mr. Gibson. If you acquit me, I do not mind who accuses. I should not like to suppose that you thought me unmaidenly. Anything would be better than that; but I can throw all such considerations to the wind when true — true — friendship is concerned. Don't you think that one ought, Mr. Gibson?'

If it had not been for the thing at the back of her head, he would have done it now. Nothing but that gave him courage to abstain. It grew bigger and bigger, more shapeless, monstrous, absurd, and abominable, as he looked at it. Nothing should force upon him the necessity of assisting to carry such an abortion through the world. 'One ought to sacrifice everything to friendship,' said Mr. Gibson, 'except self-respect.'

After much shameful and desperate shuffling and equivocating, he braced himself to take the bull by the horns, or in this case the girl by the chignon.

'If I might say a word, — ' he began.

'You may say anything,' she exclaimed.

'If I were you I don't think — '

'You don't think what, Mr. Gibson?'

He found it to be a matter very difficult to approach. 'Do you know, I don't think the fashion that has come up about wearing your hair quite suits you, — not so well as the way you used to do it.' She became on a sudden very red in the face, and he thought that she was angry. Vexed she was, but still, accompanying her vexation, there was a remembrance that she was achieving victory even by her own humiliation. She loved her chignon; but she was ready to abandon even that for him. Nevertheless she could not speak for a moment or two, and he was forced to continue his criticism. 'I have no doubt those things are very becoming and all that, and I dare say they are comfortable.'

'Oh, very,' she said.

'But there was a simplicity that I liked about the other.'

Could it be then that for the last five years he had stood aloof from her because she had arrayed herself in fashionable attire? She was still very red in the face, still suffering from wounded vanity, still conscious of that soreness which affects us all when we are made to understand that we are considered to have failed there, where we have most thought that we excelled. But her woman's art enabled her quickly to conceal the pain. 'I have made a promise,' she said, 'and you will find that I will keep it.'

'What promise?' asked Mr. Gibson.

'I said that I would do as you bade me, and so I will. I would have done it sooner if I had known that you wished it. I would never have worn it at all if I had thought that you disliked it.

'I think that a little of them is very nice,' said Mr. Gibson. Mr. Gibson was certainly an awkward man. But there are men so awkward that it seems to be their especial province to say always the very worst thing at the very worst moment.

She became redder than ever as she was thus told of the hugeness of her favourite ornament. She was almost angry now. But she restrained herself, thinking perhaps of how she might teach him taste in days to come as he was teaching her now. 'I will change it to-morrow,' she said with a smile. 'You come and see to-morrow.'

Upon this he got up and took his hat and made his escape, assuring her that he would come and see her on the morrow. She let him go now without any attempt at further tenderness.

Poor Arabella, red in face and in tears, realizes that the fish she imagined she had hooked had escaped. Worse, the fish now begins to tell himself that after all the younger sister is fresher, more spirited and more attractive, and after confessing as much to her mother, becomes engaged to Camilla, leaving Arabella prostrate and her sister triumphant. But even that situation does not last. The weak-minded reprobate, finding himself bound to a woman with a spirit and a temper that frightens him, is driven to postponing the wedding day from week to week and in the end writing her a cowardly letter confessing he has made a dreadful error, is not in love with her and cannot marry her. How, after threatening him with a carving knife, she drives him back to the welcoming arms of Arabella, is there for all to read, and well worth the reading.

In the midst of the reverend gentleman's tribulations a storm blows up between Dorothy and her aunt which threatens to break up their partnership. Sore enough when she finds herself unable to force her niece to become attached to Mr Gibson, she is driven to fury when she finds that Brooke Burgess, nephew of old Barty Burgess with whom she is at daggers drawn over a family will, after a visit to Aunt Stanbury has won Dorothy's heart and she his. When, trembling in her shoes, she confesses the fact to her aunt, the balloon goes up! Her aunt, who had been in bed seriously ill during Brookes's visit, accuses her niece of 'immodesty' and carrying on behind her back. Dorothy, knowing her innocence, protests through her tears, but her aunt is adamant. "I won't have it!" she declares and repeats. So Dorothy packs her bags and leaves, returning to live with her mother and sister. But beneath her crusty exterior and hard words her aunt has become genuinely fond of her and misses her more than she likes to admit. Of course she could not bring herself to write direct and ask the girl back again: age and dignity forbade such weakness. Instead, after hectoring her faithful long-suffering Martha, she concocts a typically convoluted feminine scheme to bring about the desired result. Martha is to go over to the Stanburys at Nuncome Putney with "a nice fore-quarter of lamb . . . . in a basket . . . . done up clean in a napkin." On no account, Martha is instructed, is she to let it be thought that the gift is for her sister-in-law: it is for Dorothy.

The whole chapter (66, entitled delightfully 'Of A Quarter Of Lamb') is a masterpiece in miniature, a splendid example of Trollope's uncanny and unrivalled genius of sexual transmogrification, the ability to put himself inside the skin of a woman, and an old spinster at that.

Of course, the soft-hearted Dorothy is unable to hold out against her aunt's appeal: with the result that Miss Stanbury, touched by her niece's devotion, after a severe battle with herself allows her better nature to take over and gives her belated blessing to the engagement between her niece and her heir, Brooke Burgess.

To conclude. As though the two themes were not enough, we are given a third minor one which is just as skilfully blended with the other two, and moreover gives Trollope scope for some satirical but not ill-natured observations on Americans. The Hon. Charles Glascock, following the failure of his proposal to Nora Rowley, Emily Trevelyan's sister, goes to Florence where his old father, Lord Peterborough, is dangerously ill. On the journey he falls in with Trevelyan, then travelling about aimlessly, trying to forget his misery, and two American sisters, Olivia and Caroline Spalding, their uncle being the American Minister at Florence and their cousin the American Secretary of the Legation. By the time they reach their destination Glascock has become very friendly with them indeed, and it follows naturally that he is introduced to and becomes acquainted with their uncle and cousin and their circle.

Mr. Spalding was a man who at home had been very hostile to English interests. Many American gentlemen are known for such hostility. They make anti-English speeches about the country, as though they thought that war with England would produce certain triumph to the States, certain increase to American trade, and certain downfall to a tyranny which no Anglo-Saxon nation ought to endure. But such is hardly their real opinion. There, in the States, as also here in England, you shall from day to day hear men propounding, in very loud language, advanced theories of political action, the assertion of which is supposed to be necessary to the end which they have in view. Men whom we know to have been as mild as sucking doves in the political aspiration of their whole lives, suddenly jump up, and with infuriated gestures declare themselves the enemies of everything existing. When they have obtained their little purpose, — or have failed to do so, — they revert naturally into their sucking-dove elements. It is so with Americans as frequently as with ourselves, — and there is no political subject on which it is considered more expedient to express pseudo-enthusiasm than on that of the sins of England. It is understood that we do not resent it. It is presumed that we regard it as the Irishman regarded his wife's cuffs. In the States a large party, which consists chiefly of those who have lately left English rule, and who are keen to prove to themselves how wise they have been in doing so, is pleased by this strong language against England; and, therefore, the strong language is spoken. But the speakers, who are, probably, men knowing something of the world, mean it not at all; they have no more idea of war with England than they have of war with all Europe; and their respect for England and for English opinion is unbounded. In their political tones of speech and modes of action they strive to be as English as possible. Mr. Spalding's aspirations were of this nature. He had uttered speeches against England which would make the hair stand on end on the head of an uninitiated English reader. He had told his countrymen that Englishmen hugged their chains, and would do so until American hammers had knocked those chains from off their wounded wrists and bleeding ankles. He had declared that, if certain American claims were not satisfied, there was nothing left for Americans to do but to cross the ferry with such a sheriff's officer as would be able to make distraint on the great English household. He had declared that the sheriff's officer would have very little trouble. He had spoken of Canada as an out-lying American territory, not yet quite sufficiently redeemed from savage life to be received into the Union as a State. There is a multiplicity of subjects of this kind ready to the hand of the American orator. Mr. Spalding had been quite successful, and was now Minister at Florence; but, perhaps, one of the greatest pleasures coming to him from his prosperity was the enjoyment of the society of well-bred Englishmen in the capital to which he had been sent. When, therefore, his wife and nieces pointed out to him the fact that it was manifestly his duty to call upon Mr. Glascock after what had passed between them on that night under the Campanile, he did not rebel for an instant against the order given to him. His mind never reverted for a moment to that opinion which had gained for him such a round of applause, when expressed on the platform of the Temperance Hall at Nubbly Creek, State of Illinois, to the effect that the English aristocrat, thorough-born and thorough-bred, who inherited acres and title from his father, could never be fitting company for a thoughtful Christian American citizen. He at once had his hat brushed, and took up his best gloves and umbrella, and went off to Mr. Glascock's hotel.

For a considerable time thereafter Mr Glascock is being constantly buttonholed by the minister and made to listen to nasal asseverations as to the perfection of American institutions and their "God's gifts of free intelligence, free air and free soil." But Trollope's most cutting observation is reserved for the creation of 'the Republican Browning' as he styles a certain literary lady of the name of Wallachia Petrie, who happens to be Caroline Spalding's guide, philosopher and friend. Miss Petrie is imbued not only with poetry but with the deepest of convictions that America is the only country fit to live in, and that Britain and the British are decadent and on the verge of extinction. She has no time for the male sex either. Independence and sex equality is her motto. When she begins to suspect that her dear young Caroline is on the verge of falling for an English aristocrat, viz. the Hon. Glascock, the future Lord Peterborough, her feelings can be easily imagined. Caroline is lectured remorselessly.

'Caroline,' said the poetess with severe eloquence, 'can you put your hand upon your heart and say that this inherited title, this tinkling cymbal as I call it, has no attraction for you or yours? Is it the unadorned simple man that you welcome to your bosom, or a thing of stars and garters, a patch of parchment, the minion of a throne, the lordling of twenty descents . . . . the hero of a scutcheon, whose glory is in his quarterings, and whose worldly wealth comes from the sweat of serfs whom the euphemism of an effete country has learned to decorate with the name of tenants?'

In a duologue with Mr Glascock concerning 'clowns and courtiers' she throws at him:

'Ah — h, — but the clown will not spare the courtier, Mr. Glascock. I understand the gibe, and I tell you that the courtier shall be spared no longer; — because he is useless. He shall be cut down together with the withered grasses and thrown into the oven, and there shall be an end of him.' Then she turned round to appeal to an American gentleman who had joined them, and Mr. Glascock made his escape. 'I hold it to be the holiest duty which I owe to my country never to spare one of them when I meet him.'
'They are all very well in their way,' said the American gentleman.
'Down with them, down with them!' exclaimed the poetess, with a beautiful enthusiasm.
In the meantime Mr. Glascock had made up his mind that he could not dare to ask Caroline Spalding to be his wife. There were certain forms of the American female so dreadful that no wise man would wilfully come in contact with them. Miss Petrie's ferocity was distressing to

him, but her eloquence and enthusiasm were worse even than her ferocity. The personal incivility of which she had been guilty in calling him a withered grass was distasteful to him, as being opposed to his ideas of the customs of society; but what would be his fate if his wife's chosen friend should be for ever dinning her denunciation of withered grasses into his ear?

It would be too much indeed, if in this American household he were to find the old vices of an aristocracy superadded to young republican sins!

Nevertheless, he soon discovers that Caroline, although of the same nationality as Miss Petrie, is a very different kettle of fish, and after hesitations and second thoughts on both sides they become engaged: on which the disappointment, despair and eloquent reproaches and diatribes of Wallachia Petrie swell to bursting point. On one specific occasion Lady Rowley, Nora Rowley's mother, is made the bewildered butt of Miss Petrie's eloquence, which she considers to be 'American bunkum.' But the beauty and humour of the incident lies in this: Lady Rowley, still suffering from her daughter's refusal of Mr Glascock's hand and her insistence on being in love with such a commoner as Hugh Stanbury, and in addition bewildered by all these Americans and their relationships, is under the impression that it is to the detested Miss Petrie that Mr Glascock has pledged his name and title and wealth. This is more than she can bear, and she later observes to her husband:

"You have no conception of the sort of woman that man is going to marry . . . . A horrid American female, as old as I am, who talks through her nose, and preaches sermons about the rights of women. It is incredible! And Nora might have had him just for lifting up her hand." But the final touch comes in the last paragraph of the chapter.

Lady Rowley took her candle and went to bed, professing to herself that she could not understand it. But what did it signify? It was, at any rate, certain now that the man had put himself out of Nora's reach, and if he chose to marry a republican virago with a red nose it could now make no difference to Nora. Lady Rowley almost felt a touch of satisfaction in reflecting on the future misery of his married life.

But Trollope does not fall into the mistake of making Wallachia Petrie no more than a Dickensian caricature, proved by one important final passage which takes the form of a spirited defence of her friend by Caroline. In reply to her fiancé's half humorous, "Doesn't she bully you horribly?" she answers: "Of course she bullies me . . . and I cannot expect you to understand as yet how it is that I love her . . . . If I were in distress tomorrow, she would give everything she has in the world to put me right . . . And she would give everything she has in the world to set the world right . . . . Her philanthropy is all real. Of course she is a bore to you."

"I am very patient."

"I hope I shall find you so — always. And of course she is ridiculous in your eyes. I have learned to see it, and to regret it; but I shall never cease to love her."

Trollope is never altogether one-sided. He realizes there are always two sides to every coin. Wallachia Petrie, in fact, is the prototype of Henry James' Henrietta Stackpole — the brusque, acrimonious, captious, independent spinster journalist, studying the British aristocracy and way of life with an American bias. Indeed the similarity is so striking that it is difficult to believe that James was not influenced by this novel of

Trollope's, knowing as we do that he expressed admiration of it.* And strangely, *Portrait of a Lady* was written exactly a decade after Trollope's and in Florence, the city in which Wallachia Petrie lives, moves and has her being.

He Knew He Was Right, with its huge canvas crowded with memorable scenes and characters, tragedy, humour and wide-ranging observation, can rightly be regarded, as it is by many, as one of its author's most masterly creations. Yet in his *Autobiography* he could write of it: 'I do not know that in any literary effort I fell more completely short of my own intention . . . . I look upon the story as being nearly altogether bad' — perhaps the most crying example of his utter lack of self-estimation. Not only did he not know how good it was, he did not know either that after having been recognized by the foremost critics as 'the unchallenged leader of contemporary novelists, the despot of the lending libraries,' from now on his popularity with his public and his price with his publishers were to be one slow decline, and that after *The Eustace Diamonds* his novels, with one or perhaps two exceptions, were to show a falling off of quality.

THE VICAR OF BULLHAMPTON

Michael Sadleir rates the novel as being among Trollope's best; and in his essay on Trollope in *The House of Fiction* Henry James singles it out for special praise. With respect, and with due deference to the famous Latin tag on men and opinions, I cannot agree with them. It has its good points and moments, and the overall merit of comparative brevity; and if we skip quickly over what is to us with our present ethics and *mores*, the dreadful Preface with its naïve 'for want of a truer word that shall not in its truth be offensive' as a 'castaway', we must admit that the first chapter is one of the most succinct and promising of all his books. The Wiltshire village of Bullhampton, with its vicarage, church, mill, river, rivalry between Primitive Methodists and the respectable Church of England, Squire Gilmore, the vicar, Mary Lowther — most of the chief protagonists, in fact, are set before us vividly and tersely, making us anticipate a first-class story. But this standard is not maintained; the novel loses itself in a mass of trivia and sentimentality. Indeed one can in truth say of it what the young Henry James said mistakenly of that infinitely greater novel, *The Belton Estate*, namely, that it is 'a work prepared for minds unable to think . . . organically stupid . . . utterly incompetent to the primary function of a book of whatever nature — namely, to suggest thought.'

The main weakness is that Trollope, in his middle-class Victorian innocence, had no notion of the nature or language of a girl who has been seduced, thrown out by her father and become what he euphemistically terms a 'castaway'; (and we are carefully left in ignorance of the circumstances of her seduction or who her seducer was). He makes her

---

*His words on it in *The House of Fiction* aptly sums it up. He writes: 'The long, slow progress of the conjugal wreck of Louis Trevelyan and his wife . . . . arrives at last at an impressive completeness of misery. . . . Touch is added to touch, one small, stupid, fatal aggravation to another; and as we gaze into the widening breach we wonder at the vulgar materials of which tragedy sometimes composes itself.'

story read as though she were a naughty girl who has played truant from Sunday-school or church. When the vicar visits her and asks her, "Are you living in sin now, Carry?" Trollope, with incredible naïveté goes on: 'She sat silent, not that she wouldn't answer him, but that she did not comprehend the meaning of his question.' And when, later, desperate and starving, Carry creeps back one summer evening to her old home at the mill and is let secretly in at the window by her mother and sister unknown to her father, and she spends the night in her sister's bed, we have to stomach: "Carry," she whispered when her sister was undressed, "will you kneel here and say your prayers as you used to?" Carry, without a word, did as she was bidden, and hid her face upon her hands in her sister's lap.'

Other minor weaknesses abound. The whole episode of the murder of Trumbull by Sam Brattle's shady companions and the chapters devoted to their eventual capture and trial, as too the whole narrative of the building of the typically ugly, red brick Primitive Methodist chapel right against the beautiful old church and the feud so occasioned, are trivia.

All this is a pity, because the novel contains three excellently drawn characters worthy of a better setting. These are the vicar himself, old Jacob Brattle, the miller, and, though to a less degree, the heroine, Mary Lowther. Michael Sadleir is just in describing the Revd Frank Fenwick 'as Trollope's ideal of what a parson should be, and with that ideal the world will sympathise.' Of all the clerics Trollope has given us he is the most sympathetic and human. Generous, humane, genial, forgiving, impetuous to the point of imprudence, a practising Christian in thought, word and deed, he wins our hearts. It is he who tries to soften old Brattle's heart towards his cast-off daughter; who defends Sam Brattle against the insinuations of the Marquis of Trowbridge that Sam is involved in the murder, and snubs him so roundly that he incurs his wrath and the petty revenge of the chapel; who alone in all Bullhampton stands up for Carry Brattle and pleads for her forgiveness; who pays for her lodgings and stands bail for her brother — all of which makes him suspect in the eyes of the local Pharisees.

Old Brattle is a well-observed portrait of a genuine, hard-headed, uncommunicative, stern, unshakeable countryman. He refuses to show it, but under his hard exterior his heart is broken by the 'fall' of his favourite adored daughter and the shady comings and goings of his younger son Sam to whom he looks for the continued existence of the mill which is his livelihood. A professed agnostic and not caring who knows it, his honesty is acknowledged by Trollope when he remarks that Brattle had never attended church when things were prospering with him, and did not now weaken in his unbelief when his life was hit by tragedy. His outburst to the vicar after he has been persuaded to allow Carry to live with them again, though he can hardly bring himself to speak to her (chapter 63 — 'The Miller Tells His Troubles') is, all the more on account of his normal taciturnity, most moving, and eloquent in that natural manner in which country folk, when driven to it, can be eloquent.

Mary Lowther, while not of the calibre of these characters or other heroines such as Lily Dale, Mary Thorne or Lucy Robarts, at least has a mind of her own, and comes as a relief from those young women who can never accept a man at his first asking either because they don't know their own minds or through Victorian prudery. Loved by both the wealthy steadfast Squire and the more volatile impecunious Captain Walter Marrable, she has no hesitation in preferring the latter, to the dismay and head-shaking of all her friends. Her outspoken direct acceptance of his unexpected and somewhat violently confessed love wins the reader's heart at once. But then follow the typically Trollopian complications, and it is here that he makes, for him, two bad psychological blunders. Marrable finds that even the small remnant he had expected from his spendthrift father's fortune is not to be his, and that therefore to go to India with his regiment is his only means of livelihood, and to take Mary in such circumstances is impossible. Although they still love each other, they mutually agree to break off their engagement. But just before leaving, Marrable learns that because of the ill-health of his uncle and his cousin, neither of whom is expected to live long, he will come in for their estate and modicum of affluence. Because of this he abandons his original intention and arranges to stay in England. He then writes to Mary to inform her of these important events, but gives no hint of a possible renewal of their engagement. Now no lover, least of all a lover such as Captain Marrable, could never have 'said nothing in his letter.' He would be full of it, along with new plans for their future. Trollope, we suspect, is doing what he does so often to the deleteriousness of his story, i.e. prolonging the dilemma of the lovers partly to keep the reader guessing, and partly to spin out his pages.

His second error occurs when, seeing no hope of her re-engagement and marriage to Walter, Mary, badgered by her friends and moved in spite of herself by Gilmore's genuine passion for her, accepts him — but on her own proclaimed terms, viz., that though she is fond of him and admires him, she does not love him; that Walter still has her heart; and that if he wanted her and could marry her she would "go to him at once." After anxious debate with himself he accepts her on those terms, so deeply is he in love with her and so convinced he can bring her to love him in the end. Then of course comes the inevitable crunch. Walter Marrable comes into his inheritance and asks her to be his wife. She has to go back on her plighted word (a terrible thing for a woman in those days) and to confess it to her friends and to — Gilmore. She does the first, but she is afraid of him and his steadfast intensity, and she plays the coward, begging their mutual friend the vicar to do the thing for her. Much against his will, but as ever always willing to help a friend, he does as she asks, anticipating only too well what the other's reaction will be. He is right. In a fury Gilmore tells his friend he will accept no such message from anyone except Mary herself, and demands to see her. Forced to accede, she meets him, and in the course of the interview he loses control of himself and returns wrong for wrong in words which make all future relationship between them impossible. It is curtains for Gilmore. Now Trollope's fault is surely this: Mary's strength of character has been shown. Although she has been foolish and done the wrong thing in allowing herself to become engaged to Gilmore, remembering her frankness with him and the terms under which she accepted him, she has enough right on her side to go quietly to him, remind him of those terms and tell her she has now been given the opportunity to follow the dictates of her heart. Her funk at facing the issue herself and faint-hearted attempt to get the vicar to do her job for her is quite out of character.

Despite its weaknesses and faults the novel is not dull, flat, stale and altogether unprofitable. But like the wandering minstrel in *The Mikado* it is 'a thing of shreds and patches,' and hardly to be given a place among Trollope's best efforts.

A final word. Analysing Mary Lowther's state of mind following the breaking off of her engagement to Walter Marrable and prior to her pact with Gilmore, Trollope goes into an interesting and very relevant discourse on the position and desires of women in his day.

> But poor Mary was, in truth, very wretched. When a girl asks herself that question, — what shall she do with her life? it is so natural that she should answer it by saying that she will get married, and give her life to somebody else. It is a woman's one career — let women rebel against the edict as they may; and though there may be word-rebellion here and there, women learn the truth early in their lives. And women know it later in life when they think of their girls; and men know it, too, when they have to deal with their daughters. Girls, too, now acknowledge aloud that they have learned the lesson; and Saturday Reviewers and others blame them for their lack of modesty in doing so, — most unreasonably, most uselessly, and, as far as the influence of such censors may go, most perniciously. Nature prompts the desire, the world acknowledges its ubiquity, circumstances show that it is reasonable, the whole theory of creation requires it; but it is required that the person most concerned should falsely repudiate it, in order that a mock modesty may be maintained in which no human being can believe! Such is the theory of the censors who deal heavily with our Englishwomen of the present day. Our daughters should be educated to be wives, but, forsooth, they should never wish to be wooed! The very idea is but a remnant of the tawdry sentimentality of an age in which the mawkish insipidity of the women was the reaction from the vice of that preceeding it. That our girls are in quest of husbands, and know well in what way their lines in life should be laid, is a fact which none can dispute. Let men be taught to recognise the same truth as regards themselves, and we shall cease to hear of the necessity of a new career for women.

And following this he makes Mary compare in her mind the different states of her spinster aunt and Mrs Fenwick, the vicar's wife — the former a 'starved, thin, poor life which, good as it was in its nature, reached but to a few persons, and admitted but of few sympathies;' the latter, with her husband and family and obligations, so happy, busy and contented. And here Trollope has hit a huge nail on the head. That he is right about women's instinct for marriage, a home and a family still holds good, let Women's Lib be never so generally and rightly accepted; and at the same time he deals a blow against the sentimentality of his day which begrudged women the right to seek to be wooed, to reciprocate love on equal terms, seeing it as damnable and an artificial code of 'mawkish insipidity,' mock modesty and prudery. At the same time he was unable to foresee, and in all probability would not have accepted even if he could have done so, that women would come to claim complete parity with men and that laws would be passed insisting on this, and that by their new-found education, rights and initiative they could do most of men's work and be wives and mothers at the same time. Let us not ask too much of him. The little, if not enough for present day standards, is something. No survey of his novels can fail to bring home to the thoughtful reader that he was full of compassion for women. Time and time again, in example after example, he reveals this through the tragedies and frustration of their circumscribed lives, by their dependence on men and the callous treatment they receive not only from society but often from their own families. His understanding of their nature and needs is unique. Women should be grateful to Trollope.

SIR HARRY HOTSPUR OF HUMBLETHWAITE

One's first reaction after reading the novel is to wonder what made Trollope write it, opposed as it is in every way to the type of story he had written so far or indeed to any he was ever to write. Was it the itch experienced by every worthwhile writer to try something different, to conquer new worlds, to show his public and posterity that he was not just a depictor of social comedy, a portrayer of comfortable or uncomfortable clerics and their limited world? Whatever the reason, the novel stands alone among his works as a stark unrelieved tragedy. *The Small House at Allington*, as I have already observed, is a tragedy, but the betrayal of Lily Dale was only one episode in that long bustling story which had its moments of comedy, and Lily, though stricken, did not die. *He Knew He Was Right* is tragic in essence but is relieved by the comedy of Aunt Stanbury and her circle. But here the withers are wrung. From the first chapter to the last there is no relief from the impending tragedy which awaits.

The scene is set for the most part in the fells of Cumberland, and Michael Sadleir is right in pointing out that the description of Humblethwaite Hall is 'the most arresting description of a big country house in the whole of Trollope's work.' The long-drawn family tragedy begins in the very first chapter. Sir Harry Hotspur, type of the genuine old English aristocrat, going back to Henry VIII, and whose main ambition is to pass on the title to a son and heir, has already suffered an irreparable blow in the death of his only son. Left with an only daughter, he had stipulated in his new will that she should inherit on the condition that her husband, whoever he might be, should take the name of Hotspur; and his greatest hope was that she should marry worthily and be happy: his greatest fear that she should marry unworthily. Thus when a distant relative, George Hotspur, turns up, Sir Harry is delighted and is prepared to give him every encouragement. But then he comes to hear stories about George that make him change his mind. The young man is a spendthrift and gambler, and had been driven to 'selling out' his commission in the army under dubious circumstances. Sir Harry and his wife, Lady Elizabeth, try to warn Emily against him and urge the cause of the irreproachable Lord Alfred Gresley. Too late, alas! True to life, Emily has already given her heart to the reprobate and will have nothing to do with the virtuous Lord Alfred. The black sheep has greater charm than the white! No warnings on the part of her parents can make her change her mind. Like every woman blinded by love she is prepared to overlook his sins and tells herself they have been exaggerated. During a short visit to Humblethwaite, George proposes to her and she only too willingly accepts him. But being a good, dutiful, religious, Victorian girl she tells him: "I will be true to you, but of course we cannot be married unless Papa consents." And George felt 'he had done a good stroke of business . . . Here was everything that fortune could give! Love her? Of course he loved her . . . And how jolly they would be together when they got hold of their share of that £20,000 a year! And how jolly it would be to owe nothing to anybody! . . . ' But Sir Harry refuses his consent. He has been making further enquiries and discovered shameful facts about George's life which make him feel he simply dare not trust his daughter's future to such a man. There is a violent quarrel between them. But George is crafty as well as unprincipled. Far from denying his vices he confesses to them, taking the line that, having been thrown upon the world among rich people when he was poor, he had been foolish and extravagant; but now, engaged to Emily, he intended to reform. Somewhat mollified, Sir Harry goes so far to promise to think the matter over and, if he finds George's debts honourable, to pay them off.

But a still further delve into his life by Boltby, Sir Harry's lawyer, lays bare yet more unpalatable and unforgivable facts. Not only is George a gambler, a spendthrift, a haunter of racecourses and in debt all round, but he has cheated a man out of money at cards and has a mistress — Mrs Morton, an actress. This is too much for Sir Harry. Much against his will — for he loves her dearly — he passes Boltby's letter of such information over to his daughter, telling her that now he can never give her his assent to her marriage. Now, surely, the unhappy father tells himself, she will see him for what he is and give him up. But Emily is one of those ferociously strong-willed pious victims of love who, even when forced to perceive that the man they have chosen is everything that is bad, only become more obstinate and feel themselves marked out to pluck their particular brand from the burning. There is an interval of weeks during which father and daughter behave like strangers to one another, and the family are at sixes and sevens. At last, unable to bear this estrangement, Sir Harry begins to vacillate. There is a moving scene with his daughter in which she begs him to give George another chance. Sir Harry relents, and George is invited to Humblethwaite. It is while he is there that two important moves in the complex game are made. The first is instigated by Mr Boltby who, having no daughter to plead with him and knowing George's true character, is determined to have him exposed for what he is. He proposes to Sir Harry that he makes an offer to George to pay all his debts and make him an annuity on condition that he submits a written promise to give up Emily for good. But George, seeing the trap, does not fall into it, to the grudging satisfaction of Sir Harry. The second move comes from Emily herself, and proves a bad blunder. In the chapter 'Emily Hotspur's Sermon' Trollope brilliantly exposes her dilemma and her character.

> To be didactic and at the same time demonstrative of affection is difficult, even with mothers towards their children, though with them the assumption of authority creates no sense of injury. Emily specially desired to point out to the erring one the paths of virtue, and yet to do so without being oppressive.
>
> 'It is so nice to have you here, George,' she said.
>
> 'Yes, indeed; isn't it?' He was walking beside her, and as yet they were within view of the house.
>
> 'Papa has been so good; isn't he good?'
>
> 'Indeed he is. The best man I know out,' said George, thinking that his gratitude would have been stronger had the Baronet given him the money and allowed him to go up to London to settle his own debts.
>
> 'And Mamma has been so kind! Mamma is very fond of you. I am sure she would do anything for you.'
>
> 'And you?' said George, looking into her face.
>
> 'I! — As for me, George, it is a matter of course now. You do not want to be told again what is and ever must be my first interest in the world.'
>
> 'I do not care how often you tell me.'
>
> 'But you know it; don't you?'
>
> 'I know what you said at the waterfall, Emily.'

'What I said then I said for always. You may be sure of that. I told Mamma so, and Papa. If they had not wanted me to love you, they should not have asked you to come here. I do love you, and I hope that some day I may be your wife.'

She was not leaning on his arm, but as she spoke she stopped, and looked steadfastly into his face. He put out his hand as though to take hers; but she shook her head, refusing it. 'No, George; come on. I want to talk to you a great deal. I want to say ever so much, — now, to-day. I hope that some day I may be your wife. If I am not, I shall never be any man's wife.'

'What does some day mean, Emily?'

'Ever so long; — years, perhaps.'

'But why? A fellow has to be consulted, you know, as well as yourself. What is the use of waiting? I know Sir Harry thinks I have been very fond of pleasure. How can I better show him how willing I am to give it up than by marrying and settling down at once? I don't see what's to be got by waiting.'

Of course she must tell him the truth. She had no idea of keeping back the truth. She loved him with all her heart, and was resolved to marry him; but the dross must first be purged from the gold. 'Of course you know, George, that Papa has made objections.'

'I know he did, but that is over now. I am to go and live at Scarrowby at once, and have the shooting. He can't want me to remain there all by myself.'

'But he does; and so do I.'

'Why?'

In order that he might be made clean by the fire of solitude and the hammer of hard work. She could not quite say this to him. 'You know, George, your life has been one of pleasure.'

'I was in the army, — for some years.'

'But you left it, and you took to going to races, and they say that you gambled and are in debt, and you have been reckless. Is not that true, George?'

'It is true.'

'And should you wonder that Papa should be afraid to trust his only child and all his property to one who, — who knows that he has been reckless? But if you can show, for a year or two, that you can give up all that — '

'Wouldn't it be all given up if we were married?'

'Indeed, I hope so. I should break my heart otherwise. But can you wonder that Papa should wish for some delay and some proof?'

'Two years!'

'Is that much? If I find you doing what he wishes, these two years will be so happy to me! We shall come and see you, and you will come here. I have never liked Scarrowby, because it is not pretty, as this place is; but, oh, how I shall like to go there now! And when you are here, Papa will get to be so fond of you. You will be like a real son to him. Only you must be steady.'

'Steady! by Jove, yes. A fellow will have to be steady at Scarrowby.' The perfume of the cleanliness of the life proposed to him was not sweet to his nostrils.

She did not like this, but she knew that she could not have everything at once. 'You must know,' she said, 'that there is a bargain between me and Papa. I told him that I should tell you everything.'

'Yes; I ought to be told everything.'

'It is he that shall fix the day. He is to do so much, that he has a right to that. I shall never press him, and you must not.'

'Oh, but I shall.'

'It will be of no use; and, George, I won't let you. I shall scold you if you do. When he thinks that you have learned how to manage the property, and that your mind is set upon that kind of work, and that there are no more races, — mind, and no betting, then, — then he will consent. And I will tell you something more if you would like to hear it.'

'Something pleasant, is it?'

'When he does, and tells me that he is not afraid to give me to you, I shall be the happiest girl in all England. Is that pleasant? — No, George, no; I will not have it.'

'Not give me one kiss?'

'I gave you one when you came, to show you that in truth I loved you. I will give you another when Papa says that everything is right.'

'Not till then?'

'No, George, not till then. But I shall love you just the same. I cannot love you better than I do.'

He had nothing for it but to submit, and was obliged to be content during the remainder of their long walk with talking of his future life at Scarrowby. It was clearly her idea that he should be head-farmer, head-steward, head-accountant, and general workman for the whole place. When he talked about the game, she brought him back to the plough; — so at least he declared to himself. And he could elicit no sympathy from her when he reminded her that the nearest meet of hounds was twenty miles and more from Scarrowby. 'You can think of other things for a while,' she said. He was obliged to say that he would, but it did seem to him that Scarrowby was a sort of penal servitude to which he was about to be sent with his own concurrence. The scent of the cleanliness was odious to him.

George has enjoyed the fleshpots too long and too well for such a settling down to appeal to him; and in any case, isn't his mistress there for the asking? By her overdone lecturing, oppressive righteousness and above all her quixotic, foolish, unreasonable, egregious refusal to give him the kiss he asks for — in other words to use the most powerful woman's weapon, her sex appeal, to rouse his desire — she loses him and a great deal of the reader's sympathy too, tell himself as he may that her protected Victorian upbringing and ignorance of men made it impossible for her to accept the fact that such men are irreclaimable.

Once back in town his debts mount and his debtors become more and more threatening, with imprisonment and disgrace looming. His mistress, with a woman's common sense and, in her situation, a devilish knowledge of what is to be gained, persuades him that his only hope of escape and of living in peace of mind is to accept the Hotspur/Holtby terms, and at her dictation he writes the shameful letter renouncing all claim to Emily and the title. This tolled the final bell for Emily who, broken-hearted, simply fades away, and losing all will to live, dies.

The novel is one of unswerving, unmitigated tragedy, terse and even brutal in its delineation of opposing forces of weakness and strength, good and evil, and like several more of his novels, is a reminder to the critics that Trollope is something more than just an easy-going transcriber of cosy domesticity. If it contains no particularly subtle or memorable piece of characterization (and much more, I feel, could have been made of George Hotspur who, as a study in shoddy charm, is no more than a pale reflection of Anne Brontë's Arthur Huntingdon), it is flawless in its construction, powerful in its intensity, and should be on every Trollopian's bookshelf.

RALPH THE HEIR

Quite apart from its merits and demerits this is arguably the adroitest in construction of all the novels. In writing of *The Claverings* I compared Trollope with a chess master. The metaphor, appropriate enough for that novel, is even more apropos here. In his study of Trollope, Sadleir gives us advance lay-outs of two of the novels, viz. *Sir Harry Hotspur* and *The Way We Live Now*. Whether these are two of many or the only examples known, he does not say; but whether available or not, I cannot believe that Trollope could have written *Ralph the Heir* without the aid of a preliminary outline. The threads are too complicated, the timing of events and change of prospects too intricate to have been done altogether impromptu.

Consider the story. The book opens by introducing one of the principal characters, Sir Thomas Underwood, and it must be said at once that he is one of the characters to be placed on the credit side of any criticism of the novel in that such a character is one of the most difficult to draw. A man who stamps about, flies into rages, domineers over his family and so on, is comparatively easy. But Sir Thomas is the reverse of that. He is a man of few words, shy of showing his emotions yet wishing he could, a solitary rather than a social being and 'yet possessed of warm affections, was by no means misanthropic . . . . and would, in truth, have given much to be able to be free and jocund as are other men.' In addition he has to carry about with him two heart-searing set-backs: the death of his wife and the humiliating loss of a political career — set-backs which have sent him curling up on himself like a suspicious hedgehog to live almost like a recluse in his lawyer's office in Southampton Buildings. Trollope also, daringly for his time, makes him an 'unbeliever', never attending church. 'The assurance of belief certainly was not his to enjoy; — nor yet that absence from fear which may come from assured unbelief.' But then of course Trollope has to add by way of blunting the shock to his readers: 'And yet none who knew him could say he was a bad man', and goes on to list his virtues. And there is a final nice touch: it has always been Sir Thomas's ambition to write a life of Francis Bacon — only he has never been able to discipline himself to getting down to it. He has made copious notes, thought out his plan of execution. Everything is ready. He has only to sit at his desk and begin. But he cannot make himself do it. The thought of the enormity of the task and the perseverance and application called for frighten him. He is too busy, he tells himself; he simply hasn't the time.

> There are men who never dream of great work, who never realise to themselves the need of work so great as to demand a lifetime, but who themselves never fail in accomplishing those second-class tasks with which they satisfy their own energies. Men these are who to the world are very useful. Some few there are, who seeing the beauty of a great work and believing in its accomplishment within the years allotted to man, are contented to struggle for success, and struggling, fail. Here and there comes one who struggles and succeeds. But the men are many who see the beauty, who adopt the task, who promise themselves the triumph, and then never struggle at all. The task is never abandoned; but days go by and weeks; — and then months and years, — and nothing is done. The dream of youth becomes the doubt of middle life, and then the despair of age. In building a summer-house it is so easy to plant the first stick, but one does

not know where to touch the sod when one begins to erect a castle. So it had been with Sir Thomas Underwood and his life of Bacon. It would not suffice to him to scrape together a few facts, to indulge in some fiction, to tell a few anecdotes, and then to call his book a biography. Here was a man who had risen higher and was reported to have fallen lower, — perhaps than any other son of Adam. With the finest intellect ever given to a man, with the purest philanthropy and the most enduring energy, he had become a byword for greed and injustice. Sir Thomas had resolved that he would tell the tale as it had never yet been told, that he would unravel facts that had never seen the light, that he would let the world know of what nature really had been this man, — and that he would write a book that should live. He had never abandoned his purpose; and now, at sixty years of age, his purpose remained with him, but not one line of his book was written.

Trollope's remarks on this may, I think, be taken as being at once a dig at those aesthetically 'pure' writers who wait on inspiration and reject the perspiration which creative work entails, and a little pat on the back for himself and other writers such as Scott and Dickens who are prepared to shackle themselves to their desks and write regardless.

As some compensation Sir Thomas has two sources of pleasure: a charming residence, Popham Villa, on the bank of the Thames, and two charming daughters, Patience and Clarissa, to look after him when he is there — which he is very infrequently. Patience, the elder, is fair and rather plain; Clary is dark and beautiful and has more go about her. Sir Thomas also has — and here the Trollope-loved complicated family connections and associations begin — a ward, young Ralph Newton, heir to the Newton estate. As with the Claverings, the names and relationships of the Newtons are so intermingled and involved that I propose to summarize them here for the benefit of the reader.

Gregory Newton, Squire of Newton Priory.
Ralph Newton, his illegitimate and only son.
Ralph Newton, elder son of the late Ralph Newton, the Squire's younger brother.
Gregory Newton, younger son of the same, a parson.

Thus because of the bar sinister, Ralph, the Squire's son, cannot be the heir to his name and estate which now by law must be entailed on his cousin Ralph Newton, known as 'Ralph the Heir', to the grief and vicious anger of the Squire who is prepared to do anything short of murder to change the situation. As an added complication the late Ralph Newton on his deathbed had asked Sir Thomas Underwood, purely out of friendship, for there was no relationship, to become guardian of his son Ralph, and 'with many doubts' the lawyer had consented. And as early as the fourth chapter, just to add a still further complication, from the West Indies comes a lately orphaned niece of Sir Thomas's, the beautiful Mary Bonner, to live with the Underwoods.

Thus the scene is set for endless misunderstandings and love affairs, both abortive and successful, happy and unhappy. And at the outset we are confronted with two of Trollope's favourite gambits: a woman who loves a man who is unworthy of her, and two men of the same family who are poles apart in character, the worse one being the rightful claimant to wealth and honours. This latter is, of course, 'Ralph the Heir', admirably described to Mary Bonner by Patience Underwood as "a gentleman at large who does nothing;" while the illegitimate Ralph is a steady-going admirable young man. Clary falls for the casual, unprincipled Ralph who, after kissing her and professing love, forgets all about her. Gregory Newton, the parson, desperately in love with Clary, is made to sigh in vain.

Then for a side issue there is Neefit the breeches maker and his daughter Polly, the latter a rare character in Trollope and indeed in Victorian fiction generally, she being a tradesman's daughter, as straight and forthright as they come, afraid neither of her father nor Ralph Newton nor any man. There is too her suitor, the ungainly, unattractive but utterly sincere Ontario Moggs. Like Sir Thomas Underwood he is a unique venture in characterization for Trollope. The son of a master bootmaker and ferocious self-made capitalist (there is no more ferocious capitalist than your self-made successful business man) Moggs is a socialist, and his greatest urge and delight is to make inflammatory speeches to friends and co-workers inciting them to strike against their bosses in the name of Purity and the Rights of Labour; and in a letter to his dear Polly he tells her he sees no reason why women should not 'understand politics as well as men' and have the franchise and the right to vote. With such a hopeful beginning to Moggs's career the reader begins to think an Alton Locke or Felix Holt is about to make his appearance on the scene, and to prepare for some serious political thought and action. (After all, the first volume of Marx's *Das Kapital* had been published four years previously.) But disappointingly, Trollope does no more than let himself be carried away in his description of the Percycross elections by recollections of his own experience as a frustrated candidate for Beverley, and Moggs is made to appear little more than a thwarted naïve idealist. Which is really only another way of saying that Trollope is at his best as a narrator of the domestic, personal scene where ambitions and emotions are kept within that scope. Thus when he returns to the Newtons and their affairs the interest revives. Will the two Underwood girls and their cousin become three Mrs Newtons, as Clary secretly hopes? The complicated moves in the love game are calculated to a nicety. At the precise time when Ralph (the heir), in desperations over his debts, has reluctantly consented to sell his birthright to his uncle, the Squire, at the height of joy now that he can pass his estates on to his own son, is killed by a fall from his horse. Trollope could never resist an opportunity to describe a hunt, and in some cases one feels he has done it merely to add interest and give action to the story. But here he makes it alter the whole course of the narrative. By the Squire's death before the agreement has been signed and sealed, his son loses all right to the inheritance and his scapegrace nephew becomes legally the new 'lord of the manor'.

Ralph's follies, however, do not end with this unexpected and to him providential event. Made confident of success by his new-gotten wealth, he offers himself and his fortunes to Mary Bonner, only to be humiliatingly rejected. His lack of consideration and faith nearly break poor Clary's heart. But unlike Emily Hotspur in their similar circumstances, her nature is more normal, more human. The fact that he could, after professing love for her, offer his hand to her cousin makes her see his true worth, and though shattered, with time the wound heals and she learns to despise him; and so when later he has the nerve to come back to her, his confessions of weakness and mistaken affection fall on deaf ears and he is sent away with a flea in his ear. Who is there left for him to offer himself and his manor to? We take leave of him with his casual half-hearted marriage to a fashionable society woman. And so parson Gregory Newton, so long turned down by Clary, finds his pertinacity rewarded. (The scene of his final declaration and her acceptance is beautifully done.) Then, as the other Ralph and Mary Bonner come together at last after long separation and uncertainty, two of the Underwood girls do become Newtons. Patience, the plain one, is left to look after papa (and that too is life all over) who, having at last made up his mind to leave his London chambers and live at home, may also make up his mind to get down to his projected Baconian labours.

Surprisingly, Sadleir's only critical reference to the novel is to praise the election episodes as being 'unsurpassed in English fiction,' and to pronounce the rest as 'rather flaccid stuff.' *Quot homines, tot sententiae.* True, the story has its flaccid moments and its prolixities, but taken as a whole, while it cannot be classed among Trollope's major efforts, it is far better stuff than Sadleir allows. The plot alone is an excellent one and skilfully handled — so much so that Charles Reade stole it without Trollope's permission for his play, *Shilly Shally*, so occasioning a violent quarrel between the two novelists. And as I have already commented, the timing and the whole manipulation of it is adroit to a degree, holding the reader by its possibilities. Good average Trollope might well sum it up.

THE EUSTACE DIAMONDS

Although this novel is always catalogued as the third of the so-called 'political' or 'Palliser' series, this is merely because some of the characters appearing in the first two (viz. *Can You Forgive Her?* and *Phineas Finn*) are either mentioned or make brief appearances in it, and it can, in fact, be read as being complete in itself. Criticism has generally conceded that it is one of Trollope's best — a fair enough judgement, I believe. If the second half had been up to the first it would have been among his very best, the character of Lizzie Greystock alone ensuring as much.

The opening chapter reveals the born novelist and manipulator of narrative. The novel is to literature much as the symphony or sonata is to music. In these large-scale forms the composer has not only to create themes but, more importantly, he has to organize them in such a way that the whole movement grows out of them, perfect in balance and design. So with a novel. For just as a symphony or sonata or any large-scale composition is more than a succession of themes, so a novel is more than a series of situations, actions, reflections, conversations, descriptions and what have you. Any composer can think up themes just as any writer can imagine characters and situations. The whole art, in either case, is to organize the various ingredients into a satisfying harmonious whole: to create in fact a cohesive work. This elusive art is perhaps best summed up in one word — craftsmanship. Craftsmanship produces that highest and most difficult essence to achieve in any art — perfection of form. And in this no novelist surpasses Jane Austen. With her there is not a scene, a character, a word too many. She knows exactly where she is going.

Except in rare instances this cannot be said of Trollope or of any other British novelist, especially nineteenth century ones, with their bondage to the three-volume novel, their moralizing, their admonitions to the reader, their mania for plots and sub-plots. The *Eustace Diamonds* is one of Trollope's most typical novels, containing as it does a great deal of his strength and some of his weakness, and perfectly illustrates my thesis. It begins splendidly, with none of the unnecessary long-winded laying out of background that mars the openings of — to take only two examples — *The American Senator* and *Doctor Thorne*. We are told at once all we need to know about Lizzie Eustace, the main character, and how she came into possession of the famous diamonds which were to become of such importance to so many people and the *raison d'être* of the novel itself, and we are introduced to most of the actors in the drama who are connected with her either as relations or as coming under her influence in some way.

Lizzie Eustace (née Greystock) is undeniably one of the most life-like and fascinating female characters in fiction: beautiful, brimming over with vitality, irresistible to men and completely dependent on them for the needs of her romantic heart and silly head, utterly unscrupulous and unstable, a schemer, a liar, a poseuse — in fact a thorough vixen as more than one character describes her. And yet we find this butterfly who is so audacious in her scheming and so frail in the carrying out of her little plots so fascinating that like all the men who suffer at her hands, even her legal opponents, we would hate to see her broken on any wheel. Strictly, she deserves all she doesn't get; but we have to shake our heads and say to ourselves "What a woman!" and half hope that, like such women, she will get away with it — which of course she does. Trollope, one gathers, in creating her was worried that comparisons and references would be made to that other vixen — Thackeray's Becky Sharp. There are odd points of contact, but he need not have concerned himself. Becky is an open parasite on society, brazenly using her sex appeal to plunder men, and wages her own battles with audacious self-sufficiency. Lizzie is much more subtle and much more feminine, constantly appealing to the very men she is taking in to help her, alluring them against their better judgement to support her and if one fails her, turning without heart or conscience to another.

Like the true novelist he is Trollope brings out the character of the young widow through her words and actions, but at least twice in the course of the novel he allows himself asides to analyse her nature and conduct. Such analyses are dangerous for a novelist, and it must be admitted that on occasions he discourses on his characters in a way that is both repetitive and unconvincing — padding, in fact. But here they are flashes of insight which illuminate Lizzie's very nature. The first occurs in chapter XIV.

There existed in her bosom a sort of craving after confidential friendship, — but with it there existed something that was altogether incompatible with confidence. She thoroughly despised Augusta Fawn, and yet would have been willing, — in want of a better friend, — to press Augusta to her bosom, and swear that there should ever be between them the tenderest friendship. She desired to be the possessor of the outward shows of all those things of which the inward facts are valued by the good and steadfast ones of the earth. She knew what were the aspirations, — what the ambition, of an honest woman; and she knew, too, how rich were the probable rewards of such honesty. True love, true friendship, true benevolence, true tenderness, were beautiful to her, — qualities on which she could descant almost with eloquence; and therefore she was always shamming love and friendship and benevolence and tenderness. She could tell you, with words most appropriate to the subject, how horrible were all shams, and in saying so would not be altogether insincere: — yet she knew that she herself was ever shamming, and she satisfied herself with shams.

The second occurs in chapter XXVI.

Lizzie had declared that she would not touch Lord Fawn with a pair of tongs, and in saying so had resolved that she could not and would not now marry his lordship even were his lordship in her power. It had been decided by her as quickly as thoughts flash, but it was decided. She would torture the unfortunate lord, but not torture him by becoming his wife. And, so much being fixed as the stars in heaven, might it be possible that she should even yet induce her cousin to take the place that had been intended for Lord Fawn? After all that had passed between them she need hardly hesitate to tell him of her love. And with the same flashing thoughts she declared to herself that she did love him, and that therefore this arrangement would be so much better than that other one which she had proposed to herself. The reader, perhaps, by this time, has not a high opinion of Lady Eustace, and may believe that among other drawbacks on her character there is especially this, — that she was heartless. But that was by no means her own opinion of herself. She would have described herself, — and would have meant to do so with truth, — as being all heart. She probably thought that an over-amount of heart was the malady under which she specially suffered. Her heart was overflowing now towards the man who was sitting by her side. And then it would be so pleasant to punish that little chit who had spurned her gift and had dared to call her mean! This man, too, was needy, and she was wealthy. Surely, were she to offer herself to him, the generosity of the thing would make it noble. She was still dissolved in tears and was still hysteric. 'Oh, Frank!' she said, and threw herself upon his breast.

Lizzie so dominates the novel, in fact, that the other characters — her various assortment of lovers — Lord Fawn, Frank Greystock and the Revd Emilius, along with her unedifying circle of friends — Lord George, John Eustace, Mrs Carbuncle, Sir Griffin Tewett — are shadowy beside her, and like moons take their shape and size and colour from the light she sheds on them rather than from any sufficiency in themselves. Lucy Morris, to whom Frank Greystock has pledged his solemn word, is simply the Victorian pattern of meek female devotion and fidelity, and in her simple sincerity a foil to Lizzie. Lord Fawn, still in pursuit of a wife with means, and Lizzie's first lover, is so pompous, literal-minded, prosaic and wooden that he is screamingly funny. The ways in which Trollope conveys this, without any crude Dickensian exaggerations and posturings, are very subtle, and the scene in which he proposes to her and gets into difficulties with his hat touch the comic sublime. Lizzie's cousin, Frank, is more complex. He is 90% in love with Lucy Morris, governess to Lady Fawn's young daughters; but his family are all against his committing himself in that quarter since Lucy is neither rich nor beautiful, and money is essential to his mode of life. The remaining 10% of his affections lie at the pretty feet of his fascinating cousin mainly because she is both beautiful and rich. Lizzie of course encourages him, being a little in love with him and altogether in need of his help in her intricate involvements (he is a barrister), until she finds she can have Lord Fawn, and even then she keeps him dangling. Trollope's acute knowledge of human nature is nowhere better revealed than in his analysis of Greystock's hesitations in bringing himself to propose to Lucy Morris.

The reader, who has read so far, will perhaps think that Frank Greystock was in love with Lucy as Lucy was in love with him. But such was not exactly the case. To be in love, as an absolute, well-marked, acknowledged fact, is the condition of a woman more frequently and more readily than of a man. Such is not the common theory on the matter, as it is the man's business to speak, and the woman's business to be reticent. And the woman is presumed to have kept her heart free from any load of love, till she may accept the burthen with an assurance that it shall become a joy and a comfort to her. But such presumptions, though they may be very useful for the regulation of conduct, may not be always true. It comes more within the scope of a woman's mind, than that of a man's, to think closely and decide sharply on such a matter. With a man it is often chance that settles the question for him. He resolves to propose to a woman, or proposes without resolving, because she is close to him. Frank Greystock ridiculed the idea of Lady Fawn's interference in so high a matter as his love, — or abstinence from love. Nevertheless, had he been made a welcome guest at Fawn Court, he would undoubtedly have told his love to Lucy Morris. He was not a welcome guest, but had been banished; and, as a consequence of that banishment, he had formed no resolution in regard to Lucy, and did not absolutely know whether she was necessary to him or not. But Lucy Morris knew all about it.

Moreover, it frequently happens with men that they fail to analyse these things, and do not make out for themselves any clear definition of what their feelings are or what they mean. We hear that a man has behaved badly to a girl, when the behaviour of which he has been guilty has resulted simply from want of thought. He has found a certain companionship to be agreeable to him, and he has accepted the pleasure without inquiry. Some vague idea has floated across his brain that the world is wrong in supposing that such friendship cannot exist without marriage, or question of marriage. It is simply friendship. And yet were his friend to tell him that she intended to give herself in marriage elsewhere, he would suffer all the pangs of jealousy, and would imagine himself to be horribly ill-treated! To have such a friend, — a friend whom he cannot or will not make his wife, — is no injury to him. To him it is simply a delight, an excitement in life, a thing to be known to himself only and not talked of to others, a source of pride and inward exultation. It is a joy to think of when he wakes, and a consolation in his little troubles. It dispels the weariness of life, and makes a green spot of holiday within his daily work. It is, indeed, death to her; — but he does not know it. Frank Greystock did think that he could not marry Lucy Morris without making an imprudent plunge into deep water, and yet he felt that Lady Fawn was an ill-natured old woman for hinting to him that he had better not, for the present, continue his visits to Fawn Court.

And later, in the chapter called 'What Frank Greystock thought about marriage', after Lizzie has taken the initiative and avowed her passion for him in a way Victorian readers must have considered shameless and damnable but for us is magnificent, we are given an even finer analysis of his emotions.

With one exception the other major characters may be described as adequately credible without need of any specific reference. That exception is Lucinda Roanoke. Did Trollope, in creating this lonely, cynical, sullen, unhappy girl (she is only eighteen), mean her as a protest against the Victorian traffic in female flesh that went on under the guise of marriage for money, for comfort, for security — marriage at any price as being the only tolerable future for thousands of Victorian women even at the cost of all self-respect? Futher, was he so ahead of his time as to portray in her a lesbian — if an unconscious one? One dare scarcely believe so; but to post-Freudian generations her conduct is otherwise hardly credible. A handsome girl (and Trollope always speaks of her as handsome, never as the more femininely usual beautiful) does not normally go about hating everyone in general and men in particular and not caring whether she lives or dies. Pursued by the lecherous uncouth Sir Griffin Tewett who, finding her to be 'the handsomest woman he had ever seen . . . . did desire to make her his wife', she allows herself against her own will for financial reasons and because she is being badgered by her aunt, Mrs Carbuncle, on whom she is utterly dependent, to accept him. Harassed by her want of means and desperate for some sort of life of her own, knowing that his feelings for her, far from being love, are dominated by sensuality and a determination to have his own way in everything and to master her in mind and body, she becomes engaged to him, telling herself that, alone in the world and without any hope in the future, she can be no worse off married to the brute than remaining single. This is the extraordinary scene in which she accepts his offer of marriage.

He now hesitated for a moment. Perhaps it might be better. Should she take him at his word there would be no going back from it. But Lord George knew that he had proposed before. Lord George had learned this from Mrs. Carbuncle, and had shown that he knew it. And then, too, — he had made up his mind about it. He wanted her, and he meant to have her. 'It requires no more thinking with me, Lucinda. I'm not a man who does things without thinking; and when I have thought I don't want to think again. There's my hand; — will you have it?'

'I will,' said Lucinda, putting her hand into his. He no sooner felt her assurance than his mind misgave him that he had been precipitate, that he had been rash, and that she had taken advantage of him. After all, how many things are there in the world more precious than a handsome girl. And she had never told him that she loved him.

'I suppose you love me?' he asked.

'H'sh! — here they all are.' The hand was withdrawn, but not before both Mrs. Carbuncle and Lady Eustace had seen it.

Mrs. Carbuncle, in her great anxiety, bided her time, keeping close to her niece. Perhaps she felt that if the two were engaged, it might be well to keep the lovers separated for a while, lest they should quarrel before the engagement should have been so confirmed by the authority of friends as to be beyond the power of easy annihilation. Lucinda rode quite demurely with the crowd. Sir Griffin remained near her, but without speaking. Lizzie whispered to Lord George that there had been a proposal. Mrs. Carbuncle sat in stately dignity on her horse, as though there were nothing which at that moment especially engaged her attention. An hour almost had passed before she was able to ask the important question, 'Well; — what have you said to him?'

'Oh; — just what you would have me.'

'You have accepted him?'

'I suppose I was obliged. At any rate I did. You shall know one thing, Aunt Jane, at any rate, and I hope it will make you comfortable. I hate a good many people; but of all the people in the world I hate Sir Griffin Tewett the worst.'

'Nonsense, Lucinda.'

'It shall be nonsense if you please; but it's true. I shall have to lie to him, — but there shall be no lying to you, however much you may wish it. I hate him!'

And in the next chapter (XXVII) we are treated to an even franker and more suggestive scene.

As soon then as the wheels of the carriage were no longer heard grating upon the road, Lucinda, who had been very careful in her dress, — so careful as to avoid all appearance of care, — with slow majestic step descended to a drawing-room which they were accustomed to use on mornings. It was probable that Sir Griffin was smoking somewhere about the grounds, but it could not be her duty to go after him out of doors. She would remain there, and, if he chose, he might come to her. There could be no ground of complaint on his side if she allowed herself to be found in one of the ordinary sitting-rooms of the house. In about half an hour he sauntered upon the terrace, and flattened his nose against the window. She bowed and smiled to him, — hating herself for smiling. It was perhaps the first time that she had endeavoured to put on a pleasant face wherewithal to greet him. He said nothing then, but passed round the house, threw away the end of his cigar, and entered the room. Whatever happened, she would not be a coward. The thing had to be done. Seeing that she had accepted him on the previous day, had not run away in the night or taken poison, and had come down to undergo the interview, she would undergo it at least with courage. What did it matter, even though he should embrace her? It was her lot to undergo misery, and as she had not chosen to take poison, the misery must be endured. She rose as he entered and gave him her hand. She had thought what she would do, and was collected and dignified. He had not, and was very awkward. 'So you haven't gone to church, Sir Griffin, — as you ought,' she said, with another smile.

'Come; I've gone as much as you.'

'But I had a headache. You stayed away to smoke cigars.'

'I stayed to see you, my girl.' A lover may call his lady love his girl, and do so very prettily. He may so use the word that she will like it, and be grateful in her heart for the sweetness of the sound. But Sir Griffin did not do it nicely. 'I've got ever so much to say to you.'

'I won't flatter you by saying that I stayed to hear it.'

'But you did; — didn't you now?' She shook her head, but there was something almost of playfulness in her manner of doing it. 'Ah, but I know you did. And why shouldn't you speak out, now that we are to be man and wife? I like a girl to speak out. I suppose if I want to be with you, you want as much to be with me; eh?'

'I don't see that that follows.'

'By — , if it doesn't, I'll be off!'

'You must please yourself about that, Sir Griffin.'

'Come; do you love me? You have never said you loved me.' Luckily perhaps for her he thought that the best assurance of love was a kiss. She did not revolt, or attempt to struggle with him; but the hot blood flew over her entire face, and her lips were very cold to his, and she almost trembled in his grasp. Sir Griffin was not a man who could ever have been the adored of many women, but the instincts of his kind were strong enough within him to make him feel that she did not return his embrace with passion. He had found her to be very beautiful; — but it seemed to him that she had never been so little beautiful as when thus pressed close to his bosom. 'Come,' he said, still holding her; 'you'll give me a kiss?'

'I did do it,' she said.

'No; — nothing like it. Oh, if you won't, you know — '

On a sudden she made up her mind, and absolutely did kiss him. She would sooner have leaped at the blackest, darkest, dirtiest river in the county. 'There,' she said, 'that will do,' gently extricating herself from his arms. 'Some girls are different, I know; but you must take me as I am, Sir Griffin; — that is if you do take me.'

'Why can't you drop the Sir?'

'Oh yes; — I can do that.'

'And you do love me?' There was a pause, while she tried to swallow the lie. 'Come; — I'm not going to marry any girl who is ashamed to say that she loves me. I like a little flesh and blood. You do love me?'

'Yes,' she said. The lie was told; and for the moment he had to be satisfied. But in his heart he didn't believe her. It was all very well for her to say that she wasn't like other girls. Why shouldn't she be like other girls? It might, no doubt, suit her to be made Lady Tewett; — but he wouldn't make her Lady Tewett if she gave herself airs with him. She should lie on his breast and swear that she loved him beyond all the world; — or else she should never be Lady Tewett. Different from other girls indeed! She should know that he was different from other men. Then he asked her to come and take a walk about the grounds. To that she made no objection. She would get her hat and be with him in a minute.

But she was absent more than ten minutes. When she was alone she stood before her glass looking at herself, and then she burst into tears. Never before had she been thus polluted. The embrace had disgusted her. It made her odious to herself. And if this, the beginning of it, were so bad, how was she to drink the cup to the bitter dregs? Other girls, she knew, were fond of their lovers, — some so fond of them that all moments of absence were moments, if not of pain, at any rate of regret. To her as she stood there ready to tear herself because of the vileness of her own condition, it now seemed as though no such love as that were possible to her. For the sake of this man who was to be her husband, she hated all men. Was not everything around her base, and mean, and sordid? She had understood thoroughly the quick divulgings of Mrs. Carbuncle's tidings, the working of her aunt's anxious mind. The man, now that he had been caught, was not to be allowed to escape. But how great would be the boon if he would escape. How should she escape? And yet she knew that she meant to go on and bear it all. Perhaps by study and due practice she might become as were some others, — a beast of prey, and nothing more. The feeling that had made these few minutes so inexpressibly loathsome to her might, perhaps, be driven from her heart. She washed the tears from her eyes with savage energy and descended to her lover with a veil fastened closely under her hat. 'I hope I haven't kept you waiting,' she said.

'Women always do,' he replied laughing. 'It gives them importance.'

'It is not so with me, I can assure you. I will tell you the truth. I was agitated, — and I cried.'

'Oh, ay; I dare say.' He rather liked the idea of having reduced the haughty Lucinda to tears. 'But you needn't have been ashamed of my seeing it. As it is I can see nothing. You must take that off presently.'

'Not now, Griffin.' Oh, what a name it was. It seemed to blister her tongue as she used it without the usual prefix.

'I never saw you tied up in that way before. You don't do it out hunting. I've seen you when the snow has been driving in your face, and you didn't mind it, — not so much as I did.'

'You can't be surprised that I should be agitated now.'

'But you're happy; — ain't you?'

'Yes,' she said. The lie once told must of course be continued.

'Upon my word I don't quite understand you,' said Sir Griffin. 'Look here, Lucinda, if you want to back out of it, you can, you know.'

'If you ask me again I will.' This was said with the old savage voice, and it at once reduced Sir Griffin to thraldom. To be rejected now would be the death of him. And should there come a quarrel he was sure that it would seem to be that he had been rejected.

'I suppose it's all right,' he said, 'only when a man is only thinking how he can make you happy, he doesn't like to find nothing but crying.'

After this there was but little more said between them before they returned to the castle.

One can't help wondering how Trollope's readers reacted to such a love scene as that. I know of nothing in nineteenth century fiction — or, come to that, in any fiction — quite like it for savagery and the annihilation of normal human sexual feeling. After going through it the reader will feel no surprise when Lucinda, despite her iron will, breaks down under the strain and is unable to force herself to keep her plighted word. The final scene with her aunt is scarifying.

Then Lucinda and Mrs. Carbuncle were alone. 'Of one thing I feel sure,' said Lucinda in a low voice.

'What is that, dear?'

'I shall never see Sir Griffin Tewett again.'

'You talk in that way on purpose to break me down at the last moment,' said Mrs. Carbuncle.

'Dear Aunt Jane, I would not break you down if I could help it. I have struggled so hard, — simply that you might be freed from me. We have been very foolish, both of us; but I would bear all the punishment, — if I could.'

'You know that this is nonsense now.'

'Very well. I only tell you. I know that I shall never see him again. I will never trust myself alone in his presence. I could not do it. When he touches me my whole body is in agony. To be kissed by him is madness.'

'Lucinda, this is very wicked. You are working yourself up to a paroxysm of folly.'

'Wicked; — yes, I know that I am wicked. There has been enough of wickedness certainly. You don't suppose that I mean to excuse myself?'

'Of course you will marry Sir Griffin to-morrow.'

'I shall never be married to him. How I shall escape from him, — by dying, or going mad, — or by destroying him, God only knows.' Then she paused, and her aunt looking into her face almost began to fear that she was in earnest. But she would not take it as at all indicating any real result for the morrow. The girl had often said nearly the same thing before, and had still submitted. 'Do you know, Aunt Jane, I don't think I could feel to any man as though I loved him. But for this man, — Oh God, how I do detest him! I cannot do it.' . . . .

'Do you want to destroy me?' Mrs. Carbuncle said at last.

'You have destroyed me,' said Lucinda.

One's only criticism of Lucinda's character must be that we do not know enough about her to give her our full sympathy. Why is she as she is? Why has she of her own volition got herself into such a position? If she is a lesbian unknown to herself then the situation makes some sort of sense: but Trollope, even if he had this in mind did not, dared not, give any hint of it. If she is a normal woman what makes her behave in so inexplicable and unfeminine a manner? Trollope, one of whose besetting sins is to stuff his novels with too lengthy backgrounds, for once fails to provide one when most needed.

Like so many of his novels, too, even the best ones, this is over-long. One becomes rather tired of the diamonds and their mystery before they finally disappear, and does not really care much who the thieves are. Why, one asks, after the first attempt to steal them and expecting a second, doesn't the silly minx put them in the bank or hide them instead of leaving them in her desk? She surely deserved to lose them. The whole plot woven around them is in fact acceptable to an adult intelligent reader only in so far as it touches the characters who are affected by them directly or indirectly through Lizzie herself. But the story (in parts) is allowed to come too close to a whodunit for it to maintain its pristine stature, and in such episodes is not improved by feeble attempts to turn the detectives into comics.

All the same, these are blemishes which do not prevent the novel *in toto* from being one of the greats among Victorian fiction.

AN EYE FOR AN EYE

The theme — seduction and revenge — must have seemed daring and 'improper' in the eyes of the first readers of the novel. However, the fact that the 'hero' is at the same time the 'villain' and meets with more than due punishment for his sinning would have made its sexual overtones excusable to Victorian minds. 'This is what comes of playing with fire and indulging in sexual immorality' they would have told themselves, and accepted it as a moral tale.

But I don't believe Trollope had any such comfortable palliative in mind when he planned and wrote the novel. Here, he more likely felt, is a damn good story, with contrast, vacillation and weakness of will as its basic ingredients. Only some 70,000 words in length, the novel is one of the shortest in all Trollope. There are no longueurs, none of those sub-plots with their crowded characters that can seem so tediously unnecessary to the modern reader. The main characters, indeed, are few, and all play their essential role in the drama. They are: the old Earl of Scroope, his wife, their two nephews Fred and Jack Neville for the English scene, with Mrs O'Hara, her daughter Kate and the priest Father Marty for the Irish. The story is a first class piece of narrative without deviations. Indeed Trollope so concentrates on the action that there is little leisure for the subtlety of characterization of which he was such a master. The characters are just sufficiently alive and varied to be convincing and make the story credible and gripping. The inexperienced Kate, living alone with her mother in a remote corner of County Clare, and as ignorant of men as Miranda in *The Tempest*, was sure to fall fatally in love with the first eligible man that came along. Her mother, learning that he is heir to wealth and land in England, was just as sure to give her lover every encouragement and to push her into his arms. And Fred Neville, a typical spoilt army officer in peacetime with nothing better to do that shoot seagulls and seals, finding her beautiful and uncritically adoring, was equally sure to seduce her.

All this may sound somewhat cold-blooded. But in fact the situation is not as simple as that. Trollope skilfully turns it into a tug-of-war between loyalties: Fred Neville has promised his uncle, to whom he owes everything including the fact of his being the heir to the title, never to marry any woman who is "beneath him" or "not fit to be the wife of an English Earl"; at the same time he has solemnly promised the now-pregnant Kate — and more especially her tigress of a mother — that he will marry her.

Put in this brief way the young man's conduct appears to be cold-blooded villainy. But as Trollope carefully and rightly points out, he is 'not a villain — simply a self-indulgent, spoiled young man who had realized to himself no idea of duty in life', and now finds himself in the position of being "a fool if he marries her and a villain if he doesn't", as his younger but more mature brother acidly puts it when Fred in his agony of mind confesses the truth to him. Thus he has placed himself between the devil and the deep sea — with his English background and aristocratic environment for the devil, and his conscience, reinforced by the threats and reproaches of Mrs O'Hara and Father Marty, for the deep sea.

And here the roles of the priest and mother are worth considering. Trollope is deliberately ambivalent here. Father Marty, who was responsible for bringing Kate and Fred together, is neither an altogether crafty *agent provocateur* nor an innocent unworldly priest. There is little doubt but that he saw in the heir to the Scroope lands a slendid prize for a poor Catholic Irish girl (the analysis of his thinking in the chapter 'Is She To Be Your Wife?' makes this clear). But when, after the appearance out of the blue of the girl's father, the disreputable Captain O'Hara, Fred begins to make this an excuse for his get-out, Father Marty prepares to fight him tooth and nail. The scene in the O'Haras' cottage between the four of them towards the end is magnificent with its sense of the tragic end soon to come.

The mother's role too is no less equivocal. Although suspicious of Neville's intentions at first, she eventually trusts him and leaves them more and more alone together, unlike the general run of Victorian strait-laced prudent mammas. If to begin with her thoughts were — as Trollope expresses them with a frankness which must have seemed shockingly blatant to his readers — 'Men are wolves to women, and utterly merciless when feeding high their lust', she is also telling herself 'This was the girl's chance. Was she to rob her of it?' She takes the chance and pays for it.

That her revenge on the cliffs of Mohir towering over Liscannor Bay is doubly tragic in that it proves futile and double-edged is Trollope's final ironic twist. I will not spoil it for the would-be reader by revealing it. I only strongly urge him to find it out for himself.

PHINEAS REDUX

Two incidents in Trollope's life were the reasons for this, the second, of the 'political' novels of the 1870s. The first was that in 1868, carrying into practice his strongly expressed opinion that the highest ambition and honour for any Briton should be to serve his country as an MP, he contested for a possible seat in Beverley. His defeat remained a bitter blow to him for the rest of his life, and to combat it he turned to politics for his subject matter. In his own words: 'As I was debarred from expressing my opinions in the House of Commons, I took this method of declaring myself . . . and was enabled from time to time to have in this way that fling at the political doings of the day which every man likes to take, if not in one fashion then in another.'[*]

But he was to find that in the seventies literary fashions and taste were changing, and that neither critics nor public were prepared to place these so-called 'political novels' alongside his Barchester series. And for once critics and public were right.

To the second Phineas novel, then.

Having got Phineas back to Ireland and married to his simple trusting Mary, Trollope, needing to bring his hero back to England and into political harness, high society and contact with attractive women, found he had made an error of judgement. Impossible for the essentially good Phineas to go on falling for such women with a wife behind him! So he had somehow to get rid of her, and he does this by making her conveniently die in childbirth, and that is the end (his father has also died) of his Irish ties. Well, women do lose their lives giving birth, and did so much more often in those days so there is no incredibility here. And yet the reader can't help feeling that a fictional sleight-of-hand has been practised on him, and tends to resent the demise of poor Mary as too facile.

And this, I feel, typifies the whole novel — or at any rate a good deal of it. Like every mature novel of Trollope's it has its high moments, but too much is dragged in and inadequately blended with the rest.

---

[*]*Autobiography.*

Phineas, back in England as a widower, is persuaded to contest the seat for Tankerville, a mining village somewhere in Durham, and with typical Finnian luck after a recount of the votes he gets it. He is an MP once more. Between these political activities he meets up with his former would-be love, Violet, now married to Lord Oswald Chiltern, and a mother, and goes to stay with her and her husband at Harrington Hall. From them he learns that his first friend and staunchest admirer, Lady Laura Kennedy, has been driven into leaving her husband to moulder in his religious gloom at Loughlinter and is living in sad lonely seclusion with her aged father in Dresden. Discussing the rift and Laura's past loyalty to Phineas Violet observes:

"I daresay you often think of her?" said Lady Chiltern.

"Indeed I do."

"What virtues she used to ascribe to you! What sins she forgave you! How hard she fought for you! Now, though she can fight no more, she does not think of it all the less."

"Poor Lady Laura!"

"Poor Laura, indeed! When one sees such shipwreck it makes a woman doubt whether she ought to marry at all."

"And yet he was a good man. She always said so."

"Men are so seldom really good. They are so little sympathetic. What man thinks of changing himself so as to suit his wife? And yet men expect that women shall put on altogether new characters when they are married, and girls think that they can do so . . . "

After leaving the Chilterns, who, now that family life and sexual harmony have claimed them, are nothing like as interesting as they were before, he receives a long letter from Lady Laura telling him of her situation and ending 'Do come if you can' — adding the all-important feminine postcript: 'If you can learn anything of Mr. Kennedy's life and of his real condition, pray do. The faint rumours which reach me are painfully distressing.' Hard on the heels of this letter comes one from Kennedy himself begging Phineas to visit him at Loughlinter. Phineas, with his usual naïve good-heartedness, accepts both invitations. The descriptions of both interviews are among the best things in the book. He finds Loughlinter, once so gay and, for him, so full of memories, a mere shell, a ghost of itself. No one greets him. The rooms are fireless and cold, the meal, brought to him by a single depressing servant in black, sparse and tasteless. Only after that is he taken to Kennedy's room to meet his 'host'. He finds a man who has aged terribly and can speak of nothing but God and the Devil and his erring wife's duty to return to him and who, when he learns that Phineas has been invited to visit her, demands that he should "abstain from seeking her presence" and takes the poker menacingly in his hand. And when Phineas defies him and tells him that nothing will make him give up his intended visit the other screams at him, "Then you will be accursed among adulterers," and launches into a religious rodomontade, a megalomaniacal outburst of stultiloquy and imbecilic sciomachy. Convinced that the man is fast becoming a lunatic, Phineas makes good his escape and leaves early next morning without seeing him again.

The next chapter, 'The Truant Wife', takes us to Dresden. As I have already noted, every scene between Phineas and Lady Laura has so far never failed to produce the best from Trollope, and this, the penultimate one, is perhaps the finest of all, with the marvellous chapter entitled 'Königstein' in which she confesses to him that she has loved him all the time and that this love has been the real reason, quite apart from the antipathy of character, which made it impossible for her to love her husband as she should have done. At the same time she declares:

> "I must insist upon it . . . . that you shall take me now as I really am, — as your dearest friend, your sister, your mother, if you will. I know what I am. Were my husband not still living it would be the same. I should never under any circumstances marry again. I have passed the period of a woman's life when as a woman she is loved; but I have not outlived the power of loving. I shall fret about you, Phineas, like an old hen after her one chick; and though you turn out to be a duck, and get away into waters where I cannot follow you, I shall go cackling round the pond, and always have my eye upon you." He was holding her now by the hand, but he could not speak, for the tears were trickling down his cheeks. "When I was young," she continued, "I did not credit myself with capacity for so much passion. I told myself that love after all should be a servant and not a master, and I married my husband fully intending to do my duty to him. Now we see what has come of it."

And to Phineas's declaring that he knows he is unworthy of her confidence she replies:

> 'Worth has nothing to do with it, — has no bearing on it. I do not say that you are more worthy than all whom I have known. But when did worth create love? What I want is that you should believe me, and know that there is one bound to you who will never be unbound, one whom you can trust in all things, — one to whom you can confess that you have been wrong if you go wrong, and yet be sure that you will not lessen her regard. And with this feeling you must pretend to nothing more than friendship. You will love again, of course.'
>
> 'Oh, no.'
>
> 'Of course you will. I tried to blaze into power by a marriage, and I failed, — because I was a woman. A woman should marry only for love. You will do it yet, and will not fail. You may remember this too, — that I shall never be jealous again. You may tell me everything with safety. You will tell me everything?'
>
> 'If there be anything to tell, I will.'
>
> 'I will never stand between you and your wife, — though I would fain hope that she should know how true a friend I am. Now we have walked here till it is dark, and the sentry will think we are taking plans of the place. Are you cold?'
>
> 'I have not thought about the cold.'
>
> 'Nor have I. We will go down to the inn and warm ourselves before the train comes. I wonder why I should have brought you here to tell you my story. Oh, Phineas.' Then she threw herself into his arms, and he pressed her to his heart, and kissed first her forehead and then her lips. 'It shall never be so again,' she said. 'I will kill it out of my heart even though I should crucify my body. But it is not my love that I will kill. When you are happy I will be happy. When you prosper I will prosper. When you fail I will fail. When you rise, — as you will rise, — I will rise with you. But I will never again feel the pressure of your arm round my waist. Here is the gate, and the old guide. So, my friend, you see that we are not lost.' Then they walked down the very steep hill to the little town below the fortress, and there they remained till the evening train came from Prague, and took them back to Dresden.

The whole episode, together with their farewells at the railway station, is most moving. The reader will later recall Laura's profession of disinterested friendship when the two meet and part for the final time (chapter 78) as her bitterness and disappointment burst from her when he tells her of his love for Madame Goesler.

Following the scene with Lady Laura the novel moves down a long slow decrescendo of interest. The politics and the murder and the trial are slow where they are convincing and unconvincing when Trollope attempts to hurry the action on; and like the similar parts of *The Eustace Diamonds* we feel they would have been better done by Wilkie Collins. In addition there is the inevitable padding — whole chapters and episodes which would have been better left out. And adding insult to injury, we are given fleeting glimpses of characters who had played important roles in the earlier novels of the series, most notably Lizzie Eustace. But these glimpses are feeble and, we feel, purely mechanical — a sort of job at our elbow to remind us that they are still around and about. But this Lizzie Eustace is a pale shadow of the fascinating woman of *The Eustace Diamonds*, and as unconvincing as the similar resurrection of Mr Pickwick in *Master Humphrey's Clock*.

These defects, it should be said, however, stem from Trollope's very source of power — his versatility, his knowledge of so many different types and his power of creating character. He is like a batsman who as often as not gets himself out through his best shots: he uses them so much that he takes risks in order to play them when he shouldn't, and he pays the penalty. Or to continue the sporting metaphor in a line of country Trollope would understand better, he is like a horseman who, disdaining the dull safety of the road or lane, insists on putting his horse at every gate, ditch and fence until he comes a cropper. Like the cricketer and the horseman Trollope rides his luck until he too pays the penalty and comes a cropper. Jane Austen knew better. Her scope was much more limited, but more perfect.

The best parts of the novel are those dominated by Madame Goesler, one of his most convincing creations. Dark, foreign, subtle and yet forthright, she conveys by her every word and action a sense of mystery, of a romantic and tantalizingly secretive past. The reader will recall that the previous novel ended by her offering her wealth and herself to Phineas and that, engaged as he was to Mary Flood, conscience had forced him to refuse her offer. In this continuation of the action every incident between them brings them closer together until the reader is made to feel that their final union is inevitable. The scene in which he proposes and she accepts is a refreshing variation from the usual Victorian courtship in which the woman seems never to be expected to accept the man at his first offer, and then only with prudish hypocritical reluctance, and is over and done with almost before the reader has time to realize it.

> At a little before noon the next morning he knocked at her door, and was told to enter. "I didn't go out after all," she said. "I hadn't courage to face the sun."
> "I saw you were not in the garden."
> "If I could have found you I would have told you I should be here all the morning. I might have sent you a message, only, — only I didn't."
> "I have come — "
> "I know why you have come."
> "I doubt that. I have come to tell you that I love you."
> "Oh Phineas; at last, at last!" And in a moment she was in his arms.

So Phineas brings his ship home to port, and there we take our leave of him.

Upon its serialization in the *Graphic* the novel was designated by one critic as being superior to its predecessor — a view few are likely to accept today. And Henry James was surely right when he asserted briefly '*Phineas Finn* is much better.'

LADY ANNA

Trollope wrote the novel during his voyage to Australia in 1871, beginning it on the day he left Liverpool and finishing it the day before reaching Melbourne. This has nothing to do with the fact that the work is little better than a pot-boiler. With the exception of his first four, all his novels were written with the same incredible facility, including many of his finest. But for some reason known only to the mystical Genius of Inspiration, she refused to visit him during the voyage. Because she was then Victorian the theme of the story perhaps affronted her sense of propriety. For let it be known that, greatly daring for his age, Trollope has made as the mainspring of the action a debauched old earl, Lord Lovel, whose chief pleasure was seducing women and who, failing to work his wicked will on the beautiful Josephine Murray, marries her to satisfy his lust and then calmly informs her that the marriage is no marriage as he already has a wife in Italy: informing her in fact that she is only his mistress and the child she is carrying a bastard. The rest of the story is taken up in relating the desperate efforts to the point of monomania of 'Lady Lovel' to prove the legality of her marriage and so the claim of her daughter, Lady Anna, to the title. Her struggles lead to endless legal involvements, and for the climax, her attempt to murder Daniel Thwaite, the kindly benefactor of both herself and her daughter because the girl had fallen in love with him — a man who in her aristocratic eyes and ambitious hopes for her daughter to marry her cousin, the young Lord Lovel, was "a mere tradesman", a "sweaty tailor" and an obstacle to be removed.

The novel is a second-rate mechanical piece of writing and can gain no converts for this most unequal of novelists. Perhaps the most — indeed the only — interesting aspect of it to a modern reader is the way in which it highlights the pernicious, morbific, rank-peccancy of Victorian class distinction and snobbery, and its intolerance of so-called mésalliance.

To us the banal abortive attempt of the mother to kill her daughter's lover seems a ludicrous exaggeration. To Trollope's contemporaries it was nothing of the sort. In fact readers (particularly women) wrote to him deploring his permitting the tailor to marry Lady Anna as an affront to decent, social convention; and a guess that a good percentage of them would have preferred to have him removed is not likely to be far wrong. In fact in his *Autobiography* Trollope was driven to write

> . . . . everyone found fault with me for marrying her to the tailor . . . . The horror which was expressed to me at the evil thing that I had done in giving the girl to the tailor was the strongest testimony I could receive of the merits of the story.

There can be no doubt but that in the opposed characters of Lady Lovel, the out-and-out aristocrat, and Daniel Thwaite, the socialistic, aristocrat-hating, irreligious working-class man, Trollope was taking a swingeing blow at the hollow pretensions of the upper classes in their claims to be divinely appointed controllers of the destiny of their country and arbiters of the lives and conditions of what Marx at that very time had described as 'the toiling ignorant masses'. In a happier moment, and with the blessing of his normal inspiration, the novel might have been a classic depicting the bitter class struggle being waged in Britain at that time, a savage satire on nobility endowed by birth, and on the creed of inheritance. Lacking these premises the novel cannot be described as being other than a failure.

HARRY HEATHCOTE OF GANGOIL

Along with *Nina Balatka, Linda Tressel* and *The Golden Lion of Granpère* this story (we cannot call it a novel) would have been more suitably placed among the *Tales of All Countries* than given a separate volume in its own right. Indeed, it is a stretch of tolerance to call it fiction at all, and would have been a far better piece of writing if Trollope had been content to leave it undramatized and published it simply as *Travelling Sketches* like those published by Chapman & Hall in 1866. It could then have been enjoyed as a vivid description of Australian bush life instead of condemnation and oblivion as an unsatisfactory hybrid. His inability to say No to a publisher or editor must be blamed in this instance.

He and his wife had sailed to Australia in 1871 to visit their son Frederic who had opted to leave home and try his luck over there in much the same way as John Caldigate in the later novel of that name, wanting to see how he was faring and at the same time for Anthony to write a travel book on Australia and New Zealand for which he was under contract. As usual, he wrote furiously as he travelled around, noting such things as the relentless heat, drought and fetid wind, the constant threat of unfriendly neighbours, bush fires started accidentally or deliberately, and the quarrels and bad blood between the 'squatters' and the 'free selectors'.

A year after his return home he was approached by the editor of the *Graphic* magazine for a long Christmas story. Now as we have already seen (v. *Orley Farm*) he detested the materialistic celebration of Christmas as indulged in by the average English family. 'Nothing can be more distasteful to me than to have to give a relish of Christmas to what I write. I feel the humbug implied by the nature of the order', he wrote, placing himself in this as in almost everything on the furthermost horizon from Dickens. On the other hand his intense professional pride as a writer able to supply any demand — to say nothing of the monetary return — would not let him turn down any advantageous offer. (In this instance £450). He therefore reluctantly accepted the editorial invitation and the result was *Harry Heathcote*, written in a month, and based on his Australian travel sketches. All he did was to introduce and give names to some of the characters he had either met or been told of by his son; a 'hero', a revengeful squatter, a bush fire, Christmas over there as a contrast with it in England, a thin sketch of a love affair, and the thing was done. The story is one of the best examples of an unabashed pot-boiler from a great novelist. Of its merit as a historic document of Australian pioneering life in the nineteenth century it may have its merits: as a work of fiction, none.

THE WAY WE LIVE NOW

More than one critic has voted this novel as being Trollope's greatest. While I cannot whole-heartedly concur (for one thing I do not believe there can be 'the greatest work' of so varied, important and prolific a writer, and in any case so much depends on personal taste) I agree it must be placed among his half-dozen outstanding achievements, and I can well understand the reasons for the opinion of such critics. For one thing it is the prime novel to give the lie to that all too common opinion of Trollope as a writer of a smug cosy rural society out of the backwash of disturbing political events and social change and unease, and indifferent to the harsher realities of contemporary society — an opinion I have already condemned in my Foreword. This is the novel before all others which should be put into the hands of those who consider Trollope to be no more than a gifted recorder of a past age of rural tranquillity and having no 'significance for' (their favourite criterion) our time. Here now is a Trollope with a pen dipped, not in his usual ink, but in acid, describing, like Balzac, a society composed not of clerics and backwater custom-clinging citizens, but a London world of financiers, crooks, big business tycoons and their parasitic hangers-on. There is swindling and decadence everywhere. Even the literary world is made to stink with its sterile editors of influential magazines and their hacks handing out puffs or snubs according to whim and circumstance.

It is, I think, worth prefacing a review of the novel by a brief glance at the society which Trollope was attacking. By the middle of the nineteenth century, and more especially during its second half, a new middle class was emerging which was slowly but finally to take over from the aristocracy as the power in the land. Even religion was to feel the change as the preaching of the Wesleys began to make its impact, and the Chapel to rival the Church for moral power. The ambition of this new class was to make itself as rich, comfortable and respectable as possible, to resist change, and to believe Britain as being the favoured nation of the Almighty (a state roughly approximating to present-day America.) Thus every virtue, through excess, became a vice. Religion became religiosity with a literal interpretation of Scripture (Mrs Proudie's rigid Sabbatarianism is an example of this); nakedness, whether in life or art, had to be covered; sex and the normal functionings of the body became taboo. Which in turn meant that prostitution and pornography flourished underground, and art in any form was tolerated only if it made satisfactory returns in money. Respectability became the first essential of living. Everyone went to church as a matter of course no matter what their private beliefs and conduct. To profess irreligion overtly was to put oneself beyond the pale of 'decent society'.*

By the middle of the century this overriding ambition of Victorian society for money-making at all cost, with its attendant ever-growing gap between rich and poor, master and man, employer and employed and growing scourge of unemployment all leading to hatred and class struggle, began to find expression in literature. The year 1844 saw the appearance of Engels' *The Condition of the Working Man in England*, to be

---

*See *Ayala's Angel* and my comment on this aspect (p. 179.)

followed by Kingsley's *Yeast* and *Alton Locke*, Elizabeth Gaskell's *Mary Barton* and *North and South*, and still later the protesting voices of Mill and Arnold and climaxing in the works of Marx. And it was typical of the religious atmosphere of the time that (with the exceptions of Marx and Engels, of course) these writers' answer to all social problems was, not economic, but a vague Socialism based on Christianity and general education which, it was their belief, would soften the hearts of the employers and make them humane. It was left to Gissing in the 1880s and 90s with his novels *The Nether World*, *Demos*, *The Emancipated* and to others* to expose the ignorance and poverty of the working class and to point to the futility of religion and education (as then practised, at least) to improve their lot.

Trollope's *The Way We Live Now*, while making no attempt to imitate the Gaskell and Kingsley novels, does latch on to a symptom peculiar to the second half of the century during which a change occurred in the social climate. The early to mid-century capitalist, although proud of his 'brass' and independence, had nevertheless, thanks to his Puritan upbringing, been thrifty and careful in his spending. But as that Puritanism began to fade and the screw of religion to be loosened, the new moneyed class began to yearn towards a display of their wealth. Lavish entertainment, parties, balls, concert and theatre-going became the fashionable thing. Wealth had to be seen to be believed. Wealth meant popularity, even power, so that wealth obtained by any means whatsoever became society's obsession, the business man's shibboleth.

It is this aspect and characteristic which is the prime mover, the be-all and end-all of Trollope's novel, embodied in the characters of the financier Melmotte and his hangers-on. But Trollope does not limit himself to exposing and castigating the financial world: he hits at the literary world of London with its corruption and charlatanism as well.

The novel in fact opens savagely with three letters of masterly subtlety written by Lady Carbury, a literary dilettante. Trading on her social status, feminine charm and marriageable condition (she is a widow), she throws herself on the good will of her 'dear friends' Nicholas Broune, Alfred Booker and Ferdinand Alf, editors of *The Morning Breakfast Table*, *The Literary Chonicle* and *The Evening Pulpit* respectively, for puffs for her new book *Criminal Queens*. Her approach to and relationship with these editorial gentlemen are an excoriating exposure of the back-scratching (or the opposite) that goes on in London literary circles. Of course, these editors are careful not to take the responsibility on themselves for whatever criticism may appear in their columns: they are not as simple as that. They employ their own chosen reviewers to do their dirty work for them.

> In spite of the dear friendship between herself and Mr. Alf, one of Mr. Alf's most sharp-nailed subordinates had been set upon her book, and had pulled it to pieces with almost rabid malignity. One would have thought that so slight a thing could hardly have been worthy of such protracted attention. Error after error was laid bare with merciless prolixity. No doubt the writer of the article must have had all history at his finger-ends, as in pointing out the various mistakes made he always spoke of the historical facts which had been misquoted, misdated, or misrepresented, as being familiar in all their bearings to every schoolboy of twelve years old.

---

*See above all Jack London's *The People of the Abyss* (1902) for an excoriating account of his experiences in the East End of London.

The writer of the criticism never suggested the idea that he himself, having been fully provided with books of reference, and having learned the art of finding in them what he wanted at a moment's notice, had, as he went on with his work, checked off the blunders without any more permanent knowledge of his own than a housekeeper has of coals when she counts so many sacks into the coal-cellar. He spoke of the parentage of one wicked ancient lady, and the dates of the frailties of another, with an assurance intended to show that an exact knowledge of all these details abided with him always. He must have been a man of vast and varied erudition, and his name was Jones. The world knew him not, but his erudition was always there at the command of Mr. Alf, — and his cruelty. The greatness of Mr. Alf consisted in this, that he always had a Mr. Jones or two ready to do his work for him. It was a great business, this of Mr. Alf's, for he had his Jones also for philology, for science, for poetry, for politics, as well as for history, and one special Jones, extraordinarily accurate and very well posted up in his references, entirely devoted to the Elizabethan drama.

There is the review intended to sell a book, — which, comes out immediately after the appearance of the book, or sometimes before it; the review which gives reputation, but does not affect the sale, and which comes a little later; the review which snuffs a book out quietly; the review which is to raise or lower the author a single peg, or two pegs, as the case may be; the review which is suddenly to make an author, and the review which is to crush him. An exuberant Jones has been known before now to declare aloud that he would crush a man, and a self-confident Jones has been known to declare that he has accomplished the deed. Of all reviews, the crushing review is the most popular, as being the most readable. When the rumour goes abroad that some notable man has been actually crushed, — been positively driven over by an entire Juggernaut's car of criticism till his literary body be a mere amorphous mass, — then a real success has been achieved, and the Alf of the day has done a great thing; but even the crushing of a poor Lady Carbury, if it be absolute, is effective. Such a review will not make all the world call for the 'Evening Pulpit', but it will cause those who do take the paper to be satisfied with their bargain. Whenever the circulation of such a paper begins to slacken, the proprietors should, as a matter of course, admonish their Alf to add a little power to the crushing department.

Mr Broune, a bachelor, who had sentimental thoughts of Lady Carbury, treated her better, as too did Mr Booker in return for a kind review the lady had given to a work of his own. Nevertheless:

It grieved his inner contemplative, intelligence that such rubbish should be thrown upon him; but in his outside experience of life he knew that even the rubbish was valuable, and that he must pay for it in the manner to which he had unfortunately become accustomed. So Mr. Booker himself wrote the article on the 'Criminal Queens' in the 'Literary Chronicle,' knowing that what he wrote would also be rubbish. 'Remarkable vivacity.' 'Power of delineating character.' 'Excellent choice of subject.' 'Considerable intimacy with the historical details of various periods.' 'The literary world would be sure to hear of Lady Carbury again.' The composition of the review, together with the reading of the book, consumed altogether perhaps an hour of Mr. Booker's time. He made no attempt to cut the pages, but here and there read those that were open. He had done this kind of thing so often, that he knew well what he was about. He could have reviewed such a book when he was three parts asleep. When the work was done he threw down his pen and uttered a deep sigh. He felt it to be hard upon him that he should be compelled, by the exigencies of his position, to descend so low in literature; but it did not occur to him to reflect that in fact he was not compelled, and that he was quite at liberty to break stones, or to starve honestly, if no other honest mode of carrying on his career was open to him. 'If I didn't, somebody else would,' he said to himself.

But Trollope is subtle in his characterization of Lady Carbury. Although she makes up to editors, plays on their emotions and gives herself airs as an authoress, this is all done for the sake of her son, Felix. Felix Carbury is, with Rawdon Crawley and Arthur Huntingdon, one of the most vivid portraits of sheer worthlessness in fiction. Of course his emotional mother, although quite undeluded as to his character and mode of life, worships the ground he treads on and is prepared to sacrifice herself and her daughter Henrietta to his everlasting demands for money which he gambles away. For him she is prepared to sit up writing half the night, beg editors for puffs, give literary evenings which she can't really afford, and see Henrietta married to anyone with money. After all, what was a Victorian daughter? An encumbrance to be married off, and parents thanked their stars if they had only one or two to worry about, and not half a dozen (as Jane Austen knew: v. *Pride and Prejudice*). And the man she worries Henrietta's life out to get herself engaged to is her cousin, Roger Carbury, a landowner in Norfolk who is deeply in love with her though she does not love him, her heart being given to Paul Montague, his closest friend, who has neither money nor property.

But this is only the beginning. Enters the gigantic figure of Augustus Melmotte, the dominant character of the novel, who proceeds to cast his colossal shadow over the destinies of all the protagonists directly or indirectly, either uniting them or disuniting them in one single motive: that of becoming rich. His origins are mysterious, a fact which makes him all the more magnetic.

> It was at any rate an established fact that Mr. Melmotte had made his wealth in France. He no doubt had had enormous dealings in other countries, as to which stories were told which must surely have been exaggerated. It was said that he had made a railway across Russia, that he provisioned the Southern army in the American civil war, that he had supplied Austria with arms, and had at one time bought up all the iron in England. He could make or mar any company by buying or selling stock, and could make money dear or cheap as he pleased. All this was said of him in his praise, — but it was also said that he was regarded in Paris as the most gigantic swindler that had ever lived; that he had made that City too hot to hold him; that he had endeavoured to establish himself in Vienna, but had been warned away by the police; and that he had at length found that British freedom would alone allow him to enjoy, without persecution, the fruits of his industry. He was now established privately in Grosvenor Square and officially in Abchurch Lane; and it was known to all the world that a Royal Prince, a Cabinet Minister, and the very cream of duchesses were going to his wife's ball. All this had been done within twelve months.
>
> There was but one child in the family, one heiress for all this wealth. Melmotte himself was a large man, with bushy whiskers and rough thick hair, with heavy eye-brows, and a wonderful look of power about his mouth and chin. This was so strong as to redeem his face from vulgarity; but the countenance and appearance of the man were on the whole unpleasant, and, I may say, untrustworthy. He looked as though he were purse-proud and a bully.

The above quotation shows that Trollope has at last learned that lengthy descriptions of people à la Scott, Hardy and himself too frequently, are pointless. One or two salient features are enough, and we get it with the 'wonderful look of power about his mouth and chin' along with the vulgarity of the rest suggestive of the weakness which was eventually to bring about his downfall.

Such a meteoric rise to power, Trollope suggests, is impossible without dubious dealings. Under their breath men (even those who fawn on him) refer to him as 'a swindler buying his way into society.' They are, partly at any rate, right, for he is determined to show the world that he can make the smug self-superior idle English aristocracy look small and jump to the crack of his whip. They do. The Longestaffes, the Nidderdales, the Grendalls, the Grassloughs, all poverty-stricken gamblers and spongers under their snobbish class-consciousness, jump on to the Melmotte bandwagon, and duchesses attend the dinners he forces his nonentity of a wife and his daughter Marie to organize. Trollope is scrupulously fair. He may have his knife in the callous business tycoon, but he does not pull his punches against the aristocracy and landed gentry either. His description of Adolphus Longestaffe, squire of Caversham in Suffolk and Pickering Park in Sussex, is superb in its bite.

> Mr. Longestaffe was a tall, heavy man, about fifty, with hair and whiskers carefully dyed, whose clothes were made with great care, though they always seemed to fit him too tightly, and who thought very much of his personal appearance. It was not that he considered himself handsome, but that he was specially proud of his aristocratic bearing. He entertained an idea that all who understood the matter would perceive at a single glance that he was a gentleman of the first water, and a man of fashion. He was intensely proud of his position in life, thinking himself to be immensely superior to all those who earned their bread. There were no doubt gentlemen of different degrees, but the English gentleman of gentlemen was he who had land, and family title-deeds, and an old family place, and family portraits, and family embarrassments, and a family absence of any usual employment. He was beginning even to look down upon peers, since so many men of much less consequence than himself had been made lords; and, having stood and been beaten three or four times for his county, he was of opinion that a seat in the House was rather a mark of bad breeding.

And to get out of debt by trying to sell one of his properties and disembarrass the other, he too is prepared to sell to Melmotte and wait humiliatingly in his office until the financial giant is ready to receive him. Roger Carbury, squire of Carbury Manor, is the one man of probity who cannot be bought, who represents the best characteristics of the old-style gentry and openly protests against the onslaught of financial corruption that is degrading London society. It is not Melmotte himself so much he despises. His own words to Lady Carbury when she tries to excuse her son Felix's probable marriage to Marie Melmotte and confesses she can understand he should not like "those people", express his feelings: "I don't dislike them. How should I dislike people that I never saw? I dislike those who seek their society simply because they have the reputation of being rich." And when she protests that she is hoping for the marriage because of her anxiety to see her prodigal son settled and no longer "a disgrace to the name and to the family," he replies:

> 'You will never get me to say that I think the family will be benefited by a marriage with the daughter of Mr. Melmotte. I look upon him as dirt in the gutter. To me, in my old-fashioned way, all his money, if he has it, can make no difference. When there is a question of marriage, people at any rate should know something of each other. Who knows anything of this man? Who can be sure that she is his daughter?'
> 'He would give her her fortune when she married.'
> 'Yes; it all comes to that. Men say openly that he is an adventurer and a swindler. No one pretends to think that he is a gentleman. There is a consciousness among all who speak of him that he amasses his money not by honest trade, but by unknown tricks, — as does a card-sharper. He is one whom we would not admit into our kitchens, much less to our tables,

on the score of his own merits. But because he has learned the art of making money, we not only put up with him, but settle upon his carcase as so many birds of prey.'

But his bitterest and finest condemnation comes later when he has heard of the attempted elopement of Marie with Felix and is discussing it with his friend Hepworth.

> 'You think Melmotte will turn out a failure.'
> 'A failure! Of course he's a failure, whether rich or poor; — a miserable imposition, a hollow vulgar fraud from beginning to end, — too insignificant for you and me to talk of, were it not that his position is a sign of the degeneracy of the age. What are we coming to when such as he is an honoured guest at our tables?'
> 'At just a table here and there,' suggested his friend.
> 'No; — it is not that. You can keep your house free from him, and so can I mine. But we set no example to the nation at large. They who do set the example go to his feasts, and of course he is seen at theirs in return. And yet these leaders of the fashion know, — at any rate they believe, — that he is what he is because he has been a swindler greater than other swindlers. What follows as a natural consequence? Men reconcile themselves to swindling. Though they themselves mean to be honest, dishonesty of itself is no longer odious to them. Then there comes the jealousy that others should be growing rich with the approval of all the world, — and the natural aptitude to do what all the world approves. It seems to me that the existence of a Melmotte is not compatible with a wholesome state of things in general.'

It is through the Longestaffes, even more than through Melmotte, that Trollope reveals an aspect of Victorian family life as revolting as anything done by Samuel Butler without any of the latter's partisan, shrill, exaggerated ferocity, without any apparent wish to attack the conformities of the society he is describing, but which in its very urbanity and objectivity is as horrifying an exposure to any perceptive reader. I refer to the heavy parental pressures and control, the boredom, the internicine feuds, the petty tyranny, the rivalries and jealousies: above all, with daughters, the everlasting, wearing, soul-destroying struggle to escape from parental moral blackmail and despotism by marriage with anybody at any cost. Sophia Longestaffe, the elder daughter, feels herself smugly superior to Georgina, her younger sister, because she has hooked a man while 'Georgey' is left stranded. In this poor girl we get one of the most harrowing and pathetic examples of the unloved, desperate spinster in fiction. Crushed by her callous father, grumbled at by her ineffectual mother, crowed over by her sister, when her father refuses to make his customary return to London and society from their dull country estate and she sees all hope of meeting any possible husband frustrated, being a spirited girl she defies the family, takes the law into her own hands and gets herself invited by Madame Melmotte to live with them even though she loathes and despises them and loses her friends because of it. But anything is better than being out of the marriage mart. When younger, she had turned down more than one proposal, not considering the makers of them fashionable or rich enough for her high-flown ambitions. But now at thirty she is learning to become less choosey, and in desperation she accepts the offer of a certain Ezekiel Brehgert, 'a fat, greasy man of fifty' who is not only a widower with a couple of teenage children, but a Jew. In spite of his accredited wealth, at the idea of such 'a humiliating alliance' (the *Jew* especially sticks in their throat) her family and friends profess themselves outraged, and combine to boycott her and make her life hell. Her father forces an interview with the man, who is decent and honourable enough in all conscience, and forbids the marriage. Forced to choose between breaking off the engagement or being ostracized by her family and that London society for which she craves, she chooses the former — a choice made somewhat easier by her learning that Brehgert is not quite as rich as she had supposed when he confesses to her that if she marries him she will have to do without his 'luxurious villa at Fulham' and content herself with one house. Forced now to live in the dull home in the country with the family, she has to endure the triumphant hymeneals of her sister, the callous indifference of her father and the irritating twittering of her mother. Finally, driven to desperation, and determined at all costs not to be left on the spinster shelf, she runs off with Mr Batherbolt, the curate of the next parish, and after deliberately missing her sister's wedding she returns a month later as Mrs Batherbolt.

Superficially her story has the Jane Austen ring about it: the spinster in search of a husband. But it is far removed from the Austen gentle badinage and irony — a few false moves, a tolerant laugh and wedding bells. This is no social comedy. The frustration, the anger, the despair, the victimization of the girl are thrown up in fierce outline together with the domestic relationships and society which are the cause of them. Georgina is far from being a likeable character. Her snobbery, imposed on her from her upbringing, is to a large extent the cause of her marriage failures and embittered spirit. Nevertheless one is driven to feeling profound pity for her.

But to return to the central figure, Melmotte. His greatest financial success, his most dazzling triumph, comes when the American Hamilton K. Fisker, another would-be big business tycoon and US robber baron, 'smoking a very large cigar which he kept constantly turning in his mouth, and half of which was inside his teeth', and speaking 'with a fine, sharp nasal twang', persuades Melmotte to come in with his American company in launching a gigantic project: no less than the formation of the Great South Central Pacific and Mexican Railway, supposedly to run from Salt Lake City, through New Mexico and Arizona, and terminate at Vera Cruz. The company is floated, shares are advertised and the vast new commercial balloon is inflated. 'The City' is intoxicated by this modern South Sea Bubble. All Melmotte's business acquaintances and hangers-on buy shares with the conviction that they are to make themselves rich beyond the dreams of avarice. Trollope's pen is vitriolic.

On Saturday, the 19th April, Fisker was to leave London on his return to New York, and on the 18th a farewell dinner was to be given to him at the club. Mr. Melmotte was asked to meet him, and on such an occasion all the resources of the club were to be brought forth. Lord Alfred Grendall was also to be a guest, and Mr. Cohenlupe, who went about a good deal with Melmotte. Nidderdale, Carbury, Montague, and Miles Grendall were members of the club, and gave the dinner. No expense was spared. Herr Vossner purveyed the viands and wines, — and paid for them. Lord Nidderdale took the chair, with Fisker on his right hand, and Melmotte on his left, and, for a fast-going young lord, was supposed to have done the thing well. There were only two toasts drunk, to the healths of Mr. Melmotte and Mr. Fisker, and two speeches were of course made by them. Mr. Melmotte may have been held to have clearly proved the genuineness of that English birth which he claimed by the awkwardness and incapacity which he showed on the occasion. He stood with his hands on the table and with his face turned to his plate blurted out his assurance that the floating of this railway company would be one of the greatest and most successful commercial operations ever conducted on either side of the Atlantic. It was a great thing, — a very great thing; — he had no hesitation in saying that it was one of the greatest things out. He didn't believe a greater thing had ever come out. He was happy to give his humble assistance to the furtherance of so great a thing, — and so on. These assertions, not varying much one from the other, he jerked out like so many separate interjections, endeavouring to look his friends in the face at each, and then turning his countenance back to his plate as though seeking for inspiration for the next attempt. He was not eloquent; but the gentlemen who heard him remembered that he was the great Augustus Melmotte, that he might probably make them all rich men, and they cheered him to the echo. Lord Alfred had reconciled himself to be called by his Christian name, since he had been put in the way of raising two or three hundred pounds on the security of shares which were to be allotted to him, but of which in the flesh he had as yet seen nothing. Wonderful are the ways of trade! If one can only get the tip of one's little finger into the right pie, what noble morsels, what rich esculents, will stick to it as it is extracted!

When Melmotte sat down Fisker made his speech, and it was fluent, fast, and florid. Without giving it word for word, which would be tedious, I could not adequately set before the reader's eye the speaker's pleasing picture of world-wide commercial love and harmony which was to be produced by a railway from Salt Lake City to Vera Cruz, nor explain the extent of gratitude from the world at large which might be claimed by, and would finally be accorded to, the great firms of Melmotte & Co. of London, and Fisker, Montague, and Montague of San Francisco. Mr. Fisker's arms were waved gracefully about. His head was turned now this way and now that, but never towards his plate. It was very well done. But there was more faith in one ponderous word from Mr. Melmotte's mouth than in all the American's oratory.

There was not one of them then present who had not after some fashion been given to understand that his fortune was to be made, not by the construction of the railway, but by the floating of the railway shares. They had all whispered to each other their convictions on this head. Even Montague did not beguile himself into an idea that he was really a director in a company to be employed in the making and working of a railway. People out of doors were to be advertised into buying shares, and they who were so to say indoors were to have the privilege of manufacturing the shares thus to be sold. That was to be their work, and they all knew it. But now, as there were eight of them collected together, they talked of humanity at large and of the coming harmony of nations.

It was not, I am sure, merely for the sake of variety that Trollope introduced the two American characters Fisker and, later, Mrs Hurtle. He had travelled in the States, and his observant eye and ear had taught him something of the Yankee mentality. Financial success and the power it brings were their gods, and they were prepared to put on a pinnacle any man, however low-born, ignorant and illiterate, who achieved this be-all and end-all: in fact, the lower born, more ignorant and illiterate he was the more they rejoiced, approved and applauded as a puff to their country's 'democracy', freedom and initiative at the expense of the British version of these virtues, making it and its aristocrats and intellectuals look old-fashioned and decadent and 'not worth a dime'. Trollope was a genial, kindly, tolerant man, prepared to accept anyone in a friendly spirit whatever his nationality. There was no Podsnappery about him. As I have already commented, his very first books together with his character Phineas Finn show a sympathy with and understanding of the Irish quite remarkable for his time. Similarly with Americans. He was not prepared to regard them *a priori* as objects of opprobrium and dislike or, like Dickens, make them subjects for caricature. He had one of the most essential of a novelist's gifts — objectivity, so that, as in *The American Senator*, he was able to portray their good points. But his acute perception of character told him that the claims of American big business that their aim in making vast fortunes was primarily for the betterment of the human race, was sheer bunkum, a pious cover-up, a gloss of hypocrisy put on thick and slab to fool most of the people most of the time. Dollars in huge quantities were their prime ambition, he saw, and was of the opinion they would sell weapons to any country wishing to wipe its neighbours out of existence so long as a profit was made from the deal. The Great South Central Pacific and Mexican Railway scheme was just another case in point: dollars first, benefit to progress and humanity a secondary euphemism. Hence the vicious irony.

With Mrs Hurtle he made an *amende honorable*. She is a forceful but attractive character, deliberately created as the typical emancipated American woman in order to make the male-dominated Englishwomen around her appear vapid. The scenes between her and her former lover, Paul Montague, are among the best in the book. She may have been divorced from a brute of a husband, or even, as rumour had it, shot him in a duel, but she is true to Paul even after he has transferred his affections to Henrietta Carbury; and the reader may be forgiven for considering him to be a fool in his choice. She deserved happiness more than he did.

To come back to Melmotte yet again. The shares of the venture sell like hot cakes, and the financier, riding the crest of his wave, swells like the frog in the fable. But in the end it proves his undoing. Intoxicated by his success and power, he decides to propose himself as the Conservative candidate for Westminster in a by-election, and support for his ambition is not slow or weak in being canvassed by 'clamorous assertions of his unprecedented commercial greatness. It seemed that there was but one virtue in the world, commercial enterprise, and that Melmotte was its prophet.' For those who know that to Trollope to become a Member of Parliament was the most signal honour an Englishman could claim, his words, his admission that such a man as Melmotte could even be considered, are bitter indeed. He succeeds in getting in by a slender majority, and takes his place in the House. But by then the bubble is about to burst. He engages in more and more vast transactions, entertains on an ever-increasing lavish scale, buys up property and, drunk with power, begins to treat his underlings, and his wife and daughter, like dirt. Rumours of swindling start and spread. Hard up for ready cash, he tries to bully his daughter into surrendering to him funds he had taken out in her name. When, looking ahead to her own future, she refuses in the teeth of threats and physical violence, he forges her name and that of a witness. The new railroad shares fall, he himself is now threatened by the law, and with ruin and dishonour staring him in the face, rather than accept imprisonment and disgrace, he kills himself.

Melmotte is not only a tremendous figure in himself: he is the pivot, the axle, round which the whole vast set of characters revolve. As I have admitted in this survey, Trollope, while great in vision, is frequently poor in design, in the carrying out of that vision, too often sacrificing it in order to fill his three volumes, improvising episodes, characters and sub-plots which are irrelevant and mere padding. Here, however, the linkages between the different strands of the story are exploited with the consummate art of the sonata movements of the great classical composers. He uses Melmotte as the spider lurking at the centre of his web drawing in all the flies, as the common chain that links the various episodes and protagonists, directly or indirectly. Lady Carbury's worthless son is loved by Melmotte's daughter, Marie, and they plan to elope, only he hasn't the guts even to do that. Georgina Longestaffe goes to live with the Melmottes and meets

Brehgert because her father has become involved in a property transaction with Melmotte. Nidderdale, Felix Carbury and the rest of the wastrels who haunt the night-clubs are shareholders in the new rail-building venture. Even the country folk of Suffolk are credible and play their part in the complex panorama. Ruby Ruggles, beloved by the tongue-tied rustic John Crump, is seduced by Felix Carbury and, thrown out by her grandfather with whom she lives, runs off to London to live as a servant with her aunt who has as a boarder Mrs Hurtle. Paul Montague is not only one of Fisker's chain gang but in love with Henrietta Carbury in rivalry with his greatest friend, Roger Carbury. Even the Catholic priest, Father Barham, who on a casual reading may appear to be unnecessary to the story, can be seen in retrospect as yet another testimony of the universal climate of corruption, the moral degradation of contemporary society. For Barham, although fully aware of Melmotte's evil genius, is prepared to go to him and beg a gift for his church. As with the rest, with him the end justifies the means. So-called religion is no better than flesh and the devil, is Trollope's message. It is his most savage crack of the scoriating whip; the last turn of the screw.

The novel, whether Trollope's greatest or not, is certainly his most ambitious, and should be put into the hands of those critics who persist in telling us that, a later Jane Austen, he accepts unquestioningly the ethics of his time and is good only as escapism from the frightening world of reality. Socialists too should rejoice in it. In no other English novel have the less desirable aspects of capitalism and the whole Victorian ethos been so savagely and so unforgettably unmasked.

THE PRIME MINISTER

Politics, depending on one's own interest or lack of it and the state of the country and parties, can be either the most temper-trying and vital of obsessions, or a bore. For many, this boredom can become even more complete when the political scene is shifted into the past, i.e. it has become a part of history. To others this same shift enhances it. *Quot homines, tot sententiae*. Presented skilfully, history can be made as interesting as fiction, whether done as 'straight' history or as historical romance. But to introduce contemporary politics in a general sense into a novel is to court disaster. And in the last two novels of the Palliser series Trollope not only courts it: he marries it. He completely fails to understand that politics as such in a novel can only be made interesting through personality — by which I mean through the characters themselves. We are made interested in the Irish tenant-right issue brought up in *Phineas Finn*, for example, not so much because of the intrinsic rights and wrongs of it, but simply because Phineas's career hangs by it; and such political issues as are raised in the earlier novels are interesting to us because we see them through the eyes of interesting people such as George Vavasor, Lady Laura, Palliser himself and Lady Glencora. But in these later novels too often we are expected to be held in thrall by the political parties' ups and downs as thrown at us by men who are little more than constantly repeated names — the Barrington Erles, the Rattrays, Robys, the

Bonteens and the rest — about whom the reader knows little and cares less. The situation is similar to that when we learn from the daily media — and how we are made to learn! — of the accidents, tragedies and farces occurring the world over every day. We say to ourselves "What a shame!" and give them a passing moment's thought, then probably turn to something which interests us personally far more, even if it is only the latest cricket scores or Wimbledon results. But if someone we know is involved in some reported accident or tragic affair, then we sit up and take notice. The whole art of fiction lies in that difference, that contrast. Personality, character, must come first and throw their grip on the reader. If we cannot interest ourselves in the protagonists of the story then the whole thing becomes leather and prunella. And the greater part of *The Prime Minister* is just that. "What makes everybody and everything so dead?" Sir Orlando Drought asks Mr Boffin as they walk together from the House after a dull session. One would like to pass the question over to its 'onlie begetter'!

But this is only the general malaise of this novel. There are more special and particular points which mar it too. Now that Burgo Fitzgerald is out of the way, their three children 'arrived' and middle age coming on, the Pallisers themselves inevitably settle down to humdrum married life. They still have their differences, but they are trivia. The Duke now being Prime Minister, Lady Glencora, to match his grandeur and keep him in the forefront of public speculation, decides to turn the huge dull castle of Omnium into a splendid gathering place for the élite of the day; so she tears the place apart, does it all up and invites hundreds of guests. But in doing so she completely miscalculates her husband's reactions. Being fundamentally a shy retiring man, and dull and uncommunicative in private life, he fails to appreciate, and even resents, her attempts to bolster his position, while the constant hordes of visitors and the changes being made to the hall of his forefathers revolt him. So there are rows; but these rows are mere domestic bickers in which the reader can feel little involvement. Furthermore, the Duke is bored by his job which involves no real brainwork such as he loves, and he spends his time secretly longing to be Chancellor again so that he can wear himself out over the problems of decimal coinage and, being bored, he himself is boring. Glencora too is losing the pristine vitality of her youth and her fascinating dangerous ingenuousness, and is only half the personality she originally was; and as the Duke shines only by her reflected light anyway, and her light is now dim, the whole set-up is depressingly mediocre indeed.

Intermixed with all this is the Lopez story. This, recounting the infatuation of Emily Wharton for the half-Portuguese adventurer Ferdinand Lopez, although in parts containing some of the most interesting episodes of the book, is not altogether convincing. That such a girl, totally kept down by her typically 'heavy' Victorian father and with no worldly experience, should fall for a handsome plausible adventurer is true enough to life. And her awakening from her romantic dream to the grim truth that she has married herself to a callous selfish brute is well done, even if it cannot compare with the similar tale of emotional disintegration portrayed by Anne Brontë in *The Tenant of Wildfell Hall*. What is unconvincing is the linkage between the Lopez story and the Pallisers via the election at Silverbridge. One simply cannot believe that an aristocrat like Lady Glencora would take Lopez seriously or allow herself to be caught in the trap which exposes her to her husband's just wrath. Nor — though the question must remain not proven — do men of Lopez's nature throw themselves under trains when their luck is out. Their motto rather is 'cut and come again', and they generally end up philosophical paupers or very wealthy men.

In any case, whatever sympathy one may feel for Emily Wharton is dissipated by her behaviour and her character. The Victorian novelists have given us some pretty dreadful 'heroines', but of them all none — not even Amelia Sedley, Agnes Wickfield, Eleanor Bold, Rachel Ray or Laura Pendennis — can hold a candle to her. As a daughter, although she stands up to her dogmatic father and admits her love for the detested Lopez, the meekness of her replies to his refusals to allow her to accept or so much as see the man make one long to strangle her. As a wife, in their quarrels, and particularly in the one over Arthur Fletcher's perfectly innocent letter, she can let him get away with the most unjust accusations and contemptible sneers ("You are a child, my dear, and must allow me to dictate to you what you ought to think in such a matter as this.") with scarcely a murmur of protest. As a widow she wears her mourning weeds until even her respectable Victorian friends are sick of the sight of them. And though at long last she realizes she has come round to love her constant lover, Arthur Fletcher, she cannot bring herself to encourage him because 'It was forbidden her, she believed, by all the canons of womanhood, even to think of love again. There ought to be nothing left for her but crape and weepers . . . . A woman, she told herself, had no right to a second chance in life, after having made such a shipwreck of herself in the first.' One can only feel sorry for Arthur Fletcher and wonder what so sensible a man can see in her.

After closing the book and going over the novel in one's mind one finds it difficult to recall a single memorable scene. And that, I think, must be the ultimate judgement on it — that, and perhaps the thought that the novel is hardly worth the £2,500 he was paid for it.

In all fairness to Trollope there is one subtle mitigating aspect of the novel which helps to redeem it and should not be omitted in any discussion of it, and this is the depiction through the career of Palliser (now the central character) of the irony of political life. Not only does he fail as Prime Minister because of his refusal to sacrifice his code of honour, but he is unaware that by his very principles of equality and justice he is helping to destroy the Liberal Party he represents. The narrative might fail, but Trollope's political acumen and ironic sense never did.

IS HE POPENJOY?

I can only describe the novel with this absurd and off-putting title as, if not quite the worst, at any rate one of the silliest Trollope wrote. Writing it can only be accounted a waste of time and genius. This story, whose plot turns on whether the son of the Marquis of Brotherton — indubitably the most revolting human being Trollope ever gave us, not even excepting Hugh Clavering or Louis Scatcherd — born in mysterious circumstances in Italy of an Italian Marchesa, is legitimate or illegitimate and so entitled or not entitled as the eldest son to be called Lord Popenjoy, is a theme which can have no interest for any adult mind. Moreover Trollope makes the marquis's character and behaviour so inexplicably inhuman as to be beyond credibility. He turns his mother, three sisters and younger brother, Lord George Germain, out of their family home for no other reason than that he has decided to come to England and live there for a time with his Italian wife and child. He insults everyone he meets, has no culture, no interests, and finds life such a bore that he does not care whether he lives or dies; and when finally, following the death of his young son and separation from his wife, he does die at the age of forty-four, alone and unloved in his Como cottage, all his family and acquaintances sigh with relief, Lord George becomes the Marquis and his wife Lady George Germain, and their son the real and only Popenjoy. The whole conception is sheer triviality.

This is a pity in that the novel contains some good characterization. The Dean of Brotherton, a carbon copy of Archdeacon Grantly in some ways, is especially sympathetic and convincing as a militant worldly churchman. His daughter Mary is well drawn too, and the gradual progression from her initial maiden inanity to married self-assurance and the development of a mind of her own which enables her to stand up to her prig and bore of a husband, Lord George, has the true Trollope touch. But these apart, the rest are puppets. We might perhaps except Adelaide De Baron, Lord George's first love who, after turning him down, tries to make the best of both worlds by marrying an older man for money and then doing her cold-blooded best to seduce him after he is married to Mary. Her frank amorality and vitality come as a refreshing change from the dull sobriety of most of the others, and probably shocked many of the book's first readers.

Finally, weakening and padding the book even further, Trollope introduces the Baroness Banmann and 'an American female', *Doctor* Olivia Q. Fleabody, who unamicably organize and run a 'Rights of Woman Institute: Established for the Relief of the Disabilities of Females', which by 'friendly tongues to friendly ears' was called The College or The Institute; 'but the irreverent public was apt to speak of the building generally as the "Female Disabilities".' Olivia Q. Fleabody, with her spectacles, tunic and trousers, is of course a caricature of the new-style aggressive loud-voiced anti-male American female. Nevertheless, it is all pointless and feeble and dragged in as satire merely to proclaim the writer's contempt for the ideals of Women's Lib. As he had already shown in previous novels Trollope deprecated the Victorian males' trampling on and tyrannous authority over their womenfolk as strongly as anyone and more strongly than most; but though he was prepared to demand equality of respect for women he had no time for the more aggressive who went about preaching for the right to do all that men did. To him women had equal place and rights, but these as wives and mothers and in the home.

The novel is not one to recommend to anyone expressing a wish to begin reading Trollope or even to extend their knowledge of him.

THE AMERICAN SENATOR

A first impression after reading the novel may well make us wonder why Trollope gave it its off-putting title which he insisted on retaining in the teeth of his publisher's attempts to make him change it. Would not *Arabella Trefoil* have been more apt in that the title would have been that of its most important and outstanding character? But reflection should help us to understand the point Trollope was making, namely, to let us see through the eyes of a foreigner (and no foreigner is more foreign than your American when it comes to English matters) customs and manners which, sacrosanct to us, seem absurd to an intelligent outside observer. And so through the eyes of Elias Gotobed, Senator of Mikewa, 'who had never been in England before and was especially anxious to study the British Constitution and to see the ways of Britons with his own eyes', Trollope is able to make us smile not only at the Senator's bewilderment over such anomalies as fox hunting, election of MPs, the sale and purchase of church livings, royalty and aristocracy, the House of Lords, the antediluvian heating systems in ducal mansions and stately homes and other shibboleths of the British, all of which seem to the worthy man as incomprehensible as cricket or our monetary system, £.s.d., and to be monstrous anachronisms in a modern world in which America alone presumes perfection, but also to make us consider in turn whether such anomalies should not be first laughed at and then done away with. This is typical of Trollope's fair-mindedness, objectivity and ironic sense. He was always able to see both sides of the coin.

Further, it must be said in defence of Trollope's characterization that he does not fall into the error of Dickens in *Martin Chuzzlewit* by making the American a caricature. He is perfectly credible, and tries to be fair-minded in his observations and criticisms; but in going around with his constant and earnest queries and determination to be given the facts and nothing but the facts, and giving the impression that everything is so much better done and run in the States, he only succeeds in setting British backs up. The love-hate relationship and clashing traditions between the two countries, who scarcely have the same language in common, is well brought out in chapter 51 — 'The Senator's Second Letter.'

> The Senator was, in truth, unhappy as he returned to town. The intimacy between him and the late Secretary of Legation at his capital had arisen from a mutual understanding between them that each was to be allowed to see the faults and to admire the virtues of their two countries, and that conversation between them was to be based on the mutual system. But nobody can, in truth, endure to be told of shortcomings, either on his own part or on that of his country. He himself can abuse himself, or his country; but he cannot endure it from alien lips. Mr. Gotobed had hardly said a word about England which Morton himself might not have said; but such words coming from an American had been too much even for the guarded temper of an unprejudiced and phlegmatic Englishman. The Senator, as he returned alone to London, understood something of this; and when a few days later he heard that the friend who had quarrelled with him was ill, he was discontented with himself and sore at heart.
>
> But he had his task to perform, and he meant to perform it to the best of his ability. In his own country he had heard vehement abuse of the old country from the lips of politicians, and

had found at the same time almost on all sides great social admiration for the people so abused. He had observed that every Englishman of distinction was received in the States as a demigod, and that some who were not very great in their own land had been converted into heroes in his. English books were read there; English laws were obeyed there; English habits were cultivated, often at the expense of American comfort. And yet it was the fashion among orators to speak of the English as a wornout, stupid, and enslaved people. He was a thoughtful man, and all this had perplexed him;

And later in chapter 77, 'The Senator's Lecture', we have:

When an intelligent Japanese travels in Great Britain or an intelligent Briton in Japan, he is struck with no wonder at national differences. He is on the other hand rather startled to find how like his strange brother is to him in many things. Crime is persecuted, wickedness is condoned, and goodness treated with indifference in both countries. Men care more for what they eat than anything else, and combine a closely defined idea of meum with a lax perception as to tuum. Barring a little difference of complexion and feature the Englishman would make a good Japanese, or the Japanese a first-class Englishman. But when an American comes to us, or a Briton goes to the States, each speaking the same language, using the same cookery, governed by the same laws, and wearing the same costume, the differences which present themselves are so striking that neither can live six months in the country of the other without a holding up of the hands and a torrent of exclamations. And in nineteen cases out of twenty the surprise and the ejaculations take the place of censure. The intelligence of the American, displayed through the nose, worries the Englishman. The unconscious self-assurance of the Englishman, not always unaccompanied by a sneer, irritates the American. They meet as might a lad from Harrow and another from Mr. Brumby's successful mechanical cramming establishment. The Harrow boy cannot answer a question, but is sure that he is the proper thing, and is ready to face the world on that assurance. Mr. Brumby's paragon is shocked at the other's inaptitude for examination, but is at the same time tortured by envy of he knows not what. In this spirit we Americans and Englishmen go on writing books about each other, sometimes with bitterness enough, but generally with good final results. But in the meantime there has sprung up a jealousy which makes each inclined to hate the other at first sight. Hate is difficult and expensive, and between individuals soon gives place to love. 'I cannot bear Americans as a rule, though I have been very lucky myself with a few friends.' Who in England has not heard that form of speech, over and over again? And what Englishman has travelled in the States without hearing abuse of all English institutions uttered amidst the pauses of a free-handed hospitality which has left him nothing to desire?

Here Trollope gets to the nub of the matter. No one is more critical of his own country than your true-born Englishman. Among his own kind he is prepared to curse the climate, denigrate the plumbing and sanitation, run down the hotels and boarding-houses, defame the House of Lords, vilify the House of Commons, lampoon our MPs, condemn the whole legal system, decry Royalty and declare the country is going to the dogs. But let a breath of similar criticism come from a foreigner and he bristles at once. And our (to some) hypocritical self-criticism and derogation and national dislike of overt patriotism and flag waving or anything that smacks of smugness and self-glorification, puts many Americans out of count with us. Trollope understood this clearly, so that when at the end the Senator makes his carefully compiled and, to his thinking, fair-minded speech, drawing his audience's attention to various British anomalies, eccentricities and short-comings, he is sent away with a large flea in his ear. The poor man, who bore no animus against us, simply had not understood that such criticism, if made at all, should be done in a light-handed, half-humorous way. But the Senator was an intelligent and serious man, and much too heavy-handed!

So much understood, one may perhaps waive criticism of the novel's title. But unfortunately one cannot do the same with the tedious needlessly detailed introductory chapters. Of all 'the 48' this, I think, in this regard is the worst. The first two chapters, devoted to explaining the genealogies of the Morton and Masters families is enough to drive a reader into a state of utter frustration and bewilderment. One can only marvel how the author himself was able to invent and remember the interminably long and complex relationships of the characters, and to credit him with a computer mind. As I commented earlier when reviewing *Doctor Thorne*, I have never been able to accept his own self-defence in the matter. Novelists, of course, must know their characters' blood and bone before achieving any convincing creation, but that is no justification why their readers should be regaled with lengthy laborious details of their antecedents which include descriptions of the mannerisms and doings of ancestors who are in their graves before the time of the story commences. Besides, many of Trollope's own novels belie his defence and make it very lame indeed: one need mention only *Barchester Towers*, *The Small House*, *The Belton Estate* and *Harry Hotspur* as proof. That all this criticism should have to be made about the novel is a pity because, like *Daniel Deronda*, it is worth reading for the sake of one character alone: in the case of George Eliot's novel that of Gwendolen Harleth, in this of Trollope's Arabella Trefoil. She and her story form the peaks of the narrative, and Arabella must be reckoned among the most fascinating of Trollope's gallery of women. She is a sort of amalgam of Alexandrina De Courcy, Lizzie Eustace and Lucinda Roanoke, and in many ways an anticipation of Gwendolen Harleth. Beautiful and attractive to men, but by nature and circumstance cold, selfish and calculating, and moreover unstable in that she is the only offspring of an unhappy marriage and divorced parents and forced to live in near poverty with a mother she despises, she is driven to seeing possible prey in every rich unmarried man she meets. On her arrival in England from the States she is supposed to be 'conditionally' engaged to John Morton (the 'conditions' being of course monetary), British attaché in Washington and Squire of Bragton Park. But on being given the hospitality of his mansion, which has become somewhat dilapidated during his long absence, and seeing him for the first time among his own people, many of whom are more 'aristocratic' than himself, she finds both the man and his estate less to be coveted than she had imagined. And when soon afterwards she and her mother are invited by Lord Rufford to spend a few days at Rufford Hall, she senses a challenge and a new hope. But she has to tread warily. Her supposed fiancé is becoming a little touchy by her coolness towards him, and her problem is to keep him dangling while she goes searching for a more affluent lover. To jump at Lord Rufford's invitation, presented via John Morton himself, would be tactless and sure to arouse resentment and suspicion. With feminine duplicity and cunning, therefore, she forces her mother, whom she completely dominates (Gwendolen Harleth again. One is forced to ask: did George Eliot, whom we know to have admired Trollope, find her inspiration for her heroine in Arabella? There are differences, of course, but also remarkable parallels) to accept the invitation in their name, thus placing the onus on her. The chapter describing their arrival at Rufford Park ends tersely: 'Then they turned in at Lord Rufford's gates; and as they were driven up beneath the oaks through the gloom, both mother and daughter thought how charming it would be to be mistress of such a park.' The few days spent there strengthen her resolution.

During all this time not a word had been said of John Morton, the master of Bragton, the man to whose party these new comers belonged. Lady Augustus and Arabella clearly understood that John Morton was only a peg on which the invitation to them had been hung. The feeling that it was so grew upon them with every word that was spoken, — and also the conviction that he must be treated like a peg at Rufford. The sight of the hangings of the room, so different to the old-fashioned dingy curtains at Bragton, the brilliancy of the mirrors, all the decorations of the place, the very blaze from the big grate, forced upon the girl's feelings a conviction that this was her proper sphere. Here she was, being made much of as a new comer, and here if possible she must remain. Everything smiled on her with gilded dimples, and these were the smiles she valued. As the softness of the cushions sank into her heart, and mellow nothingness from well-trained voices greeted her ears, and the air of wealth and idleness floated about her cheeks, her imagination rose within her and assured her that she could secure something better than Bragton. The cautions with which she had armed herself faded away. This, — this was the kind of thing for which she had been striving. As a girl of spirit was it not worth while to make another effort even though there might be danger? Aut Caesar aut nihil. She knew nothing about Caesar, but she declared to herself that she would be Lady Rufford before the tardy wheels which brought the Senator and Mr. Morton had stopped at the door.

The emotional situation begins to clarify itself, to come to a head.

In the meantime the conversation between Lord Rufford and Arabella was very different in its tone, though on the same subject. He was certainly very much struck with her, not probably ever waiting to declare to himself that she was the most beautiful woman he had ever seen in his life, but still feeling towards her an attraction which for the time was strong. A very clever girl would frighten him; a very horsey girl would disgust him; a very quiet girl would bore him; or a very noisy girl annoy him. With a shy girl he could never be at his ease, not enjoying the labour of overcoming such a barrier; and yet he looked to be able to feel that any female intimacy which he admitted was due to his own choice and not to that of the young woman. Arabella Trefoil was not very clever, but she had given all her mind to this peculiar phase of life, and, to use a common phrase, knew what she was about. She was quite alive to the fact that different men require different manners in a young woman; and as she had adapted herself to Mr. Morton at Washington, so could she at Rufford adapt herself to Lord Rufford. At the present moment the lord was in love with her, as much as he was wont to be in love.

The nub of Rufford's character lies in those last words — *as much as he was wont to be in love*. Rufford is not a romantic young man ready to fall for the first attractive woman. He is thirty, mature and experienced, and moreover one of those British sporting types (Jane Austen drew one in John Thorpe in *Northanger Abbey*) who thought more of their horses and hunting than women. He is perfectly aware that any unmarried young woman in England would give her eyes to have him, with his wealth and his title, and while willing to indulge in a little gentle flirtation, has no intention of being hooked. He knows that Arabella is after him, and she knows that he knows; but she cannot afford to wait, to play her game wisely and patiently. With Rufford on the stage and Morton in the wings she has to rush her fences, and it is this, combined with his temperament, that brings about her downfall. The climax comes when they meet for the second time at her uncle's place. Knowing his passion for hunting she has ridden out with him and taken part in a hunt, and after a long and tiring day, quite exhausted, she returns home alone with him in a post-chaise. It is now or never, and she is prepared to throw everything on the die.

'Afraid of gloves?' said he, drawing nearer to her. They might pull him as they liked by his coat-tails, but as he was in a postchaise with her he must make himself agreeable. She shook her head and laughed as she looked at him through the gloom. Then, of course, he kissed her.

'Lord Rufford, what does this mean?'

'Don't you know what it means?'

'Hardly.'

'It means that I think you the jolliest girl out. I never liked anybody so well as I do you.'

'Perhaps you never liked anybody?' said she.

'Well; — yes, I have; but I am not going to boast of what fortune has done for me in that way. I wonder whether you care for me?'

'Do you want to know?'

'I should like to know. You have never said that you did.'

'Because you have never asked me.'

'Am I not asking you now, Bella?'

'There are different ways of asking, — but there is only one way that you will get an answer from me. No; — no. I will not have it. I have allowed too much to you already. Oh, I am so tired.' Then she sank back almost into his arms, — but recovered herself very quickly. 'Lord Rufford,' she said, 'if you are a man of honour let there be an end of this. I am sure you do not wish to make me wretched.'

'I would do anything to make you happy.'

'Then tell me that you love me honestly, sincerely, with all your heart, — and I shall be happy.'

'You know I do.'

'Do you? Do you?' she said, and then she flung herself on to his shoulder, and for a while she seemed to faint. For a few minutes she lay there, and as she was lying she calculated whether it would be better to try at this moment to drive him to some clearer declaration, or to make use of what he had already said without giving him an opportunity of protesting that he had not meant to make her an offer of marriage. He had declared that he loved her honestly and with his whole heart. Would not that justify her in setting her uncle at him? And might it not be that the duke would carry great weight with him; — that the duke might induce him to utter the fatal word though she, were she to demand it now, might fail? As she thought of it all she affected to swoon, and almost herself believed that she was swooning. She was conscious, but hardly more than conscious, that he was kissing her; — and yet her brain was at work. She felt that he would be startled, repelled, perhaps disgusted, were she absolutely to demand more from him now. 'Oh, Rufford; — oh, my dearest,' she said as she woke up, and with her face close to his, so that he could look into her eyes and see their brightness even through the gloom. Then she extricated herself from his embrace with a shudder and a laugh. 'You would hardly believe how tired I am,' she said putting out her ungloved hand. He took it and drew her to him and there she sat in his arms for the short remainder of the journey.

He has fallen into her net — or so she imagines; but she is to learn with bitter tears that men like Lord Rufford are not caught so easily. As Trollope observes pithily: 'Miss Trefoil must have thought that kissing and proposing were the same thing. Other young ladies have, perhaps, before now made such a mistake. But this young lady had had much experience, and should have known better.' That night, in his bedroom, Lord Rufford began seriously considering his relationship and his feeling towards Arabella.

'He liked her well enough, but was certainly not in love with her. I doubt whether men are ever in love with girls who throw themselves into their arms. A man's love, till it has been chastened and fastened by the feeling of duty which marriage brings with it, is instigated mainly by the difficulty of pursuit' — another aspect Arabella had overlooked. A man hates the idea of being pursued, and when he thinks that this is what is happening he does what all animals do in like circumstances — he escapes. When the household rises next morning it is to discover that Lord Rufford, on the pretext of having to see a horse at Stamford, has gone.

Arabella understands the real reason very well, and swears to herself that, alone and unaided and friendless as she is, she will force him to keep his 'word', have him at any cost. "I have not done with him yet," she tells her mother fiercely when the latter dares to suggest she should give up the pursuit. The narration of her pursuit, climaxing in her forcing her way into Rufford Hall alone and confronting him (an unheard-of audacity for the time) is fascinating, and makes the rest of the episodes and characters tame by comparison.

Thus baldly outlined, her conduct and character must seem despicable beyond dispute. But Trollope puts in subtle mitigating touches: her fury with her mother who had surreptitiously negotiated an £8,000 payment from Lord Rufford as a peace offering ("And you did not spit at him!" she rages as she tears up the piece of paper); her genuine remorse and grief when John Morton dies, leaving her '£5,000 and his watch and chain and rings;' nor does he fail to let the reader understand that she is what she is not by her own nature alone but by the society which breeds her and her type.

> When Arabella Trefoil got back to Portugal Street after her visit to Rufford, she was ill. The effort she had made, the unaccustomed labour, and the necessity of holding herself aloft before the man who had rejected her, were together more than her strength could bear, and she was taken up to bed in a fainting condition. It was not till the next morning that she was able even to open the letter which contained the news of John Morton's legacy. When she had read the letter and realized the contents, she took to weeping in a fashion very unlike her usual habits. She was still in bed, and there she remained for two or three days, during which she had time to think of her past life, — and to think also a little of the future. Old Mrs. Green came to her once or twice a day, but she was necessarily left to the nursing of her own maid. Every evening Mounser Green called and sent up tender enquiries; but in all this there was very little to comfort her. There she lay with the letter in her hand, thinking that the only man who had endeavoured to be of service to her was he whom she had treated with unexampled perfidy. Other men had petted her, had amused themselves with her, and then thrown her over, had lied to her and laughed at her, till she had been taught to think that a man was a heartless, cruel, slippery animal, made indeed to be caught occasionally, but in the catching of which infinite skill was wanted, and in which infinite skill might be thrown away. But this man had been true to her to the last in spite of her treachery!
>
> She knew that she was heartless herself, and that she belonged to a heartless world; — but she knew also that there was a world of women who were not heartless. Such women had looked down upon her as from a great height, but she in return had been able to ridicule them. They had chosen their part, and she had chosen hers, — and had thought that she might climb to the glory of wealth and rank, while they would have to marry hard-working clergymen and briefless barristers. She had often been called upon to vindicate to herself the part she had chosen, and had always done so by magnifying in her own mind the sin of the men with whom she had to deal. At this moment she thought that Lord Rufford had treated her villainously, whereas her conduct to him had been only that which the necessity of the case required. To Lord Rufford

she had simply behaved after the manner of her class, heartless of course, but only in the way which the 'custom of the trade' justified. Each had tried to circumvent the other, and she as the weaker had gone to the wall. But John Morton had believed in her and loved her. Oh, how she wished that she had deserted her class, and clung to him, — even though she should now have been his widow! The legacy was a burden to her. Even she had conscience enough to be sorry for a day or two that he had named her in his will.

And what should she do with herself for the future? Her quarrel with her mother had been very serious, each swearing that under no circumstances would she again consent to live with the other. The daughter of course knew that the mother would receive her again should she ask to be received. But in such case she must go back with shortened pinions and blunted beak. Her sojourn with Mrs. Green was to last for one month, and at the end of that time she must seek for a home. If she put John Morton's legacy out to interest, she would now be mistress of a small income; — but she understood money well enough to know to what obduracy of poverty she would thus be subjected. As she looked the matter closer in the face the horrors became more startling and more manifest. Who would have her in their houses? Where should she find society, — where the possibility of lovers? What would be her life, and what her prospects? Must she give up for ever the game for which she had lived, and own that she had been conquered in the fight and beaten even to death? Then she thought over the long list of her past lovers, trying to see whether there might be one of the least desirable at whom she might again cast her javelins. But there was not one.

With her departure from the scene (with more hope of some happiness than was permitted to Becky Sharp or Gwendolen Harleth) the remainder of the story, i.e. the Senator's lecture and the long-delayed come-together of Reginald Morton and Mary Masters, seems anticlimax. The novel stands or falls by Arabella Trefoil. With Becky Sharp, Gwendolen Harleth and Moll Flanders she forms that great fictional quartet of women without a heart, who though fundamentally frigid, make men their prey, flout society and cut their way through life at the expense of all who happen to stand in their path. As in life, Arabella, like the others, finds the game not worth the small candle it brings her.

The creator's opinion of his characters is always worth knowing. In a reply to a friend who had praised the novel Trollope replied:

I have been, and still am, very much afraid of Arabella Trefoil . . . . The critics have to come, and they will tell me that she is unwomanly, unnatural, turgid, the creation of a morbid imagination . . . . But I swear I have known the woman . . . . all the traits, all the cleverness, all the patience, all the courage, all the self-abnegation — and all the failure . . . . Will such a one as Arabella Trefoil be damned, and if so, why? Think of her virtues: how she works, how true she is to her vocation, how little there is of self-indulgence, or idleness. I think that she will go to a third class heaven in which she will always be getting third class husbands.

And in fact the novel leaves her in a third class heaven as the wife of a young British Minister in Patagonia, still dreaming of Lord Rufford.

Although not one of his greatest novels, *The American Senator* can be recommended as being one of the best of Trollope's last phase.

THE DUKE'S CHILDREN

This, the last of the Palliser novels, is by far the least readable of the series, and is in fact one of the dullest and least inspired ever to come from Trollope's pen: so much so that it could almost pass for a pastiche done by a talented imitator. Reading it, one is made to think of a tennis champion of former days who tries to make a come-back. His tactics and knowledge of the game are as superb as ever, but his reactions are now slower and his stamina unequal to the demands made on it. One has the feeling too that with Lady Glencora (his own favourite character) gone from the scene, Trollope has lost heart in this attempt to wind the series up. The whole thing seems an effort. The Duke, from being at least a human being in the earlier novels, degenerates into a stupid old-fashioned pompous bore. His treatment of his son Silverbridge because he wants to enter Parliament as a Conservative instead of the invariable family Liberal, and of his daughter Lady Mary, because she has fallen in love with a decent young man who has no money, is so priggish, bigoted and narrow-minded that one longs to kick him. And the whole narrative is so ponderous, the dialogue so stilted, that one cannot care a brass farthing whether Silverbridge marries or does not marry the American girl, or Lady Mary get her Tregear. The characters talk and act like puppets, and the story never gets off the ground.

"You are nothing but a pack of cards!" one cries with Alice. In his essay 'Anthony Trollope' (1883) Henry James, who rated him highly, dismissed all his political novels as 'distinctly dull'. This is not true of the first three titles, but is partially true of the fourth, and altogether true of the penultimate and ultimate ones. Personally, I would advise readers to forget these latter and finish the series with *Phineas Finn*.

For, bluntly, Trollope now, in the last years of the seventies and with nearly 40 novels behind him, was creatively on the downward slope. Ironically his state was luminously analysed for the benefit of posterity in chapter XII of his *Autobiography* headed 'On Novels and the Art of Writing Them'. Solemnly offering 'advice to writers of fiction' he declares:

> I have from the first felt sure that the writer, when he sits down to commence his novel, should do so, not because he has to tell a story, but because he has a story to tell. The novelist's first novel will generally have sprung from the right cause. Some series of events, or some development of character, will have presented itself to his imagination — and this he feels so strongly that he thinks he can present his picture in strong and agreeable language to others . . . . But when that first novel has been received graciously by the public . . . . then the writer, naturally feeling that the writing of novels is within his grasp, looks about for something to tell in another. He cudgels his brains, not always successfully, and sits down to write, not because he has something which he burns to tell, but because he feels it to be incumbent on him to be telling something . . . .
>
> So it has been with many novelists, who, after some good work . . . have distressed their audience because they have gone on with their work till their work has become simply a trade with them . . . . They have at last become weary of that portion of a novelist's work which is of all the most essential to success. That a man as he grows old should feel the labour of writing to be a fatigue is natural enough. But a man to whom writing well has become a habit may write

well though he be fatigued. But the weary novelist refuses any longer to give his mind to that work of observation and reception from which has come his power, without which work his power cannot be continued . . . . There comes a time when he shuts his eyes and shuts his ears . . . . The things around cease to interest us, and we cannot exercise our minds upon them. To the novelist thus wearied there comes the demand for further novels. He does not know his own defect, and even if he did he does not wish to abandon his own profession. He still writes; but he writes because he has to tell a story, not because he has a story to tell. What reader of novels has not felt the 'woodenness' of this mode of telling? The characters do not live and move, but are cut out of blocks and are propped against the wall . . . . The reader can never feel — as he ought to feel — that only for that flame in the eye, only for that angry word, only for that moment of weakness, all might have been different. The course of the tale is one piece of stiff mechanism in which there is no room for a doubt.

Here in a nutshell is the explanation of the failure of so many potential novelists, and of the failure not only of *The Duke's Children* but of almost all the novels to come. For even the best of them have the touch of his genius only in isolated episodes. He was becoming 'the weary novelist' indeed.

JOHN CALDIGATE

The novel is partly the result of his Australian visit of 1871, and shows that wherever he travelled Trollope kept his eyes open and his observation alert.

David Caldigate and his son John live alone together in the former's 'moderate country house', Folking, near Cambridge, and on his 'moderate income of £3,000 a year'. (This information is typical Trollope. As in Jane Austen, people's incomes are always known and the figures given.) There are only the two of them because David Caldigate's wife and two young daughters had died before the story commences. (In passing one may remark that there seems little point in placing him in this tragic position unless it is to give a reason and some excuse for his harsh unsympathetic character.) He and his son do not hit it off. He is disappointed that young John, when on holiday from Harrow, does not take any interest in his father's attempts to inculcate him with his Liberal principles but prefers to go round shooting rats and rabbits and, more especially, to spend his time at his Uncle Babington's where there is a pony to ride, boating on the lake and 'three fine bouncing girl cousins who made much of him.'

After finishing at Harrow John goes to Cambridge where he makes friends with the unstable Dick Shand and gets into debt. On hearing from John's tutor that he cannot take his degree until he pays his debts, old man Caldigate's anger boils over; he pays his son's debts but expels him from his home and heart. While he is consoling himself at the Babingtons, Aunt Polly, assuming him to be his father's only possible heir, deliberately puts him into an equivocal position *vis-à-vis* her eldest daughter Julia and inveigles him into make a half-promise of marriage to her. From the Babingtons he pays a visit to Mr Bolton, a banker and friend of his father, with the purpose of fixing the financial transaction by which he is 'bought out' by his father and to be paid a sum of money instead of waiting for the family estate to revert to him on the old man's death. While there he meets the banker's daughter, Hester, and is so taken with her that he vows to himself he will somehow or other make her his wife.

His intention, now that he has a sum of ready money to hand, is to invest it in a fortune-making bid as a gold miner in Australia. His friend Dick Shand agrees to throw his lot in with him, being something of a scapegrace and having nothing to lose.

At chapter 5, with the description of the voyage to New South Wales in 'The Goldfinder', the preliminary English scenes end and the story takes on a different atmosphere and a new momentum. It is here that Trollope's observant much-travelled eye comes into its own, noting how life on board ship is so 'completely a life of itself, governed by its own rules'; its friendships, animosities, class distinctions, cliquishness. Turning from the general to the particular, Dick Shand becomes interested in a 'mysterious' Mrs Smith and determines to unravel the mystery. But before long she gets into conversation with Caldigate who, Hester or no Hester, finds her so fascinating that he comes under her spell and completely ousts Shand, who sulks and takes umbrage. And indeed she is fascinating. There is none of the usual Victorian feminine coyness about her. She talks to him as equal to equal. The dialogue scintillates. We learn that she is a widow and travelling to Australia on her own, but with what purpose she does not divulge. She is shunned by the women, and the captain goes so far as to warn Caldigate against her — which makes their relationship all the more piquant. The intimacy deepens, and chapter VIII ('Reaching Melbourne'), describing their last days at sea is superb.

> It was on the evening of the same day, after they had sighted Cape Otway, that Mrs. Smith and Caldigate began their last conversation on board the Goldfinder — a conversation which lasted, with one or two interruptions, late into the night.
>
> "So we have come to the end of it," she said.
>
> "To the end of what?"
>
> "To the end of all that is pleasant and easy and safe. Don't you remember my telling you how I dreaded the finish? Here I have been fairly comfortable . . . . I have had you to talk to; and there has been a flavour of old days about it. What shall I be doing this time tomorrow?"
>
> "I don't know your plans."
>
> "Exactly — and I have not told you because I would not have you bothered with me when I land. You have enough on your own hands; and if I were to be a burden to you now it might be serious trouble. I am afraid poor Mr. Shand objects to me."
>
> "You don't think that would stand in my way?"
>
> "It stands in mine. Of course, with your pride and your obstinacy you would tell Mr. Shand to go to — the devil if he ventured to object to any little delay that might be occasioned by looking after me. Then Mr. Shand would go — there, or elsewhere; and all your plans would be broken up, and you would be without a companion."
>
> "Unless I had you."
>
> Of all the words he could have spoken in such an emergency these were the most foolish; and yet, at so tender a moment, how were they to be repressed?
>
> "I do think that Dick Shand is dangerous," she answered, laughing; "but I should be worse. I am afraid Dick Shand will — drink."
>
> "If so, we must part. And what would you do?"
>
> "What would I do? What could I do?" Then there was a pause.
>
> "Perhaps I should want you to marry me, which would be worse than Dick Shand's drinking. Eh?"

And here Trollope puts in a philosophical reflection based on his passion for riding and hunting which, unlike so many of his asides and those of the Victorians generally, is not a longueur and thoroughly amusing.

> There is an obligation on a man to persevere when a woman has encouraged him in love-making. It is like riding at a fence. When once you have set your horse at it you must go on, however impracticable it may appear as you draw close to it. If you have never looked at the fence at all — if you have ridden quite the other way, making for some safe gate or clinging to the dull lane — then there will be no excitement, but also there will be no danger and no disgrace. Caldigate had ridden hard at the fence . . . . and could only trust to his good fortune to carry him safe over.
>
> "I don't suppose you would want it," he said, "but I might."
>
> "You would want me, but you would not want me for always . . . I often wonder that any man is ever fool enough to marry . . . I think men only marry when they are caught. Women are prehensile things, which have to cling to something for nourishment and support. When I come across such a one as you I naturally put out my feelers."
>
> "I have not been aware of it."
>
> "Yes, you are; and I do not doubt that your mind is vacillating about me. I am sure you like me."
>
> "Certainly I like you."
>
> "And you know that I love you."
>
> "I did not know it."
>
> "Yes, you did. You are not the man to be diffident of yourself in such a matter. You must either think that I love you, or that I have been a great hypocrite in pretending to do so. Love you!" . . . . At this time it was dark; but their eyes had become used to the gloom, and each could see the other's face. "Love you!" she repeated, looking up at him, speaking in a very low voice, but yet oh so clearly, so that not a fraction of a sound was lost to his ears, with no special emotion in her face, but with her eyes fixed upon his. "How should it be possible that I should not love you? For two months we have been together as people seldom are in the world — as they can never be without hating or loving each other thoroughly. You have been very good to me who am all alone and desolate. And you are clever, educated — and a man. How should I not love you? And I know from the touch of your hand, from your breath when I feel it on my face, from the fire in your eye and from the tenderness of your mouth, that you, too, love me."
>
> "I do," he said.

Then there are critics who maintain that Trollope was never anything but flat and prosaic without a grain of poetry in him. Such a love scene as that, such a character as Mrs Smith, is absolutely unique in nineteenth century literature and must have seemed terribly shocking to the public for which Trollope wrote. For us today it makes an exhilarating change from the normal timid, bashful, sickening coy tearfulness of the average Victorian 'heroine' — so much so that we can feel nothing but regret at the later role her creator destines for her.

At Melbourne they separate, and the next three chapters draw a vivid picture of life as lived in an Australian out-back gold-mining community where every man is out for himself and existence is a coarse, depraving routine of hard work, hard drinking and hard gambling. Here Trollope shows his courageous realism and versatility. No other nineteenth century British novelist has done anything comparable. The shifty Crinkett who tries to cheat the raw newcomers; the rough diamond Mick Maggott who takes charge of the two of them, helps them to stake their claim, finds gold for them and between weeks of killing hard work has bouts of drinking himself unconscious; Mrs Henniker who runs a canteen for all these roughnecks, are all little gems of portraiture.

In all this John has not forgotten his Mrs Smith. Driven by desire of her he goes to Sydney where he finds she is doing what we would call a 'music hall turn' under the name of Mademoiselle Cettini 'without much clothes.' Unhappy and disgusted, he puts off visiting her but eventually betakes himself to her lodgings where, 'dressed with all the pretty care which a woman can use when she expects her lover', she throws herself into his arms and all his reserves vanish as he embraces and kisses her.

But with chapter XIII comes a sharp break. John 'strikes it lucky' and makes a reasonable fortune. Mrs Smith is left so to speak in mid air. Dick Shand, we are told, breaks under the strain, becomes a drunkard and is reduced to accepting any poverty-stricken job he can get; and John, after writing several affectionate letters to his father, telling him the good news of himself, follows them up in person, and in one chapter we are back in England, where the contrast between the Australian way of life and the English middle-upper class scene with its snobberies, smug self-sufficiency, easy protected lives and religious bigotry brings us up with a jerk. The earlier strands are taken up by John almost as if he had never broken them. He makes it up with his father and shares Folking with him; Hester, fancy free, is ready to fall in love with him and marry him, though not before he has wriggled free from his enforced half-promise to poor cousin Julia and mortally offended Aunt Polly in so doing. But that obstacle proves a very minor stumbling block in comparison with Hester's mother, Mrs Bolton. In her Trollope has drawn a bitter picture of religious bigotry and maternal possessiveness. She would have been antagonistic to any prospective son-in-law on principle, for Hester is her only child, her 'treasure' she intends to keep for herself; but to have her taken from her by a man notorious in the neighbourhood for his wild oats and his debts, one who had cleared out of the country in order to escape from the condemnation of all and sundry and to gamble his all on gold mining in that uncivilized Australia and who, worst sin of all in her eyes, was believed to be irreligious or at least never went to church, was something she was prepared to fight to the death of herself and the everlasting misery of her child if necessary. The social position of daughters in Victorian society is here thrust home with horrifying reality. Robert Bolton, Hester's stepbrother and an attorney, after the fullest investigation behind the scenes into Caldigate's finances and character, and learning 'that the man as to whom he was making inquiry was held in high esteem for honesty, perseverance and capacity . . . . returned to Cambridge with a feeling that *his sister ought to be allowed to make the man's acquaintance.*' (My italics.) By force of argument and feeling he eventually wins the family over into accepting Caldigate — all except Mrs Bolton of course, who continues to bully, lecture and brow-beat her daughter to try to make her break off the engagement, 'always giving as a reason the alleged fact that John Caldigate was not a true believer.' But Hester, in spite of her affection for her mother, has the spirit to hold out against her, and the marriage takes place.

But unlike so many Victorian novels in which marriage is supposed to end all feuds, plots and obstacles, here it is the beginning of trouble. Caldigate had arranged to sell his interest in his Australian mine to Crinkett; but now he receives telegrams asking him to postpone this, and subsequent letters informing him that the mine had become worked out and demanding half the money invested back. He refuses Crinkett's demands, upon which, out of the blue, comes a letter from Mrs Smith, alias Mlle Cettini — a letter of sheer blackmail threatening that unless he agrees to Crinkett's terms she will ruin his reputation by coming forward and revealing to the world that he had married her in Ahalala, for the truth of which she claims to have legal proof. In desperation Caldigate goes to Robert Bolton with the letter, denies that he ever married her, but confesses that he had promised to do so and that he had 'lived with' her. These unsavoury details of his past put the puritan-minded Bolton firmly against him. The whole story leaks out. Hester's mother is able to rejoice and say that her antagonism to the marriage has been vindicated, and never ceases to tell her daughter that she cannot now be regarded as a wife but is no better than Caldigate's mistress living in mortal sin and the mother of a bastard child. And on top of all this Crinkett and Mrs Smith arrive in England and start legal proceedings. The second half of the novel is taken up with the trial and all its legal, social and personal ramifications. John Caldigate is found guilty of bigamy and sent to prison. The Boltons rejoice, especially Hester's mother, who sees in the verdict absolute justification for her unalterable hatred for the girl's husband. But their triumph is short-lived. With an astuteness worthy of Sherlock Holmes, Trollope uses his knowledge of Post Office procedures and techniques to prove, through the person of Samuel Bagwax (an example of the silly names Trollope sometimes gives his characters and of which Henry James rightly complained) that the stamp on the envelope containing the damning evidence that Caldigate refers to Mrs Smith as his wife has been faked, thus proving that the whole evidence of the prosecution is a tissue of lies. Acute and gratifying though all this is, it must be said that this episode is dragged out far beyond an acceptable length. The side issue of Bagwax and Curlydown's daughter is totally irrelevant; but this of course is applicable to so many Victorian novels where a requisite length has to be spun out at all costs.

Apart from its quality as a piece of narrative, the novel contains some typically acute character studies, and moreover gives us a vivid impression of Victorian society on different levels. Its weaknesses are its too great length along with the unexplained and therefore unsatisfactory dichotomy in the character of Mrs Smith. She ought at least, we feel, to have been given some life and character in the second half of the story if only to vindicate her astonishing change of attitude towards her former lover. After giving her such vivid sympathetic life in the first half of the story, to make her nothing but a cheap adventuress in the second without allowing her a word to say for herself is surely an artistic blot. We almost wish, indeed, that Trollope had made her the heroine; for Hester, though she has the guts to stand by her husband and defy her family, has servile weepy moments with her monstrous mother which make a modern reader cringe. Mrs Smith, we feel, after being emotionally blackmailed and physically kidnapped would never have 'wept over her and kissed her', or have humiliated herself so far as to following her all the way to her carriage in order to kiss her hand.

And finally, to one reader at least, an overall reflection after reading this novel (and indeed other nineteenth century novels) is that our century, despite its many vices, has taken enormous strides forward on two counts: the throwing over of religiosity (at least as practised by the Victorians) and the achieving of Women's Lib.

AYALA'S ANGEL

In a sense, this novel is Trollope's greatest tour de force: in fact a double one in that (a) it is a story by a man about the lives, loves, griefs and joys of two sisters, Lucy and Ayala Dormer (b) the whole narrative deals with nothing else — or very little else — but the love affairs, flirtations and foolish actions of young people of both sexes, all so tangled and devious that before the end the reader has almost forgotten who belongs to whom in the 'pre-marital jungle.'

As far as (a) is concerned the novel is a triumph. The feminine challenge is met with the same consummate assurance as Anne Brontë met the masculine one in the first half of *The Tenant of Wildfell Hall*. As regards (b) one has to confess that the novel is nothing like as good.

The concept of the story, the main theme which in all probability came first into the author's mind and set the machinery of invention going, can be told in a few words. Lucy and Ayala Dormer are the daughters of an artist and his beautiful wife, both dead before the action begins. Lucy is the elder and more rational one of the two, whereas Ayala has all her father's romanticism, idealism, love of art and panache to the nth degree. (A similarity here with the sisters Elinor and Marianne in *Sense and Sensibility*.) Ayala, indeed, is so romantic, so 'wayward', so 'elfin-like', so full of yearnings for the ideal that she disdains all her suitors (and being beautiful she has no end of them, to the dismay of her family) as they do not measure up to the impossible superhuman ideal 'Angel of Light' her imagination has pictured to her as the one and only one to whom she can give her love: only to discover by slow, painful and humiliating degrees that this 'Angel' turns out be the third of her persistent suitors — the red-headed, positively ugly colonel with the name of Jonathan Stubbs!

Now such a theme, while suitable for a novelette, can't hope to form the substance of a 3-decker novel by itself: hence the surrounding aura of *contretemps* involving other lovers and would-be lovers, some of which is amusing in brief spells but, carried to great lengths, becomes padding and a bore. If ever a novel could be named as an example of Trollope's *over*-fertile brain, this is surely the one. While one can only admire his sheer powers of invention, one longs for more self-discipline, for the knowledge of when to stop. It is the old, old story: one has to say of it as of so many others — made half the length it would be twice as good.

The shame is, it begins so splendidly. The two sisters, on the death of their improvident artist father, are left totally unprovided for, and so it becomes urgent that some branch of the family should come to their aid. In the event their uncle, Sir Thomas Tringle, the Lombard Street millionaire business tycoon, and his wife, Emmeline, agree to take one of the girls, and another uncle, Reginald Dosett (or more accurately, his stronger-minded wife) the other. Lady Tringle, however, makes the proviso (to her misfortune, as it turns out) that they should have 'Ayala the romantic; Ayala the poetic!' as being the more beautiful and attractive. 'The matter was decided in Lady Tringle's back drawing-room.' In such casual, laconic, devastating words does Trollope depict not only the decision of a lifetime but the helpless dependence of Victorian girls — a dependence still more damningly brought home later when circumstances demand the change-over.

So Ayala goes to the Tringles and wealth and fashion and gracious living, and Lucy is left to the care of the childless, middle-class, struggling, unimaginative Dosetts. The way Lady Tringle announces the decision and the reasons for it is masterly.

> The tidings had been communicated to Lucy and to Lucy alone, by Aunt Tringle. "As you are the eldest, dear, we think that you will be best able to be a comfort to your aunt," said Lady Tringle.
>
> "I will do the best I can, Aunt Emmeline," said Lucy, declaring to herself that, in giving such a reason, her aunt was lying basely.
>
> "I am sure you will. Poor dear Ayala is younger than her cousins, and will be more subject to them."
>
> So in truth was Lucy younger than her cousins, but of that she said nothing. "I am sure you will agree with me that it is best that we should have the youngest."
>
> "Perhaps it is, Aunt Emmeline."
>
> "Sir Thomas would not have had it any other way," said Lady Tringle with a little severity, feeling that Lucy's accord had hardly been as generous as it should be. But she recovered herself quickly, remembering how much Lucy was to lose . . . .

Was to lose indeed! In the next chapter we are given a picture of life as lived by such as the Dosetts which is nightmarish in its overall petty practical littleness and sense of soul-chilling boredom. For Lucy the contrast between life as it was lived in her father's milieu and now was killing. Then there had been books to read, visitors, artists, a piano, music, intelligent conversation, an occasional visit to a concert or a theatre. Here there was no library, no piano, no music, no visitors, no young people, no going to concerts or the theatre, no intelligent conversation, no company at all except that of her morose aunt and the dubious addition of her uncle in the evening on his return from his office, when 'after their genteel dinner he would sleep a little and she would knit.' The Dosetts were in straitened circumstances, and Aunt Dosett dug a certain desperate pleasure in living as near to the poverty line as she could in order to complain; and Lucy's life (existence, rather) became one mindless boring round of helping her aunt in her domestic chores: turning sheets, mending, sewing, darning, learning how to choose the cheaper cuts of meat and to make food and clothes last. Trollope's knowledge of feminine routine and conversation is uncanny. The description might have been written by Elizabeth Gaskell. And he sums it all up with 'When a month passed by Lucy began to think that time itself would almost drive her mad . . . . It seemed to her that her whole life was a blank . . . . '

But unknown to Lucy changes are on the way. Her sole recreation, taken for the sake of exercise 'as she was becoming pale,' was a daily walk in nearby Kensington Gardens, and in the course of one of these walks she sees Isadore Hamel, a rising young sculptor she had known and felt something more than friendship for in the days when he used to visit her father. The incident as described by Trollope is a potent reminder to us of what any girl of today would consider as the intolerable 'proprieties' by which the Victorian girl was imprisoned.

> Though she saw no more than his back she was sure that it was Isadore Hamel. For a moment there was an impulse on her to run after him and to call his name . . . . It had seemed to her

that she had not an acquaintance in the world except Uncle Reg and Aunt Dosett. And now, almost within reach of her hand, was the one being in all the world whom she most longed to see. She did stand, and the word was formed within her lips; but she could not speak it. Then came the thought that she would run after him, but the thought was expelled quickly. Though she might lose him again and for ever she could not do that. She stood almost gasping till he was out of sight, and then she passed on upon her usual round.

Though a girl's future happiness might hinge on it, she must not go up to a man on her own and talk to him! But fortune favours her. Not long afterwards she meets him again, but this time he is with a friend, 'and it seemed to Lucy at once that she could only bow to him, only mutter something, and pass on. How can a girl stand and speak to a gentleman in public, especially when that gentleman has a friend with him?' So yet again because of stupid Victorian convention she makes a mess of things and loses him. No wonder women came to demand their Lib!

But something other than Isadore Hamel is about to happen too. Ayala has been sadly blotting her copybook with the Tringles. She and their daughter Augusta are continually at loggerheads and detest each other. Even worse is the fact that their son Tom, whom she can't abide, has fallen in love with her and pursues her, so that in spite of the luxury with which she is surrounded she is far from happy. There were disagreements, rows, bitter words passed on both sides. So bad became the situation, in fact, that Sir Thomas was driven to writing a short letter to Mr Dosett, and his wife a long one to Mrs D. suggesting that an exchange of girls should be made in the hope of better success. And here Trollope even more strongly than before thrusts home to us the dreadful insecurity and feudal tutelage of Victorian girls. Discussing the situation with her aunt, Lucy protests.

"However it might have been arranged at first, it aught to remain now. Even though Ayala and I are only girls, we ought not to be changed about as though we were horses . . . . "

They are *only girls*, you see. But even Aunt Dosett is moved to agree with Lucy. Later, when the sisters meet and discuss the pros and cons of the change, Ayala remarks: "But what is the good of talking about it, Lucy? You and I have no voice in it, though it is all about ourselves. As you say, we are like two tame birds, who have to be moved from one cage to another just as the owner pleases. We belong either to Uncle Tom or Uncle Dosett, just as they like to settle it. Oh, Lucy, I do so wish I were dead." So simply told; yet to a percipient reader the pathos of the situation is harrowing. Their plight is, in effect, an even more damning condemnation of the Victorian attitude to women and its whole social system than the verbal protests of the Brontës, Harriet Martineau and the later Suffragettes.

For Ayala, the romantic, idealistic and now money-spoiled, her existence with the Dosetts becomes sheer agony, (not lessened by visits from Tom Tringle who refuses to give up hope) and exacerbated by her aunt's lectures to the effect that she is a fool for turning down the offers of a young man who has prospects of wealth and means of making any girl happy. Then, just when things are at their lowest ebb for her, the gay Marchesa Baldoni, whom she had met at Rome in the course of the family's travels and liked very much, finds her and insists on taking her out and enabling her to mix with pleasant society. At a dance she meets Colonel Jonathan Stubbs, who is very taken with her and whose talk and humour she finds most attractive — only, as to being her 'Angel' the idea is laughable, he is "so ugly and red-haired, and with a name like Jonathan Stubbs!" But with constant association her fondness for him grows — which does not prevent her from refusing him three times, to the annoyance of her relations. But in the end his perseverance wins the day and she ultimately comes to realize that immaculate and perfect Angels of Light who shall be all that romantic girls dream of are simply not to be had on the planet Earth, and that they had better make do with the nearest they can come. So Ayala gets her Jonathan and Lucy her Isadore.

Had Trollope been content to make this the sole theme of his novel it would have been a very good one. But yet again the 3-decker Molech must receive its full toll of scrip and scrippage, and we have to bear with Tom Tringle and his asinine gaffes, the ditherings of Frank Houston, the puerilities of Captain Batsby and the Tringles' second daughter Gertrude who is prepared to marry anything in trousers until, like poor bewildered Sir Thomas Tringle, we are heartily sick of the whole family. Though full of delightful character sketches and searing exposures of Victorian hypocrisy, social and religious,* the novel sags through too much detail and length, and sadly cannot be placed among Trollope's best. But it is well worth reading.

COUSIN HENRY

In his essay on *Our Mutual Friend* (1865) Henry James wrote '*Our Mutual Friend* is, to our perception, the poorest of Mr Dickens's works. And it is poor with the poverty not of momentary embarrassment, but of permanent exhaustion. It is wanting in inspiration. For the last ten years it has seemed to me that Mr Dickens has been unmistakably forcing himself. *Bleak House* was forced; *Little Dorrit* was laboured; the present work is dug out with a spade and pickaxe.'

The passage could be repeated with the substitution of Trollope for Dickens, and the novels of the former from *Cousin Henry* onwards for those of the latter. The fact must be faced that after the *The Way We Live Now* Trollope wrote nothing to come up to that work, and that with the possible exceptions of *The American Senator, John Caldigate, Ayala's Angel* and *Doctor Wortle's School* — and then only in parts — the rest are merely Trollope in decay — examples of purely mechanical necessitarian production void of inspiration and life.

* For an example of the latter see chapter 26. 'It was a law at Stalham that everyone should go to church on Sunday morning. Sir Harry himself, who was not supposed to be a peculiarly religious man, was always angry when any male guest did not show himself in the enormous family pew. "I call it d . . . . indecent," he has been heard to say. But nobody was expected to go twice — and consequently nobody ever did go twice.' Trollope's opinion of such sanctimoniousness is obvious.

Why, the disgruntled reader may ask himself, did Trollope, Dickens and indeed do most writers persist in turning out work when their powers have gone? The answer is simple. To the man of creative genius creation is the prime purpose of his being, his very breath of life. Not to create, not to write, is to him a living death. Nothing else can give him a sense of fulfilment. With or without inspiration he *must* fulfil that function in life which he has come to consider his own. So he is driven to attempt work which he probably knows in his heart of hearts to be below his best. No matter: it is better than vegetation, than the complete atrophy of the mind, the surrender to infirmity. And therefore he writes . . . . writes . . . Trollope himself put this in a nutshell* once when he declared to a friend: "When I can no longer write I shall no longer want to live." So he wrote to the very end.

Cousin Henry is the first of these novels of the late seventy-eights and early eighties to be examples of this mechanical process of creation bereft of inspiration, the last glimmer of the failing candle, the final effort of the exhausted mind that will not admit defeat. It is, too, yet another example of Trollope's recurring theme, becoming almost an obsession, of entail and the complications of last will and testament; also of an attempt at some sort of psychoanalysis. The fact that in the latter aspect it fails, and cannot be counted among his better novels is a pity in that the central idea is gripping in its possibilities, and on that account alone forces the reader to peruse it to the end. Summarizing, the plot is as follows:

Old Uncle Indefer Jones (the location of the story is Welsh — Carmarthen — and the characters have Welsh names) is torn in his mind about his will. His niece, Isabel Broderick, who lives with him and looks after him and his household (he is a bachelor) has his heart; but he is hidebound by the right of male descent and feels passionately that 'the estate ought to go to a man — a Jones,' for Llanfeare had belonged to Indefer Joneses for generations. The ideal solution would be for Isabel to marry his nephew Henry Jones, the next of kin male, but she refuses even to consider becoming the wife "of a man I despise!" But all we are told of this cousin Henry is that his father had 'disgraced the family' by running off with a married woman whom he had eventually married after her divorce, and 'taken to race-courses and billiard rooms;' that despite this his son Henry had been taken into the good graces of Uncle Indefer who had had him educated at his expense and sent him to Oxford; that he had been invited to Llanfeare on several occasions where he was heartily disliked and despised by everyone as being 'sly' and 'given to lying'; that he had been sent down from Oxford 'for some offence not altogether trivial'; that, finally, Uncle Indefer 'had declared to himself and others that Llanfeare should never fall into his hands.'

But now — and this is where the story opens — being an old man, he begins to have doubts and regrets about his decision. He dislikes his nephew, loves his niece and would much prefer to leave the estate to her. But then it would no longer be in the Jones family. Isabel tells him again and again that she is utterly disinterested, will not for all Llanfeare marry the despicable Henry, and that he must act according to his conscience. He

---

* As did Flaubert. While agonizing over *Madame Bovary* he wrote in a letter: 'No matter, it is a delicious thing to write, whether well or badly — to be no longer yourself but to move in an entire universe of your own creating.'

eventually salves this by a will leaving the estate to Henry but stipulating that Isabel should be paid an income from it: on which the old man invites Henry, who is a clerk in some London office, to spend a month with them so that he can be informed of the important decision and get the feel of the estate and its tenants.

Henry comes, and is disliked even more intensely by everyone. Following his uncle's hints he proposes to Isabel who snubs him (she loves another man anyway), and so gets on his uncle's nerves that just before his death his feelings get the better of his sense of family duty and he makes a new and final will, witnessed by two of his tenants, in which he reverses his previous decision. But on his death no such will is to be found, and the only witnesses there had in fact been are the two tenants who had signed it as such. Where is the will? Had the old man had yet another change of mind and torn it up? Who was the last to see it? Had he put it somewhere? It is not with his papers and former will. Had it been hidden by someone? A sense of mystery is in the air. Mr Apjohn, the family solicitor and friend, like all the rest, dislikes Henry and had always advised, even begged, old Indefer not to do Isabel so great an injustice as to leave the estate to her cousin. Now, his suspicions raised, he institutes a search for the mysterious will, but nothing comes of it. The previous will, therefore, is read and acted on, and Henry becomes the heir. But Mr Apjohn can't rest. He senses from Henry's evasive conduct and shifty manner that he knows the whereabouts of the later will, and is determined to leave no stone unturned until either it is discovered or Henry is made to confess what he knows.

All this makes an excellent plot, has all the ingredients of another *Orley Farm*. But Trollope throws it away by the feebleness of his characterization and the flatness of the writing. Henry in particular is so abjectly spineless as to be beyond credibility and interest. All he can do while general suspicion hovers over him is to sit day after day alone in the library, his eyes turning constantly as though hypnotized towards a certain volume — one of a set of Jeremy Taylor's works, his uncle's favourite reading. Whenever he is asked by Isabel or Mr Apjohn whether he knows anything about the will, he is seen to turn 'ashy pale' and his forehead to become bedewed with drops of perspiration and every inch of him to proclaim guilt. Only when he finds that his strange behaviour is being commented on by the butler and the housekeeper does he force himself to leave the room and wander listlessly about *his* estate.

Now, true to his invariable principle of never playing with his readers, Trollope gives them the facts, which in any case they have already deduced for themselves. His uncle had placed the new will in a volume of Jeremy Taylor's 'Sermons' which he kept by his bedside, Henry had taken it away to put it back in its place and in doing so had discovered the will and left it there. Most of the rest of the story is an attempt to depict and analyse his feelings — the sense of wrong he considers his uncle has done him after first promising him the estate warring with the knowledge of the posthumous wrong he is doing his uncle by defrauding Isabel of her right as heir. But he is such an inhumanly abject figure that we can take little interest in his endless vacillations which do no more than take him on the self-same round like a donkey at the treadmill. He cannot bring himself to destroy the will and thus make himself forever secure because of vague religious fears of punishment hereafter; nor dare he confess he knows its whereabouts or even pretend he has come across it by accident. He does nothing: merely leaves it where it is and leaving everything to chance so as to seem to lessen his guilt should it ever be found. And Chance, in the form of Mr Apjohn, does the rest in a Sherlock Holmesian manner, ringing down the curtain.

Golf has been pithily described by someone evidently unimpressed by the ancient and royal game as 'a good walk ruined'. Much the same view must be taken, as a novel, of *Cousin Henry*.

MARION FAY

One of the last of the novels, this must rank as one of the feeblest. That Trollope ever came to write so dull, so utterly undistinguished a piece of fiction can only be explained by the reason I gave for the feebleness of *Cousin Henry* (q.v.) Even if he had limited the story to one volume instead of the customary pernicious three, this narrative about the loves of (a) an aristocrat (Lord Hampstead) for Marion Fay, daughter of a Quaker, and (b) his sister, Lady Frances, for George Roden, a Post Office clerk, would have been insipid. Dragged out as it is it becomes a thing of monumental tediousness and mediocrity. The narration is so flat, the characters so void of personality, the dialogue so mechanical and the whole so unreadable that if it were to be discovered that Trollope had engaged a hack to write it and merely given it a hasty revision, no one need be surprised.

If the novel was intended as a protest against Victorian snobbery and class distinction, as an attack on Anglican clergy in the character of the 'positively evil' domestic chaplain, Thomas Greenwood, or as a satire on social and religious prejudices (the belated discovery that the commoner George Roden turns out to be the son of an Italian duke to the relief and joy of those who have hitherto spurned him gives some grounds for believing this just possible), it still fails lamentably in that.

The New York *Critic* wrote of it: 'It is a disappointment that Mr Trollope can be tiresome; but very, very tiresome and unnatural he is in the story of *Marion Fay*.' Which sums it up.

DR. WHORTLE'S SCHOOL

With *An Eye for an Eye* (q.v.) this is the shortest of the novels, and an acute study of a liberal-minded man's fight against Victorian prejudice and convention. Of course, to our century the whole affair seems a storm in a teacup and one more nail in the coffin of Victorian morality. The story is simple and direct without any red herrings or sub-plots, and with *John Caldigate* arguably the best of these last novels.

The Revd Jeffrey Wortle, DD, Rector of Bowick and Principal of a prosperous Private School, is a man who, though devoutly religious, has no regard for petty conventions, being liberal-minded, masterful and at times even provocative — 'a man much esteemed by others — and by himself' as the very first sentence of the novel describes him — a sentence and description worthy of Jane Austen at her pungent best. It has always been widely supposed that in him Trollope penned a pretty true self-portrait. Into his life of decorous calm come the Revd Peacocke and his beautiful young American wife, taken on by the Doctor as usher and matron respectively for his school. So far so good. But Mrs Peacocke is rather an unusual woman, preferring to keep herself very much to herself and never accepting any of the offers from Mrs Wortle or other ladies of her circle to join them in gossip and tea-drinking; and so the suspicious scandal-mongering Mrs Stantiloup, thinking she smells a rat, decides that the absolutely unknown five years of the Peacockes spent in the uncivilized backwoods of Missouri ought to be looked into. And at this point (Chapter III, 'The Mystery') Trollope, hating all mystery and suspense because he counted them as being the despicable tools of literary cheapjacks, characteristically takes the bull by the horns.

> And now, O kind-hearted reader, I feel myself constrained, in the telling of this little story, to depart altogether from those principles of story-telling to which you probably have become accustomed, and to put the horse of my romance before the cart. There is a mystery respecting Mr. and Mrs. Peacocke which, according to all laws recognised in such matters, ought not to be elucidated till, let us say, the last chapter but two, so that your interest should be maintained almost to the end . . . . It is my purpose to disclose the mystery at once, and to ask you to look for your interest — should you go on with my chronicle — simply in the conduct of my persons . . . . Therefore put the book down if the revelation of some future secret be necessary for your enjoyment. Our mystery is going to be revealed in the next paragraph — in the next half-dozen words. Mr. and Mrs. Peacocke were not man and wife.

Then, after confessing this enormity, he goes on to recount briefly how it came about. Ella Beaufort, the daughter of a ruined planter in St Louis, had married at the age of seventeen Colonel Ferdinand Lefroy who, after a short spell of married life during which he treated her with brutal cruelty, left her to fend for herself and went off with his equally uncivilized brother, Robert, also a Colonel, to Mexico to live the life of a desperado there. It was during this period that Mr Peacocke, then Vice-President of the College of Missouri, met her and fell in love with her. But of course he was unable to marry her. Then came rumours that a Colonel Lefroy had been killed in a mêlée with the US military authorities. But which Colonel Lefroy was it — Ferdinand or Robert? Peacocke takes three months leave and goes to Mexico to find out and returns with the news that he has seen Robert and been told by him that his brother was dead. So Peacocke and Ella are free to marry. But six months after their marriage Ferdinand turns up. After declaring he doesn't believe Peacocke's story of having met his brother and accusing him of framing the whole thing in order to salve his conscience, he leaves, making vague threats, and 'from that moment they had never heard of or seen him.'

And here we come to the crux of the matter, and Trollope puts it to his readers squarely, and not perhaps without a little irony:

> Should they part? There is no one who reads this but will say they should have parted. Every

day passed together as man and wife must be a falsehood and a sin. There would be absolute misery for both in parting; — but there is no law from God or man entitling a man to escape from misery at the expense of falsehood and sin. Though their hearts might have burst in the doing of it, they should have parted . . . . That he had not done so the reader is aware. That he had lived a life of sin — that he and she had continued in one great falsehood — is manifest enough. Mrs. Stantiloup, when she hears it all, will have her triumph . . . . The Bishop will be unutterably shocked . . . . '

And Trollope ends the chapter: 'The mystery has at any rate been told, and they who feel that on this account all hope of interest is at an end had better put down the book.'

The question immediately arises: was Trollope genuinely speaking for himself here, or was he merely throwing a sop to his public? If the former, the reader can be forgiven for having to resist a desire to throw the book across the room; for our society has travelled a long way in a short time, and the contention that two people finding themselves in the position of the Peacockes should separate because 'religion' disapproves to us is laughable. But after carefully studying the pros and cons I do not believe that it is Trollope speaking, but that he is only protecting himself from a possible backwash of Victorian morality. There is no proof of this, but there are clues. When the truth of the Peacockes' relationship is finally exposed, and the Bishop and the Hon. Mrs Stantiloupe, can congratulate themselves that their worst fears have been substantiated, Trollope makes Dr Wortle say (and Wortle, remember, is almost certainly Trollope himself) that given the same situation he too "would cling to her, let the law say what it might."

Mr Puddicombe, the curate, icily correct and sticking to the letter of the religious code of behaviour, is limned as a contrast to the warm-hearted impulsive Wortle. And the Bishop, like the one who had the misfortune to be the husband of Mrs Proudie, talks and acts like a tired, near-to retiring headmaster who wants to shelve all his problems.

If Wortle is Trollope, it becomes interesting to speculate about Mrs Wortle — that timid, apologetic shadow of a woman, that echo of himself and type of Victorian wife who worships at the feet of her lord and master. Was she a portrait of his wife? We know little of Rose Trollope: only that she seems to have filled the role of the Victorian conception of a good wife — giving him two sons, making his life comfortable and easy, copying his MSS, entertaining his friends. There would seem to have been no emotional scenes, no domestic unheavals, no rifts between them, only a long calm happy partnership. Did he long on rare occasions for something more? Did Kate Field represent an unattainable ideal, a longing for young love and romance he had to crush in his middle age? Were his feelings for her more than platonic? His unrevealing *Autobiography* gives no clue, and we shall never know.

To return to the novel. When it becomes known that the Peacockes are 'living in sin' and that Dr Wortle refuses to publicly condemn them, some parents become alarmed and withdraw their boys from the school, fearful of their moral contamination and the sanctity of their souls. Both for this reason and a determination to vindicate himself and his wife, Peacocke goes back to San Francisco with Robert Lefroy (who has suddenly made appearance at the school with the purpose of blackmailing him) determined to get the truth once and for all. Mrs Peacocke, though relieved of her job as matron, is given a home in the Doctor's establishment, thereby incurring more evil rumours and encouraging spiteful tongues to hint that he has got rid of the husband in order to make love to the wife. 'Amo in the cool of the evening' as the nasty-minded press article had it. Poor Wortle was finding that whatever he did he simply couldn't win.

But eventually everything comes right. Peacocke returns with proof of Ferdinand Lefroy's death; Robert Lefroy, only too glad to lie low when Peacocke discovers he has been forging dollar notes, fades from the scene; the whole scandal dies a natural death; the school, after losing many of its boys, thrives again; and Mary, the Wortles' only child, becomes engaged to Lord Carstairs, a former pupil, and all's well that ends well.

A final comment. The courtship of Carstairs is revelatory of Victorian society and the feudal position of daughters in particular and children in general. The lad, aged nineteen, rides over to the school one afternoon in the hope of declaring himself to Mary. To his joy he finds her alone, and after a game of tennis he tells her of his feelings for her. Following a long paragraph in which Trollope gives us all the cons and doubts that flash through the girl's mind — his youth, the probable opposition of his parents, the fact that he had not yet begun his career at Oxford and would be in no position to offer her marriage for years to come — the dialogue runs:

> "Lord Carstairs," she said severely, "you ought not to have come here when papa and mamma are away."
> "I didn't know they were away. I expected to find them here."
> "But they ain't. And you ought to go away."
> "Is that all you can say to me?"
> "I think it is. You know you oughtn't to talk to me like that. Your own papa and mamma would be angry if they knew it."
> "Why should they be angry? Do you think that I shall not tell them?"
> "I am sure they would disapprove it altogether," said Mary. "In fact it is all nonsense, and you really must go away."
> Then she made a decided attempt to enter the house by the drawing-room window, which opened out on a gravel terrace . . . .

When her mother returns and discovers that the young man has been talking, alone, with her daughter, she clucks like an agitated old hen.

> "It was very unfortunate that Lord Carstairs should have come just when I was away," said Mrs. Wortle to her daughter as soon as they were alone together.
> "Yes, mamma; it was."
> "And so odd. I haven't been away from home any day all the summer."
> "He expected to find you."
> "Of course he did. Had he anything particular to say."
> "Yes, mamma."
> "He had? What was it, my dear?"
> "I was very much surprised, mamma, but I couldn't help it. He asked me — "
> "Asked you what, Mary?"
> "Oh, mamma!" Here she knelt down and hid her face in her mother's lap.
> "Oh, my dear, this is very bad; very bad indeed." . . . .

To today's generations, the parental end of which may consider themselves favoured if they are told of their children's love affairs at all, such attitudes must seem incredible enough; but Trollope goes on to give further evidence of Victorian idiocy. In his friendly letter to Dr Wortle, giving his sanction to the engagement of his son to Mary, Lord Bracy writes:

> ' . . . . However foolish it is — or perhaps I had better say unusual — that a lad should be in love before he is twenty, it is, I suppose possible . . . . '

But even this is not the end, for in the penultimate chapter Trollope keeps this for us:

> And so it came to be understood by the Doctor, by Mrs. Wortle, and by Mary herself, that Mary was engaged to Lord Carstairs . . . Poor Mary herself probably had the worst of it. No provision was made either for her to see her lover or to write to him . . . She did not in the least know when she might be allowed to see him — whether it had not been settled among the elders that they were not to see each other as real lovers till he should have taken his degree — which would be almost in a future world, so distant seemed the time . . . . '

And her disgruntled thoughts are continued in the final chapter:

> That very morning Mary had been bemoaning herself as to her hard condition. Of what use was it to her to have a lover, if she were never to see him, never to hear from him — only to be told about him — that she was not to think of him more than she could help? . . . . Her mother had told her that very morning that there was to be no meeting — probably for three years, till he should have done with Oxford . . . .

Such a state of affairs makes us understand and admire the rebellion of women like the Brontës, George Eliot, Florence Nightingale, the Pankhursts and other fighters for female rights; and we can do nothing but rejoice that a society as depicted here has received its quietus. As for the religious dilemma, Trollope himself has sized it up once and for all in this very novel when he makes Wortle — a Doctor of Divinity, remember — observe to his wife when a religious mamma hints of taking away her boy from the school because of the Peacockes: "It is often a question to me whether the religion of the world is not more odious than its want of religion." Clearly such was Trollope's own view, and after that nothing remains to be said.

KEPT IN THE DARK

The novel must be among the worst half-dozen of Trollope's output. If ever a mountain was made out of a molehill this work is just that. In its feebleness of plot and characterization it scarcely rises above the level of the average woman's magazine story. Even to Trollope's contemporaries it must have seemed an empty bubble; to us today it is a ludicrous piece of Victorian uxorious idiocy.

Cecilia Hunt, living with her mother in Exeter, is an incipient bluestocking, 'great among French and German poets', with vague yearnings for higher things than her prosaic life offers her. Surprisingly and not very convincingly she falls in love with Sir

Francis Geraldine, a man not only twenty years older than herself but typical of a certain brand of Philistine British aristocracy, who follows his pursuits of racing, shooting and women in a superior off-hand manner and allowing nothing to come between them and himself. They become engaged. Then, after the date of the wedding has been fixed, she discovers her mistake and breaks off the engagement. As Trollope has already shown us in *Can You Forgive Her?* this is an unforgivable thing for a Victorian woman to do. Outlawed more or less by her relations and her social conscience, she and mamma go abroad to avoid the one and erase the other.

Eventually she meets, likes and goes about with a Mr Western who, like her, has been the victim of an unhappy love affair, having been callously thrown over for a wealthier suitor. He is two years younger than Sir Geraldine: that is to say only eighteen years older than she! (The modern reader notes with some surprise the ease with which Victorian young women fall in love with men twice their age. Clearly this is the security virus at work.) He tells her frankly of his broken engagement, and eventually proposes to her. Before accepting him she tells herself that now is the time for being equally frank with him, but haunted by the incubus of Victorian propriety and dread lest he should despise her, she cannot bring herself to the point, and marries him with him being 'kept in the dark'.

Of course the expected unexpected happens. The man for whom Western's ex-fiancée had thrown him over turns out to be Sir Francis's cousin, Captain Walter Geraldine. Cecilia's mischief-making friend, Miss Altifioria, becomes very friendly with Sir Francis. The contretemps pile up and the dreadful secret escapes. Western is shattered. He can't bring himself to credit that his adored wife could have left him in ignorance so treacherously, and persuades himself that her secrecy hides some unspeakable evil. So convinced is he of this (the theme of *He Knew He Was Right* again) that he tells her he can no longer live with her or regard her as his wife, and leaves her.

Soon after this she finds she is pregnant. His sister, who sees what a fool he is making of himself, appears on the scene, breaks the news to him, and after a great deal of common sense sisterly talk at last succeeds in making him see reason and persuading him to go back to her. Which he does, and finds joy and solace once more — as Trollope, daringly erotic for his time expresses it — in rediscovering 'how warm and yet how cool was the touch of her lips; how absolutely symmetrical was the sweet curve of her bust; what a fragrance came from her breath!'

The one commendable bit of this deplorable book is the tail-piece, in which Trollope indulges in a little wry satire. The interfering Miss Altifioria, who has exploded the bomb and so nearly ruined the marriage, latches on to Sir Francis herself and almost brings him to the point of proposal. But he wriggles out at the last moment and she is left high and dry to the delight of the reader.

Perhaps intended, like *He Knew He Was Right*, as a study of morbid jealousy, it can only be described as a pot-boiler.

THE FIXED PERIOD

It would be difficult to decide whether this or *The Two Heroines of Plumplington* is Trollope's worst novel. The conception of an imaginary island (Britannula) in the Pacific and the sort of existence which might be led by its citizens in 1980 required, as Pope Hennessy observed, the pen of a Swift, Wells or Orwell to carry it out. Now pure inventive imagination was precisely what Trollope lacked. Reality, observation, description of everyday life, society and manners constituted his strength — or as Henry James summed it up 'His great, his inestimable merit was a complete appreciation of the usual.' The ability to escape from that life and create a world of fantasy was never his, so that such an attempt as this was doomed to failure from the start.

The only possible point of interest in it for us today is his Introduction, in which he explains the significance of the somewhat nebulous title. This Introduction, supposedly written by a survivor of the Britannulist colony, is undisguised Trollope, for in it, looking a century ahead, one of the imaginary island society's laws comes right up against a dilemma and source of bitter argument of our own time, namely, the principle of euthanasia.

After explaining that the Fixed Period is the age of 67, decided on by the Britannulist Assembly as that period of life when every citizen attaining it should of his own volition, without fuss and with honour, retire to a special Home to be given his quietus, Trollope goes on:

The Fixed Period has been so far discussed as to make it almost unnecessary for me to explain its tenets, though its advantages may require a few words of argument in a world that is at present dead to its charms. It consists altogether of the abolition of the miseries, weakness, and *fainéant* imbecility of old age, by the prearranged ceasing to live of those who would otherwise become old. Need I explain to the inhabitants of England, for whom I chiefly write, how extreme are those sufferings, and how great the costliness of that old age which is unable in any degree to supply its own wants? Such old age should not, we Britannulists maintain, be allowed to be. This should be prevented, in the interest both of the young and of those who do become old when obliged to linger on after their "period" of work is over. Two mistakes have been made by mankind in reference to their own race, — first, in allowing the world to be burdened with the continued maintenance of those whose cares should have been made to cease, and whose troubles should be at an end. Does not the Psalmist say the same? — "If by reason of strength they be fourscore years, yet is their strength labour and sorrow." And the second, in requiring those who remain to live a useless and painful life. Both these errors have come from an ill-judged and a thoughtless tenderness, — a tenderness to the young in not calling upon them to provide for the decent and comfortable departure of their progenitors; and a tenderness to the old lest the man, when uninstructed and unconscious of good and evil, should be unwilling to leave the world for which he is not fitted. But such tenderness is no better than unpardonable weakness. Statistics have told us that the sufficient sustenance of an old man is more costly than the feeding of a young one, — as is also the care, nourishment, and education of the as yet unprofitable child. Statistics also have told us that the unprofitable young and the no less unprofitable old form a third of the population. Let the reader think of the burden with which the labour of the world is thus saddled. To these are to be added all who, because of illness cannot work, and becuse of idleness will not. How are a people to thrive when so weighted? And for what good? As for the children, they are clearly necessary. They have to be nourished in order that they may do good work as their time shall come. But for whose good are the old and effete to be maintained amid all these troubles and miseries? Had there been any one in our Parliament capable of showing that they could reasonably desire it, the bill would not have been passed. Though to me the politico-economical view of the subject was always very strong, the relief to be brought to the aged was the one argument to which no reply could be given.

It was put forward by some who opposed the movement, that the old themselves would not like it. I never felt sure of that, nor do I now. When the colony had become used to the Fixed Period system, the old would become accustomed as well as the young. It is to be understood that a euthanasia was to be prepared for them; — and how many, as men now are, does a euthanasia await? And they would depart with the full respect of all their fellow-citizens. To how many does that lot now fall? During the last years of their lives they were to be saved from any of the horrors of poverty. How many now lack the comforts they cannot earn for themselves? And to them there would be no degraded feeling that they were the recipients of charity. They would be prepared for their departure, for the benefit of their country, surrounded by all the comforts to which, at their time of life, they would be susceptible, in a college maintained at the public expense; and each, as he drew nearer to the happy day, would be treated with still increasing honour.

And he continues:

Many arguments were used against us, but were vain and futile in their conception. In it religion was brought to bear; and in talking of this the terrible word 'murder' was brought into common use . . . . Murder! Did any one who attempted to deter us by the use of foul language be-think himself that murder, to be murder, must be opposed to the law? This thing was to be done by the law. There can be no other murder . . . But in truth, the difficulties which lay in our way were very stern. The philosophical truth on which the system is founded was too strong, too mighty, too divine, to be adopted by man in the immediate age of its first appearance.

And he adds: 'But I am still . . . . assured that the doctrine will ultimately prevail over the face of the civilised world, though I will acknowledge that men are not as yet ripe for it.'

Trollope, as is proved here, was years ahead of his time in this. Of course, medical science, a more progressive education and the weakened influence of religion have thrown certain spanners into Trollope's carefully thought-out theories. People nowadays are not considered as fit only for the dustbin at 65, or even 70. The normal span of life has been greatly extended since 1880 when men and women were considered decrepit at sixty; nor had an enlightened government decreed that all workers should receive a pension on retirement. But his principle, whether one agrees or disagrees with it, remains. There can be little doubt that he would have been horrified to know that hundreds of old people now, bed-ridden, helpless, useless and only too ready to lay down what Samuel Johnson called 'the load of life' are being deliberately kept alive at enormous public expense in geriatric wards in the names of kindness and religion. Euthanasia is a contemporary battlefield of clashing opinions. *The Fixed Period* proclaims openly and indisputably where Trollope's sympathies would lie on the question of voluntary euthanasia. Didn't he himself declare to a friend that he would have no wish to live when he reached the time when he no longer had the mental will and energy to write?*

As for the 'tale' itself, when the reader learns that the beneficent imagination of 'the *élite* of the selected population of New Zealand' in 1980 can invent nothing better than a steam tricycle capable of travelling at 25 m.p.h., cricket matches with sixteen players a side and a steam-bowler, and a machine for reporting speeches, he can gain some idea of its puerility. Whether the novel is taken as pure fantasy or as a forward-looking satire on social planning and the Welfare State, it is no less a failure, and interesting only as an expression of Trollope's own views.

MR. SCARBOROUGH'S FAMILY

If one were to search the invaluable Roget's *Thesaurus* for epithets most descriptive of this novel, I think 'grotesque', 'uncouth', 'bizarre', 'denaturalized', 'barbaric', 'malevolent' would run a close race for being the most apt. Why Trollope chose to write such a story at all must be asked by anyone who takes the trouble to read it. The only explanation I can give is two-fold (1) that some example had come to his notice of a peculiarly cruel case of unjust heritage (2) for some reason the whole law concerning entail and the injustices it perpetrated had so brought him to loathe it as to drive him almost obsessively to using the theme as the basis of plots. As readers must have remarked, the theme of property and inheritance with their evil results and effects on character had been a favourite subject with him even in previous novels such as *Doctor Thorne, Miss Mackenzie, Orley Farm, The Belton Estate, Sir Harry Hotspur, Ralph the Heir, Cousin Henry, Lady Anna* and *Is He Popenjoy?*

The novel under discussion could be described as one to end all such novels, its 64 chapters reading as they do like a drawn-out monstrous burlesque against primogeniture, entail, paternal authority, filial deference and all such Victorian shibboleths. For a work to merit the description of 'dexterous raillery' given to the novel by Michael Sadleir it surely needs some touches of wit and humour in addition to invective savagery. I myself can find none.

To relate to an enquirer the bare bones of this involved tale is no easy task; but, to be as succinct as possible, it runs along the following lines:

A rich old man, John Scarborough, has two sons — Mountjoy, the elder, and

---

* Clearly Trollope would have applauded Nietzsche's famous words in chapter 36 of *Twilight of the Idols* written only seven years after his (Trollope's) novel (i.e. in 1888). 'The invalid is a parasite on society. In a certain state it is indecent to go on living. To vegetate on in cowardly dependence on physicians and medicaments after the meaning of life, the *right* to life, has been lost ought to entail the profound contempt of society.' Men, he goes on to argue, should have 'the right . . . . to die proudly when it is no longer possible to live proudly. Death of one's own free choice, death at the proper time, with a clear head and with joyfulness, consummated in the midst of children and witnesses . . . . all this in contrast to the pitiable and horrible comedy Christianity has made of the hour of death.'

Augustus. The former, a wild young fellow, spends his time at gaming tables and getting into debt without making any bones about it, whereas the latter is to all appearances sober and virtuous. Mountjoy becomes at last so desperate for cash that he begins to borrow heavily from money-lenders, principally Jews, to such an extent that he mortgages part of his expectations from his father's estate on post-obits. Getting to hear of this the old man, a malevolent, ferocious individualist fearing neither God nor man, determines to teach him a lesson he will not forget and cheat the jackal creditors into the bargain. To this end he summons Mr Grey, his lawyer, and both verbally and by cleverly concocted apparently authentic documents informs him that Mountjoy is not really his heir, being illegitimate, thus making Augustus the legal heir and putting Mountjoy beyond read of his creditors and safeguarding his own property at one sweep. But having done this, he discovers that the outwardly virtuous Augustus is at heart a cold-blooded calculating young man, paying small sums to his brother to keep him out of the way, indifferent to his father's ill-health (for almost the whole of the novel he is bed-ridden after two serious operations with no hope of recovery) and even impatient for his death so that he can inherit the estate. Unfortunately for himself Augustus over-reaches himself, has rows with his father which blaze to a climax in which he tells the old man the sooner he dies and is out of the way the better. He should have had more sense, for the old man never forgets or forgives an insult, and decides to take a last crushing revenge on his son. Again he sends for Mr Grey and tells him yet another version of his past and relationship to his sons which drives the poor old man of law nearly demented with doubt. This second story is nothing less than a confession that his first story was a pure fabrication to protect his estate from Mountjoy's ravening creditors and to punish him for frittering away his wealth. He now declares that Mountjoy is in fact his legitimate elder son by a marriage with a foreign woman in some remote European country, and Augustus his second. He then makes a second and final will declaring Mountjoy his heir and cutting out Augustus altogether. Such is Mr Scarborough's 'family' and his revenge, and he dies soon afterwards.

I have more than once compared Trollope's manipulation of his plots with a game of chess, and the analogy, when allied with his gift of characterization, can be taken as a compliment to his creative skill. But here everything is sacrificed to the plot, which is bizarre anyway. The characters are puppets for whom we can feel little if any sympathy. Yet another criticism must be that in order to spin out the story all sorts of red herrings are dragged in such as the Annesley-Prosper relationship, the fatuous wooing of Prosper and Miss Thoroughbung, the vain sighings of Anderson and Grascour for Florence Mountjoy, supposedly the heroine, along with the unnecessary Harkaways, Junipers and Vignolles.

The only comment on the credit side for the novel for a prospective reader is the dubious one that at least here is a very different Trollope from that of popular belief, of Barchester — the 'pleasant, amusing and healthy' novelist of Everyman's *Dictionary of English Literature*. But as Tony Weller observed about marriage: whether it is worth while going through so much to learn so little, is a matter of opinion.

AN OLD MAN'S LOVE

This was Trollope's penultimate completed novel, and can be seen as the work of an ageing tired man. The starkness of the style and lack of detailed background in the opening chapters at first bring hopes of a new technique that is going to achieve results without indulging in the old tendency towards prolixity; but as the story continues they only succeed in bringing home to us that the writer is under strain and cannot bring himself to dotting the 'i's and crossing the 't's.

The theme is a splendid one — so good in fact that one can only regret that Trollope didn't have it when he was in his prime. Michael Sadleir suggests that this tale of the love of the fifty-year-old William Whittlestaff (an old man by Victorian standards) for his twenty-five-year-old 'ward' Mary Lawrie was a rewriting of Trollope's own repressed feelings for Kate Field. This may well be true, though of course, being the novelist he was, he made the characters and circumstances very different from the originals. There is nothing of Trollope in Mr Whittlestaff or of Kate Field in the colourless Mary Lawrie.

The theme, I repeat, is excellent. Whittlestaff, a bachelor, learns that his best friend has died leaving his daughter penniless in the care of an unsympathetic step-mother. When she too dies he invites the girl to come and live with him and his old housekeeper — an offer she gratefully accepts. The inevitable happens: he falls in love with her and asks her to marry him. She agrees, but not before telling him she has already given her heart to a young man, John Gordon, who had fallen in love with her but who, being without means, had been told to clear out by her step-mother. There had been no words of love or promises between them. All he had said, pressing her hand as he left her, was, "If I return, the first place I will come to shall be Norwich," and with that he had left her and she had not heard from him since. But still, she confessed to Mr Whittlestaff, she "thought of him." Nevertheless, he accepted her on those terms, believing that time would obliterate what he considered to be no more than a romantic memory.

But on the very day she gave him her promise John Gordon turned up. The rest of the novel is devoted to the tug-of-war between the old and young man for her love. Full of infinite possibilities as the theme is, one has to confess that Trollope's treatment leaves much to be desired. To begin with one simply does not believe that a virile, adventurous young man like John Gordon would leave a girl he loved in such a feeble uncertain way nor, after leaving her, not keep in touch with her. Just to appear out of the blue on the very day she has accepted Whittlestaff is not convincing enough, and too coincidental. We are made to feel that Trollope has manipulated events in this way so that Mary will not have any grounds for refusing him.

This, however, is a detail. The main flaw is the too-great length to which he stretches the theme. Though one of his shorter novels, it is still too long for its matter. In order to keep the tale going he introduces episodes and characters that make it sag and creak. His housekeeper, old Mrs Baggett and her wooden-legged drunken sot of a husband, Squire Hall and his daughters, the feather-headed Revd Montague Blake, Fitzwalker Tookey and his dubious Mrs are all dragged in to make the story a publishable length and could well be done without. And Whittlestaff and Mary in their mental agonies and doubts spin it out, going over and over the same ground when in reality, if the latter had had anything about her instead of being obsessed by 'the maidenly instincts which forbade her to declare her passion in his (John Gordon's) presence', all she needed to do to get herself free and out of her dilemma was to confess to Whittlestaff that she did after all love the younger man and to ask him to release her. But then there would have been only a very short story!

And that is the nub of the matter. The theme would have made a perfect *nouvelle*, calling as it does for shorter, more concentrated treatment, and would have made an ideal subject for later writers specializing in the form such as Hardy, D. H. Lawrence or Willa Cather. Hardy would have made it into one of his *Life's Little Ironies*, Lawrence have revelled in that aspect which Trollope the Victorian had sedulously to avoid, namely, the sexual implications, and Willa Cather turned it into a sympathetic study of age and youth.

Michael Sadleir refers briefly to the novel as 'that short (and wrongly disregarded) tale,' but does not give any reasons for his championing of it. All I wish to add is that if I were Trollope's publisher I would be torn by doubts as to whether to keep it in print or not. On the one hand it has psychological and autobiographical interest, and if it is one of his weaker novels there are several far worse. So I end by suggesting that the reader should make the effort, read it, and form his own judgement.

THE TWO HEROINES OF PLUMPLINGTON

Even devotees who know the map of Barsetshire by heart will be surprised to learn from no less an authority than Trollope himself that Plumplington not only exists but is 'the second town in Barsetshire', with 'a population of over 20,000 souls and three separate banks'. Where has this mysterious town sprung from, they will ask, and where do we find our author's information about it?

The answer is: in that rarest of all Trollope's novels — *The Two Heroines Of Plumplington*, that is to say, his last completed novel, written for the Christmas number of *Good Words* for 1882. But Trollope died on the 6 December, and though the story appeared in the magazine, and reprints were issued in New York soon afterwards, it did not receive book publication until 1953 when André Deutsch brought out the first edition.*

However, even the most ardent Trollope devotee can feel nothing but regret that his author should have given way to a desire to add a Postscript to *The Last Chronicle of Barset*, arguably his greatest novel. Its feebleness brings a sense of anti-climactic failure rivalled only by Dickens's equally lamentable attempt to resuscitate Mr Pickwick and Sam Weller in *Master Humphrey's Clock*. The only possible pleasure either can give is to their respective creators. For to put it bluntly, this tale of two daughters who thwart their fathers' opposition to their making a match with their chosen poor young men, is an

---

* I am indebted to John Hampden's Introduction to the novel for the above facts about it.

insult to the Barsetshire series. The veriest hack today could have churned it out as a Trollopian imitation; and the feeble attempt to remind readers of its Barset association by its references to Harry Gresham, Barchester and the Duke of Omnium only add to one's sense of outrage.

I can only conclude by imploring the reader to forget the belated and mistaken existence of this magazine pot-boiler or, if out of curiosity he insists on reading it, at least to do so before coming to *The Last Chronicle* rather than after it. In the present writer's opinion it was an error of judgement to print it. It would have been kinder to Trollope to leave it in oblivion.

THE LANDLEAGUERS

Trollope began his literary career with Ireland and its troubles, and he ended it similarly. It would have been glorious and a tremendous sense of climax if admirers could have written of this coda to his life's work: the end crowns the work. In a sense it does in that the novel, unfinished at his death, marks the last effort of that fluent pen; but in another it fails. *The Landleaguers* must join *Cousin Henry, Marion Fay,* and *Kept In the Dark* as evidence of waning powers in his later years. Like *Cousin Henry*, the novel is a great chance mostly thrown away. It opens splendidly with magnificent promise of a powerful drama, for Trollope was writing about what he knew. Stirred by the Phoenix Park murders in the May of 1882, he made two visits to Ireland despite his age and signs of failing health to see and judge events and motives for himself, and the novel is the result. The first half, — as far as the murder of the boy Florian — is first rate. The setting and characters have all the ingredients of tense drama — a drama moreover which has for us all the implications and significance and bewilderment of the Ireland of today: the warring factions, the suspicions, the resentment, the combination of religious and political fanaticism, the boycotting, the shooting, the killing of innocent people in the name of patriotism. As Trollope makes clear, the Landleaguers were the nineteenth century version of the IRA, and terrorism stalked the country no less savagely and haphazardly. With him it was a case of 'The pity of it!' for from his early days he had always, within limits, loved and sympathized with the Irish. Let his own words speak:

> And, indeed, the feeling had become common through the country that all the lawyers and judges in Ireland, — the lawyers and judges that is who were opposed to the Landleague, — could not secure a conviction of any kind against prisoners whom the Landleague was bound to support. It had come to be whispered about, that there were men in the County of Galway, — and men also in other counties, — too strong for the Government, men who could beat the Government on any point, men whom no jury could be brought to convict by any evidence; men who boasted of the possession of certain secret powers, — which generally meant murder. It came to be believed that these men were possessed of certain mysterious capabilities which the police could not handle, nor the magistrates touch. And the danger to be feared from these men arose chiefly from the belief in them which had become common. It was not that they could do anything special if left to their own devices, but that the crowds by whom they were

surrounded trembled at their existence. The man living next to you, ignorant, and a Roman Catholic, inspired with some mysterious awe, would wish in his heart that the country was rid of such fire-brands. He knew well that the country, and he as part of the country, had more to get from law and order than from murder and misrule. But murder and misrule had so raised their heads for the present as to make themselves appear to him more powerful than law and order. Mr. Lax, and others like him, were keenly alive to the necessity of maintaining this belief in their mysterious power.

And he understood the feelings of the peaceable majority who, in spite of their inmost desire to be free from British rule, preferred that to the rule of the gun.

A new and terrible aristocracy was growing up among them, — the aristocracy of hidden fire-arms. There was but little said among them, even by the husband to the wife, or by the father to the son; because the husband feared his wife, and the father his own child. There had been a feeling of old among them that they were being ground down by the old aristocracy. There must ever be such an idea on the part of those who do not have enough to eat in regard to their betters, who have more than plenty. It cannot be but that want should engender such feeling. But now the dread of the new aristocracy was becoming worse than that of the old. In the dull, dim minds of these poor people there arose, gradually indeed but quickly, a conviction that the new aristocracy might be worse even than the old; and that law, as administered by Government, might be less tyrannical than the law of those who had no law to govern them. So the people sat silent at their hearths, or crawled miserably about their potato patches, speaking not at all of the life around them.

It is this background which gives the novel its incipient power and possibilities.

Philip Jones, his two daughters Ada and Edith, and two sons Frank and Florian, own and live on their estate of Morny in County Galway. They were Protestants living on friendly terms with their Catholic neighbours except for Florian, the youngest who, though only ten, had been mixing with certain Catholics and their priests and had come home one day informing his family that he had become a convert to Catholicism, would not longer attend their church but go to mass instead. Naturally they are horrified and try by all possible means to cure him of what they consider to be his 'perversion' rather than conversion, but to no avail. Then Trollope, who saw clearly that in Ireland religion and politics were inseparable, subtly makes use of the fact to further the story. Florian's Catholic friends have so convinced him that the Protestant British are treating the Irish as little better than slaves that he is prepared to take their side even against his own family; and when the first blow is struck against them by the opening of the flood gates on Philip Jones's Ballentubber marshes, thereby ruining next year's entire crop, Florian pretends he does not know who has been responsible for the deed. But in spite of his denials his guilt shows in his young face. Edith, whom he loves most, tries to talk him into some confession, but he has been so worked on by the anti-British, anti-Protestant priest, Father Brosnan and, more potently still, by a masked Landleaguer who has made him swear on a wooden cross and under fear of death and threat of hell's flames hereafter, that no appeals can make him tell what she knows he knows. What with her relentless cross-questioning and the fear of Landleaguer reprisal if he were to mention names, Florian's life becomes a hell of uncertainty and divided loyalties. At last, ashamed of being called a traitor to his own father and family, his sense of honour wins and his opposition is broken, and he tells them the names of the ringleaders. One of them is caught and imprisoned, and Florian, after a written testimony, is taken by his father to give his evidence in court at the trial at Galway. On the way they are fired at by a masked man, and Florian is killed. "The bitterness of the Orange feud was in his blood" was all Father Brosnan had to say when he was informed of the boy's death. To him and the Landleaguers Florian had simply been "untrue to his oath and religion" and suffered the penalty. As the climax of the so-called trial the prisoner's own brother, who had been bribed to give evidence against him, is shot at point-blank range in the open courtroom.

Up to this point the story is gripping and promises well. But then Trollope indulges in a typical sub-plot, and it sinks in the quicksands of Rachel O'Mahony, her silly lovers and her attempts to become a famous singer in London; and this, together with a chapter (XLI) devoted to a dissertation on 'The State Of Ireland' — a chapter made totally unnecessary by the story itself — has the result of making the reader hardly able to feel regret that Trollope was unable to finish it.

Since we are touching on the Irish problem it might not be out of place to conclude our survey with a thought which must carry significance for us today. Fond and understanding of the Irish though Trollope was, in the last of the five articles he wrote on Ireland for John Forster's magazine *The Examiner* in 1848/49 he was driven to state: 'I find it impossible to believe that the Irish are gifted with those qualities which are required to support a stern struggle for constitutional liberty.' And in a letter to his mother in 1848 he declared:

> Here in Ireland the meaning of the word Communism — or even social revolution — is not understood. The people have not the remotest notion of attempting to improve their worldly condition by making the difference between the employer and employed less marked. Revolution here means a row . . . . I think there is too much intelligence in England for any large body of men to look for any sudden improvement; and not enough intelligence in Ireland for any body of men at all to conceive the possibility of social improvement.

We of the 1980s, seeing Ireland in the throes of yet another repeat of 'the troubles' and with bombings, murders, mutilations and savagery everyday news, may well ponder over the significance of Trollope's words.

CHRONOLOGICAL LIST OF THE NOVELS AND THEIR PUBLICATION DATES

The Macdermots of Ballycloran (3 vols, 1847)
The Kellys and the O'Kellys (3 vols, 1848)
La Vendée: An Historical Romance (3 vols, 1850)
The Warden (1 vol, 1855)
Barchester Towers (3 vols, 1857)
The Three Clerks (3 vols, 1858)
Doctor Thorne (3 vols, 1858)
The Bertrams (3 vols, 1859)
Castle Richmond (3 vols, 1860)
Framley Parsonage (3 vols, 1861)
Orley Farm (2 vols, 1862)
Rachel Ray (2 vols, 1863)
The Small House at Allington (2 vols, 1864)
Can You Forgive Her? (2 vols, 1864-5)
Miss Mackenzie (2 vols, 1865)
The Belton Estate (3 vols, 1866)
Nina Balatka (2 vols, 1867)
The Last Chronicle of Barset (2 vols, 1867)
The Claverings (2 vols, 1867)
Linda Tressel (2 vols, 1868)
Phineas Finn (2 vols, 1869)
He Knew He Was Right (2 vols, 1869)
The Vicar of Bullhampton (1 vol, 1870)
The Struggles of Brown, Jones and Robinson (1 vol, 1870)
Sir Harry Hotspur of Humblethwaite (1 vol, 1871)
Ralph the Heir (3 vols, 1871)
The Golden Lion of Granpère (1 vol, 1872)
The Eustace Diamonds (3 vols, 1873)
Lady Anna (2 vols, 1874)
Phineas Redux (2 vols, 1874)
Harry Heathcote of Gangoil (1 vol, 1874)
The Way We Live Now (2 vols, 1875)
The Prime Minister (4 vols, 1876)
The American Senator (3 vols, 1877)
Is He Popenjoy? (3 vols, 1878)
An Eye for an Eye (2 vols, 1879)
John Caldigate (3 vols, 1879)
Cousin Henry (2 vols, 1879)
The Duke's Children (3, vols, 1880)

Dr. Wortle's School (2 vols, 1881)
Ayala's Angel (3 vols, 1881)
The Fixed Period (2 vols, 1882)
Marion Fay (3 vols, 1882)
Kept in the Dark (2 vols, 1882)
Mr. Scarborough's Family (3 vols, 1883)
The Landleaguers (3 vols, 1883)
An Old Man's Love (2 vols, 1884)
The Two Heroines of Plumplington (1953)

CLASSIFICATION OF THE NOVELS

The Chronicles of Barsetshire
 The Warden
 Barchester Towers
 Doctor Thorne
 Framley Parsonage
 The Small House at Allington
 The Last Chronicle of Barset
 The Two Heroines of Plumplington

The Palliser or Political Novels
 Can You Forgive Her?
 Phineas Finn
 The Eustace Diamonds
 Phineas Redux
 The Prime Minister
 The Duke's Children

Irish Novels
 The Macdermots of Ballycloran
 The Kellys and the O'Kellys
 Castle Richmond
 An Eye for an Eye (part)
 The Landleaguers

Australian Novels
 Harry Heathcote of Gangoil
 John Caldigate (part)

Novels with a foreign setting
 La Vendée
 Nina Balatka
 Linda Tressel
 The Golden Lion of Granpère

BIBLIOGRAPHY OF WORKS ON TROLLOPE

Anthony Trollope: His Work, Associates and Literary Originals — T.H.S. Escott (1913)
The Significance of Anthony Trollope — S.van Nicholas (1925)
Trollope: A Commentary — M. Sadleir (1927)
Trollope: A Biography — M. Sadleir (1928)
Anthony Trollope — H. Walpole (1929)
Female Characters in the Works of Trollope — C.C. Koets (1933)
The Trollopes: The Chronicle of a Writing Family — L.P. and R.P. Stebbins (1945)
Trollope: A New Judgement — E. Bowen. (1946)
Anthony Trollope — B.C. Brown (1950)
Anthony Trollope: A Critical Study — A.O.J. Cockshut (1955)
A Century of Trollope Criticism — R. Helling (1956)
Anthony Trollope: Aspects of His Life and Work — B.A. Booth (1959)
Trollope: Artist and Moralist — (Chatto & Windus, London, 1971). Ruth apRoberts.
Anthony Trollope — (Cape, 1971). James Pope Hennessy.

APHORISMS FROM TROLLOPE

The American Senator
He liked her well enough, but was certainly not in love with her. I doubt whether men are ever in love with girls who throw themselves into their arms. A man's love, till it has been chastened and fastened by the feeling of duty which marriage brings with it, is instigated mainly by the difficulty of pursuit.

Mr. Scarborough's Family
Most men have some little pet tyranny in their hearts.

Ralph the Heir
The demagogue who is of all demogogues the most popular, is the demagogue who is a demagogue in opposition to his apparent nature. The Radical earl, the free-thinking parson, the squire who won't preserve, the tenant who defies the landlord, the capitalist with a theory for dividing profits, the Moggs who loves a strike, — these are the men whom the working men delight to follow.
It takes years to make a friendship; but a marriage may be settled in a week.
There are some leaps which you must take in the dark if you mean to jump at all.

The Claverings

"There are some people who never will understand what they can do, and what they can't."

"How I did respect you when you dared to speak the truth to me! Men don't know women, or they would be harder to them."

"There is no way so certain to bind a woman to you, heart and soul, as to show her that you trust her in everything."

The Bertrams

"Those who have courage to love should have courage to suffer."

The Last Chronicle of Barset

"That is to say, we think you cannot do so. People can do so many things that they don't think they can do; and can't do so many things that they think they can do."

A man who desires to soften another man's heart should aways abuse himself. In softening a woman's heart he should abuse her.

"It couldn't be that such a man should become a thief all at once. It's not human nature, sir, is it?"

"It is very hard to know what is human nature," said the squire.

The power of a woman, when she chooses to use it recklessly, is, for the moment, unbounded.

The Small House At Allington

To think of one's absent love is very sweet; but it becomes monotonous after a mile or two of a towing-path, and the mind will turn away to Aunt Sally, the Cremorne Gardens, and financial questions. I doubt whether any girl would be satisfied with her lover's mind if she knew the whole of it.

Why is it that girls so . . . . frequently ask men who have loved them to be present at their marriages with other men? There is no triumph in it. It is done in sheer kindness and affection . . . . I fully appreciate the intention, but in honest truth, I doubt the eligibility of the proffered entertainment.

Crosbie also was thinking of his departure more than he should have done during Mr Boyce's sermon . . . . It is very hard, that necessity of listening to a man who says nothing.

The little sacrifices of society are all made by women, as are also the great sacrifices of life.

We constantly talk of the thoughtlessness of youth. I do not know whether we might not more appropriately speak of its thoughtfulness. It is, however, no doubt true that thought will not at once produce wisdom. It may almost be a question whether such wisdom as many of us have in our mature years has not come from the dying out of the power of temptation, rather than as the results of thought and resolution.

Men are cowards before women until they become tyrants; and are easy dupes, till of a sudden they recognize the fact that it is pleasanter to be the victimizer than the victim — and as easy. There are men, indeed, who never learn the latter lesson.

But the fault of her face was this — that when you left her you could not remember it.

"And, above all things, never think that you're not good enough yourself. A man should never think that. My belief is that in life people will take you very much at your own reckoning."

Phineas Redux
"Men are so seldom really good. They are so little sympathetic. What man thinks of changing himself so as to suit his wife? And yet men expect that women shall put on altogether new characters when they are married, and girls think that they can do so."
"Men when they are true are simple. They are often false as hell, and then they are crafty as Lucifer. But the man who is true judges others by himself — almost without reflection. A woman can be as true as steel and cunning at the same time."

Orley Farm
"Mamma is all for a Darby and Joan life," said Sophia, laughing.
"No, I am not, my dear . . . . I don't advocate anything that is absurd. But I do say that life should be lived at home. That is the best part of it. What is the meaning of home if it isn't that?"
"We cannot bring ourselves to believe it possible that a foreigner should in any respect be wiser than ourselves. If any such point out to us our follies, we at once claim those follies as the special evidences of our wisdom."
"Perseverance in such a course will produce results. It is because we put up with bad things that hotel keepers continue to give them to us."
"As for conceit, what man will do any good who is not conceited? Nobody holds a good opinion of a man who has a low opinion of himself."
" . . . . no knowledge obtained of a friend in happiness is at all equal to that which is obtained in sorrow."
"I ask you to answer me fairly. Is not additional eating an ordinary Englishman's ordinary idea of Christmas-day? . . . . I believe that the ceremony, as kept by us, is perpetuated by the butchers and beersellers, with a helping hand from the grocers. It is essentially a material festival; and I would not object to it even on that account if it were not so grievously overdone."
It is not the prize that can make us happy; it is not even the winning of the prize, though for the one short half-hour of triumph that is pleasant enough. The struggle, the long hot hour of the honest fight, the grinding work — when the teeth are set, and the skin moist with sweat and rough with dust, when all is doubtful and sometimes desperate, when a man must trust to his own manhood knowing that those around him trust to it not at all — that is the happy time of life. There is no human bliss equal to twelve hours of work with only six hours in which to do it.
Nothing makes a man so cross as success, or so soon turns a pleasant friend into a captious acquaintance . . . . He wants pleasure and excitement, and roams about looking for satisfaction in places where no man ever found it. He frets himself with his banker's book, and everything tastes amiss to him that has not on it the flavour of gold . . . . Success is the necessary misfortune of life, but it is only to the very unfortunate that it comes early.

The Belton Estate
"(These) things always pay for themselves if they are properly done."

Doctor Thorne

"Such a life as mine makes a man a fool, and makes him mad, too. . . . I'm worth three hundred thousand pounds, and I'd give it all to be able to go to work tomorrow with a hod and mortar, and have a fellow clap his hand upon my shoulder and say: 'Well, Roger, shall us have that 'ere other half-pint this morning?' . . . when a man has made three hundred thousand pounds there's nothing left for him but to die. It's all he's good for then. When money's been made, the next thing is to spend it. Now the man who makes it has not the heart to do that."

Frank had become legally of age, legally a man, when he was twenty-one. Nature, it seems, had postponed the ceremony till he was twenty-two. Nature often does postpone the ceremony even to a much later age — sometimes altogether forgets to accomplish it.

The comic almanacs give us dreadful pictures of January and February; but in truth, the months which should be made to look gloomy in England are March and April. Let no man boast himself that he has got through the perils of winter till at least the seventh of May.

What had he not done for her, that uncle of hers, who had been more loving than any father! How was he, too, to be paid? Paid, indeed! Love can only be paid in its own coin: it knows of no other legal tender.

The Way We Live Now

Is it not singular how some men continue to obtain the reputation of popular authorship without adding a word to the literature of their country worthy of note? . . . . To puff and get one's self puffed have become different branches of a new profession.

Roger Carbury did not quite believe in the forgiveness of injuries. If you pardon all the evil done to you, you encourage others to do evil. If you give your cloak to him who steals your coat, how long will it be before your shirt and trousers will go also?

"Love is like any other luxury. You have no right to it unless you can afford it."

Phineas Finn

Perhaps there is nothing more perilous to a man's honesty than that . . . . of knowing himself to be quite loved by a girl whom he almost loves himself.

He Knew He Was Right

"What is it that we all live upon but self-esteem? When we want praise it is only because praise enables us to think well of ourselves. Everyone to himself is the centre and pivot of all the world."

"It is a great mistake . . . . to think that anybody is either an angel or a devil."

Marion Fay

A man cannot rid himself of a prejudice because he knows or believes it to be a prejudice.

Miss Mackenzie

With many women I doubt whether there be any more effectual way of touching their hearts than ill-using them and then confessing it. If you wish to get the sweetest fragrance from the herb at your feet, tread on it and bruise it.

"Men live and die from natural causes, and not from God's interposition."

"Clergymen are like women. As long as they're pure, they're a long sight purer than other men; but when they fall, they sink deeper."

Men who can succeed in deceiving no one else will succeed at last in deceiving themselves.

"You know, John," she said, "a woman can't love a man all at once."

The Vicar of Bullhampton

If search for bread, and meat, and raiment, be set aside, then beyond that, our happiness or misery here depends chiefly on success or failure in small things.

" . . . . it is so often that we want that which we have not, and find it so little worthy of having when we get it."

"It always seems to me," said Mr Gilmore, "that to be successful in love, a man should not be in love at all; or at any rate, he should hide it."

Is He Popenjoy?

. . . . there is nothing which requires so much experience to attain as the power of refusing.

There are sins as to which there is no satisfaction in visiting the results with penalties.

Everything is dull after a certain time of life, unless a man has made some fixed line for himself.

"Some people manage to live so that everybody will be the better for their dying."

Dr. Wortle's School

"It is often a question to me whether the religion of the world is not more odious than its want of religion.

INDEX OF TROLLOPE'S WORKS REFERRED TO IN THE TEXT

GENERAL INDEX